OCT 2 1 2004

FEB 2 3 2005

MAR 2 4 2005
OCT 1 6 2006

NOV 2 1 2006

DEC 1 4 2006

The Globalization of the Chinese Economy

The Globalization of the Chinese Economy

Edited by

Shang-Jin Wei

Senior Fellow holding the New Century Chair in International Economics at the Brookings Institution, USA

Guanzhong James Wen

Associate Professor at Trinity College, USA

Huizhong Zhou

Professor of Economics at Western Michigan University, USA

Edward Elgar

Cheltenham, UK • Northampton, MA, USA

© Shang-Jin Wei, Guanzhong James Wen, Huizhong Zhou, 2002

All rights reserved. No part of this publication may be reproduced, stored in a retrieval system or transmitted in any form or by any means, electronic, mechanical or photocopying, recording, or otherwise without the prior permission of the publisher.

Published by
Edward Elgar Publishing Limited
Glensanda House
Montpellier Parade
Cheltenham
Glos GL50 1UA
UK

Edward Elgar Publishing, Inc.
136 West Street
Suite 202
Northampton
Massachusetts 01060
USA

UNIVERSITY OF
TORONTO AT
MISSISSAUGA
LIBRARY

Reprinted 2003

A catalogue record for this book is available from the British Library

Library of Congress Cataloging in Publication Data
The globalization of the Chinese economy / edited by Shang-Jin Wei, Guanzhong James Wen, Huizhong Zhou.
    p.cm.
  Includes bibliographical references and index.
1. China–Foreign economic relations. 2. Globalization–Economic aspects–China. 3. Globalization–Social aspects–China. 4. Investments, Foreign–China. 5. China--Economic policy–2000- 6. China–Economic conditions–2000- 7. International economic integration. I. Wei, Shang-Jin.
II. Wen, G. (Guanzhong James) III. Zhou, Huizhong, 1947–

HF1604.G56 2002
337.51–dc21   2002021389

ISBN 1 84064 880 5

Printed in Great Britain by Biddles Short Run Books, King's Lynn

Contents

About the Editors

Shang-Jin Wei is Senior Fellow at the Brookings Institution, holding the New Century Chair in International Economics, and a research fellow at Harvard University's Center for International Development, National Bureau of Economic Research (USA) and Centre for Economic Policy Research (Europe). He holds an MS degree in finance and a Ph.D. degree in economics from the University of California at Berkeley.

Guanzhong James Wen received his Ph.D. degree in economics from University of Chicago and currently is Associate Professor at Trinity College, Hartford, Connecticut, USA. He served as President of the Chinese Economists Society in 1999–2000.

Huizhong Zhou is Professor of Economics at Western Michigan University, a visiting professor at Beijing University and Fudan University in China and a research associate at Rikkyo University in Japan. He received his Ph.D. degree in managerial economics from the Kellogg Graduate School of Management at Northwestern University.

Contributors

David F. Gates is a consultant on Asia and world economic and energy issues for the Petroleum Finance Company, an international energy consultancy in Washington, DC. Dr. Gates holds a Ph.D. in economics from Princeton University and was employed by Exxon Corporation for more than 32 years, including more than nine years resident in Japan.

D. Gale Johnson is the Eliakim Hastings Moore Distinguished Service Professor Emeritus of Economics at the University of Chicago. His area of specialization is agricultural economics and he has studied the development of China's agriculture and rural economy during the reform period of the last two decades.

Doowon Lee is Associate Professor of Economics in Yonsei University, Seoul, Korea. He received his Ph.D. in economics from Northwestern University in 1991, specializing in international trade and economic development.

Haizheng Li is Assistant Professor of Economics at Georgia Institute of Technology. He researches a variety of topics in econometric methods and labor economics, including migration choices, labor supply, returns to schooling and the incidence of social security tax.

Liu Liu is a research assistant in economics at Hopkins-Nanjing Center, Nanjing, China. Her current research interest is foreign direct investment in China.

Minquan Liu is the Providence Professor in Economics at Hopkins-Nanjing Center, Nanjing, China. His current research interests include foreign direct investment and Rural Credit Cooperatives in China.

Ding Lu, Associate Professor of Economics in National University of Singapore, holds a Ph.D. from Northwestern University. He has published three books and 16 papers in peer-reviewed international journals on the Chinese economy, telecommunications, trade and investment, and other issues.

Chen-yuan Tung is a Ph.D. candidate in international affairs at the School of Advanced International Studies, Johns Hopkins University. His expertise focuses on economic relations between Taiwan and China, Chinese economic development, and Taiwan–US–China trilateral relations.

Zhi Wang is a Senior Research Scientist at George Mason University. His major fields of study include computable general equilibrium modeling, economic integration among Pacific Rim countries, behavior of economic agents under quantity constraint, and international trade.

Guanzhong James Wen received his Ph.D. degree in Economics from University of Chicago and currently is Associate Professor at Trinity College, Connecticut, USA. He served as president of the Chinese Economists Society in 1999–2000.

Luodan Xu is Professor of Economics in Lingnan College, Zhongshan University, Guangzhou, China. One of her current research interests is foreign direct investment in China.

Guifang Yang is an economist and manager at Arthur Andersen LLP. Her research interests include the theoretical and empirical linkages among intellectual property rights, international technology transfer and economic growth, and computable general equilibrium modeling of international trade issues.

Jason Z. Yin is Associate Professor of Strategy Management and International Business at W. Paul Stillman School of Business, Seton Hall University. His research interests are in areas of strategic management, international trade and investment, business environment in China and Internet strategy.

Kevin Honglin Zhang is Assistant Professor of Economics at Illinois State University. He has published over 20 articles in leading academic journals, in addition to a book and many book-chapters.

Xiaobo Zhang is a postdoctoral fellow at the International Food Policy Research Institute. His research interest focuses on income distribution and public investment, with particular reference to China and India.

Huizhong Zhou is Professor of Economics at Western Michigan University, a visiting professor at Beijing University and Fudan University in China and a visiting research fellow at Rikkyo University in Japan. His current research interest focuses on competition in regulated industries, including telecommunications and tobacco industries.

Acknowledgements

This volume is based largely on research papers presented at an international conference held in Shanghai in July 2000. The editors would like to thank the Ford Foundation, the Asian Development Bank, the World Bank and BP Amoco for their generous support that made the conference possible. The editors would also like to thank David F. Gates for his patience, understanding and excellent work in preparing the camera-ready copy of the book.

1. A Globalizing China: An Introduction

Shang-Jin Wei, Guanzhong James Wen and Huizhong Zhou

The continued advance of the world economy demonstrates convincingly that international trade and economic integration bring greater wealth and welfare to all participating nations. However, these potential gains are not distributed evenly among different interest groups within each nation. There will be winners and losers at least in the short run. Disruption and commotion resulting from economic integration can be costly and painful when a nation makes adjustments in its economic and social structure. Therefore there is also resentment and resistance to globalization. The redistribution of costs and benefits, if not handled properly, can lead to social instability and international conflicts. Indeed the earlier rounds of economic globalization witnessed disruptions and delays in some extreme forms such as the World Wars and the Cold War. Therefore a nation that embraces economic globalization must be ready for social reforms and economic restructuring and adapt itself to uncertain developments of globalization before it can fully benefit from it.

China's long struggle for openness and economic integration, which has eventually led to its accession to the WTO recently, will prove to be an excellent example that demonstrates the distrust and resistance that a nation may hold against globalization, the benefits that it will enjoy through integration and the pain that it can suffer when exposed to world competition. Although China has made every effort to integrate itself into the world economy in the past two decades, it has a long history of closing its door to outsiders. Inheriting a great civilization that has its own values and traditions China had often looked at the rest of the world with suspicion. Its record on international integration was rather poor in its modern history. For example, before 1840, when the first Opium War forced China to open its door, China led almost all East Asian nations in following a *sakoku* policy that closed national borders to foreigners. As recently as the mid 1960s through the mid 1970s the Chinese leaders openly challenged the rationale underlying economic globalization by overemphasizing so-called self-reliance and nearly discontinuing trade with a limited number of partners that it kept during that period of time. Moving from being hostile to economic globalization China now becomes a constructive force, whose stake in preserving and promoting the existing global rules and order will grow as its trade with the rest of the world expands. The experiences of this transformation in China should provide important lessons to those economies that are facing difficult choices as to whether and how they should open their doors to the world.

The significance of China's accession to the WTO lies also in the size and potential of the Chinese economy. China used to choose to stay away from the world's efforts in enhancing exchange and cooperation in the past. Its participation in the WTO marks a new era in which all the major powers join forces for the first time to promote economic integration through free trade and market competition. Thus it is now more promising than ever that the current round of economic globalization will be sustained. China's decision to become a member of the WTO has far-reaching implications both for China itself and for the rest of the world. It signifies that China is to break away from its past practices of managed opening and controlled trade, which have become increasingly unacceptable to China's major trade partners. By accepting the rules and regulations of the WTO, China has committed itself to opening further its market and leveling most of its trade and investment barriers within two to five years. China has promised to allow foreign capital to enter gradually the sectors that it has been protecting so far, such as heavy industries, agriculture, finance and retail. These measures will surely bring tremendous benefits to the rest of the world as well as China. The significance of China's embrace of the WTO can never be overestimated. This event may be remembered as one of the most important in this century.

Given the importance of China's membership of the WTO and diverging opinions regarding the benefits and costs of China's accession to the WTO among policy makers, business practitioners and economists in China and abroad, it is high time for a dispassionate, balanced and fact-based analysis of the implications of China's accession to the WTO. This volume serves exactly that purpose. The volume is based on research papers presented at an international conference, 'Developing through Globalization: China's Opportunities and Challenges in the New Century,' held in Shanghai, 5–7 July 2000. The conference was sponsored by the Chinese Economists Society, a US-based non-profit research organization. Most authors in this volume are professors and research scholars at universities and institutions in the United States. All have an intimate knowledge of the Chinese economy and society and follow closely new developments in the country. Many of them were born and grew up in China. They share a unique combination of an outsider's broad perspective and an insider's sensitivity to details and subtleties. The analyses in this volume are intended to promote a more complete understanding of the implications of China's WTO membership for itself and the rest of the world while offering timely policy recommendations to China and its trade partners.

China's accession to the WTO will have profound impacts on the Chinese and world economies. Since 1978 China has been an important player in the global economy. By the end of 2000 China's exports were worth $249.2

billion and its imports reached \$225.1 billion. By joining the WTO China will be committed to adopt measures to liberalize trade further, including substantial reductions in tariffs and non-tariff barriers in many sectors. New opportunities for export and the expected influx of foreign goods will change and inflict profound effects on the structure of the Chinese economy. The industries that face the greatest challenges are those that are regarded as strategically important to the national economy and security, such as telecommunications, banking and financial services, and automobiles and energy. They have been monopolized by the central government and protected from competition until very recently. The challenges faced by these industries are twofold: Not only will enterprises have to improve their performance to compete with foreign companies and possibly domestic non-state rivals, but regulators or policy makers will also have to revise the rules of the game such that these conform with the WTO agreements. The chapter in this volume on industrial policy provides an overall account of the regulatory environment in which Chinese enterprises have been operating and in which foreign competitors may find themselves when they enter the Chinese market. Chapters on telecommunications and the automobile industry offer particular cases of regulated industries and changes taking place recently. Some of the conclusions derived from the analysis of these two industries can be extended to other highly regulated industries in China.

Another major impact that China's WTO membership will bring to the economy is the displacement of the labor force, especially in the agricultural sector. The rural labor force has undergone dramatic restructuring during the past two decades when the Chinese economy grew and developed rapidly. Large-scale migration from rural to urban areas has brought troubles to cities as well as cheap labor and prosperity. Moreover urban areas have their own unemployment pressure. The state sectors employ about one half of China's urban employees. Although state-owned enterprises have been improving their performance in the face of competition, they still lag behind non-state firms and many are on the brink of bankruptcy. The governments have started to dissolve failing state enterprises recently. With increased competition as a result of WTO accession one can only expect massive layoffs in the state sectors. As China's social safety net is still under construction, large-scale unemployment and displacement can cause disruptions to society. Job creation, urbanization and social security will become the center of concerns for economists and policy makers for years to come.

The membership of the WTO will bring in valuable resources to China, in particular, badly needed capital. China has already benefited greatly from foreign investment since it opened its door to the world economy in the late 1970s. It has become the largest recipient of foreign direct investment (FDI) among developing countries since 1993, receiving over \$27 billion in that year, which amounted to 35 per cent of total FDI in all developing countries.

Toward the end of 2000 the cumulative number of registered FDI projects stood at 361 500, the contracted value of FDI was $662.6 billion, and the total realized amount of FDI in China reached $344.1 billion. The inflow of foreign capital has created employment opportunities and contributed to the growth of the economy. FDI firms employed 18 million Chinese by the end of 1996, constituting 18 per cent of the total non-agricultural labor force. In 1997 19 per cent of total gross industrial output was produced by foreign affiliates. China's accession to the WTO will open the door further to foreign investors, which should benefit the Chinese economy even more.

With the accounts in the previous paragraphs as the backdrop, we organize the chapters in this volume into three parts: Part 1 provides updated accounts of recent developments in several important sectors in China, including agriculture, telecommunications and automobiles. These new developments should prove useful to policy makers and investors seeking to evaluate market conditions in traditionally regulated industries in China. The first chapter in this part offers an overview of industrial policies in China. Chapter 3 evaluates the effects of China's accession to the WTO on its agricultural sector and offers an overview of the outlook for the rural economy in the future. Chapter 4 provides a comprehensive account of the rapid growth and profound changes in telecommunications in the past 15 years or so, and Chapter 5 assesses the implications of major adjustments in the telecommunications rate structure that took effect in 2001. While both addressing regulation and competition in the telecommunications industry, the latter is more critical of regulatory arrangements of the industry than the former. The conflicting views reflect the fact that, while making great progress in opening the market for competition, the industry is still highly regulated. Chapter 6 offers a projection of the potential demand for automobiles and automobile fuel in China and evaluates the impact of the WTO on the Chinese automobile industry.

The second part of this volume addresses some of the concerns in China regarding its entry to the WTO, which include whether the opening of the Chinese economy will cause massive unemployment and increase inequalities among regions. Chapter 7, using a computable general equilibrium model, analyzes gains and losses in jobs as a result of China's entry into the WTO, while Chapter 8 examines the impact of globalization on regional inequality and identifies factors that mitigate inequalities among regions. Chapter 9 addresses a related issue, namely, migration and urbanization in China in the midst of globalization.

Part 3 evaluates the effects of increased trade and financial ties between China and the rest of the world. The first two chapters in this part analyze the effects of China's entry into the WTO on the US and Taiwan economies. They are followed by two chapters that investigate conditions facilitating foreign direct investment in China. Chapter 12 identifies factors in the host country, China; while Chapter 13 examines characteristics of investing firms from different countries. The last chapter in this part provides an assessment of the outlook for trade disputes involving China in the near future as trade between China and the rest of the world grows.

The remainder of this introduction provides an overview of each chapter.

PART 1. TRANSFORMATION IN THE CHINESE ECONOMY

The Chinese government still plays a dominant role in the economy, although that role has declined steadily from the heyday of central planning during 1949–1979. While refusing to abandon intervention in the economy, the Chinese government has increasingly recognized the importance of moving towards rule-based intervention. In 1989 China promulgated its first industrial policy. The content of the policy has evolved over time. Some of these policy specifics are inconsistent with the requirements of the WTO and will have to be jettisoned. Others are likely to be modified and remain in effect even after WTO membership. In the first chapter in this part Lu provides a review of the evolution of China's industrial policy and a timely assessment of what the business–government relationship is likely to be after entry into the WTO. China's industrial policy favors certain sectors at the expense of others. Sectoral discrimination is often accompanied by unequal treatment of foreign and domestic firms. The current policy characterizes development projects as projects to be encouraged, projects to be restricted or prohibited, and projects to be left alone. Projects to be encouraged include those that bring in new technologies in agricultural development, technologies that save energy and raw materials, and production processes that contribute to exports and that can be located in the central and western regions of the country. Foreign firms that are able to take advantage of these industrial biases can expect to do relatively well in the post-WTO China. Lu's chapter also offers information on sectors that are discouraged or prohibited, which is equally useful for understanding future foreign investment patterns in China.

Johnson's chapter deals with the agricultural sector and the rural economy. He evaluates the short-term effects of WTO accession on China's agriculture and emphasizes that economic growth, not just WTO entry, will bring about broader and more significant adjustments in the rural sector over the coming decades. Johnson points out that the much-talked-about crowding out of domestic wheat and other agricultural products by foreign products is only part of the picture. Chinese farmers will also benefit from more competitive markets for inputs – fertilizers, pesticides, seeds and machinery and improved access to credit. Compared to the adjustments in response to the WTO, the adjustments in China's rural area required by its overall economic growth are much more substantial. Johnson projects that agriculture's share of national employment will decline from the current 45 per cent to about 10 per cent by 2030. This adjustment could take many forms. Instead of migration to industrial cities, which has been restricted by the central government, the employment of rural labor could take the form of non-farm jobs located *in the rural areas*, including the so-called township-village-enterprises, which have experienced rapid growth throughout the last two decades. Restrictions on renting and sale of land use rights and on rural–urban migration, or their lack thereof, are likely to have a significant impact on the welfare of the people currently in the rural areas.

Telecommunications is one of the few high profile areas in China's entry negotiations with major WTO members. In Chapter 4 Lu provides a detailed account of the process of opening for competition in this industry. Amidst rapid growth in the past decade, dramatic measures have been taken to break state monopolization, including introducing competing operators, restructuring the dominant incumbent and separating regulatory functions from business operations. Some operations such as paging and messaging have become very competitive. Telecommunications equipment manufacturing was open for competition much earlier and is now very competitive in the global market. Major foreign equipment manufacturers have significant operations in China. However China currently prohibits foreign equity investment in telecommunications operations. When it becomes a member of the WTO, China will allow foreign firms to have up to 49 per cent ownership in telecommunications.

Zhou is more critical of the competitive conditions in the Chinese telecommunications market. He characterizes the market as one controlled by a captive regulator and a dominant incumbent. Although political competition has introduced new players into the market, price control by the regulator and the dominance in access by the incumbent has impeded competition. Against this background Chapter 5 introduces the new rate structure that is to take effect in 2001 and evaluates its impacts on the market. Under the new structure, rates for most services are lowered, especially for line leases and Internet services. Cross-subsidization from long-distance to local telephone service will be reduced, while that from urban to rural areas may increase. Access and interconnection are still highly centralized. Overall these adjustments do not represent much progress in curtailing the incumbent's market power and promoting competition.

The last chapter in this part offers an assessment of the prospects for cars and car fuel in China. The development of the automobile industry will not only boost other major industries, but also increase mobility and employment and change the life style of the people. It will also generate pollution and cause over-population and traffic congestion in urban areas. Yin and Gates offer a projection of the future demand for cars and car fuel in China based on projected income growth and the experiences of other countries in acquiring cars. Various studies suggest that the number of cars in China in 2010 will be between 10 to 30 per 1000 people. They then discuss inefficiencies in the Chinese auto industry. Two major problems of the industry are the small scale of manufacturers and the fragmentation of the market. These problems are a result of special treatment of the auto firms by the central and local governments and regional protectionism. The chapter also evaluates the effects of China's entry into the WTO on the industry and suggests how FDI can improve the efficiency of domestic auto manufacturers as well as benefit foreign producers.

PART 2. SOCIAL IMPLICATIONS

The prospect of imminent membership of the WTO has stirred up fear among many people inside China focusing on, among other things, the possibility of a sharp increase in the unemployment rate at least in the short run. The basic reason behind these concerns is the asymmetric responses to WTO entry from the Chinese import-competing sector and the export sector. The negotiations that led up WTO entry have committed China to take liberalization measures that will result in greater reductions in Chinese barriers to foreign products than in foreign barriers to Chinese exports. Consequently it seems reasonable to conclude that, within the next five years or so, there will be a greater increase in Chinese imports than exports, and a greater loss in jobs in the import-competing industries than gains in jobs from the export industries. Hence the aggregate unemployment rate will rise. This rise in unemployment could cause social and political instability, with which the Chinese government has been obsessed. In their chapter Li and Yang dispel this myth. With the aid of sector-level data and a computable general equilibrium model that relaxes the standard assumption of full employment, they demonstrate that the aforementioned concern is only partially right. It is true that the volume of imports may very well rise faster than the volume of exports. However the export sectors in China are generally more labor-intensive than its import-competing sectors: a 1 per cent increase in exports creates more jobs than jobs lost resulting from a 1 per cent increase in imports. Their model shows that, on a net basis, WTO entry will indeed create more jobs from increased exports than jobs lost to increased import competition.

Two additional elements may further alleviate fears for increased unemployment. First, if the real exchange rate is allowed to adjust, even the relative rate of growth of China's imports over exports is likely to be adjusted downward, which may provide another boost to job creation. Second, the analysis in this chapter concentrates on the effects resulting from changes in exports and imports. WTO entry will also bring more foreign firms, banks and other businesses to China.

Another concern in China is whether globalization will increase income inequality among regions. This concern has as many political implications as economic ones. Zhang and Zhang examine this question in Chapter 8 using Chinese province-level data. They find that greater participation in international trade and a larger share in inward foreign direct investment are indeed correlated with a faster growth rate. This supports casual observations that China's coastal areas are more open and grow faster. The authors offer two possible explanations: The first is comparative advantage. Coastal regions can better take advantage of the world economy and are in a better position to catch up with wealthy countries than are the inland provinces. The second has to do with government policies. By and large the government economic policies until recently have tended to favor the coastal areas. These policies include offering tax concessions and exercising liberal regulations in the so-called special economic zones and coastal open cities.

Dislocation of jobs and income inequality among regions has already created a massive wave of migration in China. A taxing task facing the government is how to approach urbanization. In his chapter Wen projects that urbanization in China will accelerate after WTO entry. The urban population may increase from 400 million, or a third of the current national population, to about 1.6 billion, or 80 per cent of the national population by the middle of this century. Wen's projection implies a more sanguine view than Johnson's on how quickly restrictions on rural–urban migration may be eased in China. If Wen is right, the speed of urbanization would be unprecedented in human history.

PART 3. LINKAGE WITH THE WORLD

With WTO membership China's exports to the US and the rest of the world will increase, while its imports from the US and the rest of the world are likely to increase as well. What does this mean for employment and output in the US and China's other major trading partners? This question can be properly answered with the aid of multi-sector models based on detailed data. Wang provides such an analysis with a computable general equilibrium model suited to this task. To make the analysis meaningful, he considers two scenarios: a world with China and Taiwan as members of the WTO adhering to liberalization measures agreed upon during the China's WTO accession negotiations, and a baseline case in which China and Taiwan are not members. The overall message for the rest of the world is moderately positive: the real growth rate of consumption in the world would be 0.02 percentage points higher each year with China's membership. The benefits are substantial when accumulated over time. For the United States real consumption would be 0.16 per cent higher by 2010 with China's WTO membership. Overall, China still benefits more than other countries.

WTO membership brings a gradual phase out of the Multi-fiber Agreement quota imposed on apparel exports from China (and other countries) to the US. Wang's analysis suggests that China is in a better position to take advantage of this phase out than are its Asian and Latin American competitors. He projects a further rise in China's market share in the US market. His projection puts China's share in the US apparel market at 40 per cent by 2010, exceeding the shares of all other Asian exporters combined.

Taiwan has been a significant direct investor in Mainland China. The cumulative realized FDI was about $24 billion by the end of 1999. Trade between the two sides of the Taiwan Strait is also significant, reaching about US $26 billion in 1999, though often through a third region such as Hong Kong. Taiwan enjoyed a huge trade surplus in the order of $17 billion that year. Tung's chapter addresses several questions on the impact of the cross-strait exchange on Taiwan. For example does Taiwan's direct investment in China drain investment from Taiwan? Does trade between the two contribute to a change in wage inequality in Taiwan? Definitive answers to these questions are hard to come by due to data constraints. Tung suggests that investment in China has not drained investment from Taiwan in general. While moving some production activities to the Mainland may reduce jobs associated with these activities, lower production costs in the Mainland help to maintain the overall profits of firms and to expand jobs in the production that stays in Taiwan. There is no evidence either to support the view that Taiwan's investment in China has worsened wage inequality back home. In fact, during the period 1987–1996, when there was an acceleration of Taiwan's investment in China, there was an improvement in the ratio of earnings by non-college graduates to those of college graduates.

For the last two decades or so China has been the largest recipient of foreign direct investment (FDI) among developing countries. By the end of 1998 the total FDI in China reached $265 billion. In his chapter Zhang provides a systemic framework to analyze determinants of FDI and its economic impacts. He then explores factors behind China's success in attracting FDI to foster economic growth and development. These factors include the size of the Chinese market, policies toward FDI, a strong central government and a large body of overseas Chinese investors. The chapter also finds that patterns of human capital may affect the distribution of foreign investment among regions.

Chapter 13 analyzes factors that affect FDI strategies from the perspective of the investors. In this chapter Liu, Xu and Liu identify important characteristics of four groups of foreign firms, overseas Chinese, Japanese, European and American, and investigate how these characteristics affect each group's investment strategies. The study is based on a survey of 405 FDI firms in Guangdong province. The findings in the study should provide a basis for assessing the effect of China's WTO membership on inward investment from various sources.

As trade between China and the rest of the world grows, trade disputes will inevitably emerge. Yin and Lee's chapter examines the prospect of trade disputes in detail. Based on historic data the authors establish a relationship between trade disputes that a country is expected to encounter and its various economic and policy characteristics. There is evidence that countries with large volumes of trade and high tariff and non-tariff barriers are more likely to be involved in disputes. Countries that export mainly primary products and products from heavy and chemical industries are less likely to have disputes, while exporters of other manufactured products such as textiles are more likely to be involved in disputes. The authors go one step further to make an estimate of the likely number of trade disputes that China may face as a member of the WTO, based on the prediction of a model that is built on statistical data on China's trade structure in 1997. This 'educated guess' suggests that China would encounter 19 cases of disputes, placing it in fifth place among all nations on that score. One could speculate that trade disputes involving China might be even higher than this in the near future as China's share in world trade rises. The authors also discuss challenges faced by China in practicing rules of law as demanded by the WTO and the implications of the newly available WTO dispute settlement mechanism for multinational firms operating in China.

PART 1

Transformation in the Chinese Economy

2. Revamping the Industrial Policies

Ding Lu

Since China promulgated its first explicit industrial policy in 1989, state intervention towards business has become more industry-oriented. National economic planning has put great emphasis on development of the so-called 'pillar industries', which consist of high-tech sectors with capital-intensive technologies. Meanwhile policies towards foreign trade and foreign direct investment have become more industry selective.

This industrial policy regime will have to adapt to changes that will be brought about by China's accession to the WTO. In this chapter we first review the contents of China's industrial policy packages and examine the policy instruments that the government has relied on to carry out these policies. We then look into the incentive implications of these policies for inter-industry resource allocation. Finally we discuss the likely changes to the industrial policy regime after China joins the WTO.

CONTENTS OF INDUSTRIAL POLICY

Industrial policy refers to government attempts to channel resources into sectors that it views as important for future economic growth. According to Johnson (1984) the aim of industrial policy is to create industries that will have a comparative advantage in international trade. Industrial policy packages usually involve government support or protection for domestic industries that are deemed to have the potential for comparative advantage but have not yet become internationally competitive on their own. The most common justification for an active industrial policy is the 'infant industry' argument, which suggests that developing countries could speed up their catching up process by selectively protecting their industries at an early stage of development. Whether or to what extent an active industrial policy is necessary and has been effective in the past in promoting development is still an issue subject to debate. Advocates of industrial policy nevertheless stress the positive role of industrial policy in helping Japan and the newly industrialized economies (NIEs) in successfully achieving rapid economic growth in the past several decades (Wade, 1990; Takahashi, 1997).

Various industrial policies pursued by Japan and the NIEs share the feature of active government intervention in resource allocation across industries. However their approach is different from the central planning approach that existed in the former Soviet block or pre-reform China. These

13

differences arise from differences in the fundamental institutions of these economies (Table 2.1).

Table 2.1: The NIE Industrial Policy Regime vs. the Central Planning System

	Industrial policy regime	Centrally planned economy
Fundamental mechanism of resource allocation	Market	Central planning
Ownership	Basically private; public finance may play pivotal role	Public (state or collective)
Decision making	Combination of state and private decisions, with private de jure right over property use protected	Centrally planned by the state
Information coordination	Market transaction guided by state policies	Administrative
Motivation and incentives	Firms: profits State: pragmatic, non-ideological	Firms: fulfillment of plans State: mostly ideological

China's rapid economic development in the past two decades has shown a distinct feature of strong government guidance. Shortly after China embarked on market-oriented reform in the early 1980s (1982), Beijing announced an ambitious plan to modernize the economy and to quadruple the nation's annual gross output within two decades (by the year 2000). Reflecting concern for the weaknesses of the economy in infrastructure and technology, this plan highlighted three 'strategic foci' for development. One was energy and transportation. The second was agriculture and the third was education and science.[1]

The explicit concept of 'industrial policy' nevertheless did not appear in official documents until the late 1980s. By that time a series of market-oriented reforms that started in 1979 had drastically changed the framework and institutions of the Chinese economy. Liberalized market forces gradually dismantled the centrally planned process and replaced the latter as the dominant mechanism of resource allocation in daily economic life. The share of the state-owned sector in the national economy was on the wane through the 1980s. At the same time, China was changing itself from a near autarchy in the 1970s to a booming exporter and an increasingly attractive host to foreign direct investment in the world economy.

Early Policies (1989–1990)

In March 1989 the State Council issued the 'Decision on the Gist of Current Industrial Policy', the first explicit and detailed official guideline for a national industrial policy.[2] The document noted four problems in China's industrial structure: (1) Production capacity of the manufacturing industries was too large for the relatively underdeveloped agricultural sector, energy and raw material industries, and transportation sector. (2) The advanced-level manufacturing was in shortage. (3) The inter-regional distribution of industries was not founded on regional (comparative) advantages. (4) Industrial concentration was too low.

The 'Decision' put forward the major principles of China's industrial policy. These include:

- Using state guidance to adjust industrial structure and coordinate demand and supply.
- Reducing production and investment in goods with excess supply, expanding production and investment in goods with shortages.
- Planning industrial priorities with consideration to market demand, industrial linkage, technological progress, capacity to earn foreign exchange, and economic efficiency.

Based on these principles, the document provided a list of industries and products that should receive priority. These included agriculture and agriculture-service industries, selected products in light industry and textiles, transportation, telecommunications, energy supplies, some important raw materials, machinery and electronic industries, high-tech industries, and exports that earn profits and foreign exchange.

The document also defined the areas of production to be suppressed and constrained. These mainly included low quality products and machinery, consumer durable goods that consumed 'excess' electricity, luxury consumer products, where the required inputs were in short supply, production modes that were obsolete, energy wasting and environmentally harmful. There was also a list of products or production activities to be banned. Accordingly the document listed the areas where the state would support investment in capital construction and technology upgrading. It also listed the areas where investment would be strictly controlled. On top of that the Decision specified that exports of high value-added manufacturing goods and domestically abundant commodities should be encouraged. Strict plans were to apply to the export of major resource commodities considered to be vital to China's national interest. Exports of goods in severe shortage in the domestic economy were also to be banned.

Later Policies (1991–1995)

In April 1991 the National People's Congress approved the Eighth Five-year Plan (1991–95) and the Ten-year Plan for National Economic and Social Development (1991–2000). Both of these plans regarded the adjustment of the industrial structure as the foremost development goal. The Ten-year Plan called for efforts to strengthen agriculture, basic industries and infrastructure facilities. It vowed to restructure and upgrade the manufacturing industry. The Plan gave priority to the development of the electronic industry and urged active promotion of the construction sector and tertiary industry.

Accordingly the Eighth Five-year Plan (1991–95) stressed the development of 12 sectors and specified output and construction targets for each. These sectors included agriculture and the rural economy, irrigation and water conservation, energy, transportation and telecommunications, raw materials, geological prospecting and weather forecasting, electronics, advanced machinery, defense and research, certain products in light industry and textiles, construction, and certain commercial services.

In regard to foreign trade the Plan took a step beyond the Seventh Five-year Plan to promote exports of manufactured goods, in particular, machinery products, electrical equipment, light industrial products, textiles and high-tech products. The Plan pledged to increase export quality and adjust the export structure toward one more reliant on higher value-added manufactured goods.

Before China concluded its Eighth Five-year Plan, the State Council promulgated 'The Outline of State Industrial Policy in the 1990s' in June 1994.[3] The 'Outline' vowed to:

- Strengthen agriculture as the foundation of the national economy.
- Beef up basic industries and infrastructure.
- Accelerate the development of the 'mainstay (or pillar) industries', which include the machinery industry, electronics industry, petroleum processing, the raw chemical materials industry, the automobile industry and the construction industry.
- Restructure foreign trade by boosting exports of certain agricultural products, home electronics appliances and other internationally competitive products; encouraging imports of crucial parts, equipment and technologies; discouraging imports of luxurious consumer goods; and gradually reducing exports of primary goods and energy intensive goods.
- Support industries using new and high technologies.

A remarkable point in the 'Outline' was its announcement of a state industrial organization policy. This policy aimed to promote 'rational competition', reap economies of scale and enhance specialization. For industries with strong scale economies, the document recommended state support for large businesses. For other industries it offered encouragement to small businesses.

This document also defined the authorities responsible for industrial policy making and the procedures for review and approval of industrial policies. The state council was authorized to set national industrial policies while the State Planning Commission (SPC) was to be in charge of designing and coordinating sectoral industrial policies. The 'Outline' required the establishment of a formal arrangement for implementing policies and a system to assess and monitor the results of the policies. All of the major state authorities in charge of planning, the fiscal budget, banking, taxation, domestic and foreign trade, customs tariffs, the security markets, state assets, business registration, etc., had to be committed to implementing state industrial policies. They had to consult with the SPC for coordination before making any major policy decisions that involved industrial development. The SPC was to work with the relevant authorities to monitor, assess, and analyze the implementation of state industrial policies. Based on the results of that process, the SPC would report to the State Council on the effects of implementation and propose amendments accordingly. The provincial governments would work out detailed local plans for implementing the 'Guideline' and file their plans to the SPC.

Based on the 'Outline', the SPC drafted sector-specific industrial policies for telecommunications, transportation, construction, electronics, machinery, petroleum processing and production of chemical materials. It also masterminded the industrial policies regarding foreign investment, foreign trade, industrial organization and technology development.

Present Policies (1996–2010)

In March 1996 China's Eighth National People's Congress approved at its fourth session 'The Outlines of the Ninth Five-year Plan for National Economic and Social Development and the Long-term Target for the Year 2010'.[4] This landmark document set a new direction for state intervention and provided a blueprint for national development into the 21st century. The 1996 'Outline' set the objectives for 2010 as follows:

- Double the 2000 GDP.
- Control population within 1.4 billion and enable people to live an 'even more comfortable life'.

- Establish 'a relatively complete socialist market economy', a macroeconomic control system with better agility and effectiveness and a regulatory framework more in compliance with the rule of law.
- Establish a modern enterprise system for state-owned enterprises and develop a number of internationally competitive large enterprises and business groups.
- Improve industrial structure by:
    - enhancing commercialization and specialization in agriculture;
    - building a group of national infrastructure projects (including the major water control projects in the Yangtze River and Yellow River such as the 'Three Gorges' project);
    - promoting pillar industries and making them the major driving force for economic growth; and
    - increasing the share of the tertiary sector in the national economy and its service functions.
- Promote a more coordinated development of the regional economies and gradually reduce inter-region development disparity.

What is noteworthy in these objectives is the emphasis on institution building for a market economy and the development of the so-called 'pillar industries'. According to the 1996 'Outline', to ensure sustainable and rapid economic growth, the key requirement is to achieve two fundamental transitions. One is the transition from the centrally planned economy to a 'socialist market economy', in which the market plays a fundamental role in resource allocation under state macro-control. The other is the transition from an extensive growth mode, which is driven by expansion of production inputs, to an intensive growth mode, which is driven by increasing efficiency and productivity.

The document classifies investment projects into three types, namely 'projects of a competitive nature', 'projects of a foundation nature', and 'projects of a public welfare nature'. In the 'competitive industries', resources should be allocated primarily by the market. The investment projects in these industries are categorized accordingly as 'projects of a competition nature', which should be funded mainly by enterprises and financed through the market. The government, however, will selectively give support to key projects in the pillar industries and to high-tech development projects. The 'pillar industries' defined in this document are industries involving machinery, electronics, petrochemicals, automobiles and construction. For these industries, the government may even play a role in 'optimizing industrial organizations' to promote economies of scale by coordinating business regrouping among large enterprises or enterprise groups. The state will continue to play a leading role in 'non-competitive industries'. The government should be the main fund provider or the leading fundraiser for the 'projects of a foundation nature'. These projects are likely to be related to infrastructure or 'basic industry' (energy supplies and raw materials). Governments 'at various levels' should be responsible for funding the 'projects of public welfare nature'.

INSTRUMENTS OF INDUSTRIAL POLICY

From the above review of China's industrial policy since 1989, we observe that, with the transition to a market economy, state intervention in cross-industry resource allocation has gradually moved away from a central planning regime to an industrial policy regime that is similar to that of the NIEs (cf. Table 2.1). However legacies of the central planning regime continue to play a role in the government's economic policy making. These legacies characterize the instruments of China's industrial policy.

As summarized by Zhang and Long (1997), China has relied on six types of industrial policy tools: central government financing and planning; empowering key industries with direct financing; preferential interest and tax rates and favorable financing for target industries; infant industry (trade) protection; pricing policies; and administrative means. In addition to these six tools there are at least two additional important measures. One is systematic guidelines to channel foreign direct investment into desired industries. Based on these guidelines the government exercises licensing and approval of investment projects. The other is the various restrictions imposed on foreign ownership, including business content and geographic scope of foreign-funded enterprises.

All of the policy instruments listed in Table 2.2 have played important roles in implementing the official industrial policy guidelines during the past decade. The relative importance of these instruments, however, has been significantly changed over the years as the whole economy has moved toward a more open and market-oriented system. Some of these policy instruments have become increasingly difficult to apply in recent years. For instance, since 1997, the Zhu Rongji administration has tried to restructure the state-owned enterprises into modern corporations with tight budget constraints and business autonomy. In this context the use of policy instruments such as direct state price controls and administrative intervention in business organizations is less appropriate.

As a founding member of the Asia-Pacific Economic Co-operation (APEC) and a rising economic power, China has made some important 'down-payments' for free trade, including tariff cuts and import quota reductions. In its bid for membership in the World Trade Organization (WTO) China has gradually cut its average tariff rate from over 40 per cent to the current 15 per cent since the early 1990s. As for non-tariff barriers, after

Table 2.2: Main Industrial Policy Instruments

Policy instrument	Evidence and examples
1. Central government financing and planning	Central government's direct investment in infrastructure projects; financial assistance to key industries; and budget assistance to projects in backward regions.
2. Administrative means	Administrative planning measures are used from time to time to implement industrial organization policy, such as issuing direct orders to close down or merge state-owned enterprises.
3. Pricing policies	State price controls over power and water supply; permitting state telecommunications companies to charge installation fees for new telephone subscribers (1980s to early 1990s).
4. Empowering key industries with direct financing	Permitting local governments or state-owned consortiums to issue construction bonds to develop energy and communications industries; granting official approval of stock market listing, IPOs or overseas financing according to industrial policies; and adopting the Building, Operating, and Transferring (BOT) model for infrastructure projects
5. Infant industry (trade) protection	Tariffs and non-tariff measures such as import duties, import quotas, import licensing, and local-content requirements (e.g. car industry).
6. Restrictions on the businesses of foreign-funded enterprises	The general prohibition on foreign firms distributing products other than those they make in China, or controlling their own distribution networks; Ban on foreign bank branches from operating RMB deposits and loans and restrictions on their business in designated cities.
7. Preferential interest and tax rates, and favorable financing	State banks' low interest loans and discriminative lending to different industries; Various industry-oriented tax incentives; 'coordinating tax' for directions of fixed capital in fixed capital investment.
8. Licensing and approval of investment projects	Since 1995, the government has periodically promulgated a Direction Guide for Foreign Investment to specify the projects to be encouraged, the ones to be allowed, the ones to be restricted, and the ones to be forbidden.

the landmark promulgation of the 'Law of Foreign Trade of the People's Republic of China' in 1994, China sped up its elimination of license requirements and quotas for most imports and embarked on a transition toward an automatic import licensing system. The Ministry of Foreign Trade and Economic Co-operation, however, promulgated in March 1999 a procedure and a directory for 114 imported commodities subject to non-automatic licensing.[5] Generally, trade protection as an industrial policy instrument has become less viable in recent years.

Relatively speaking industry-oriented tax incentives have become more important. In 1994 China launched a comprehensive tax reform unifying all enterprises' corporate income taxes at a flat rate of 33 per cent. The central government, however, announced in March 1994 that it would grant income tax exemptions and concessions to certain businesses and/or categories of incomes, including the following:[6]

- The high-tech enterprises in High-tech Industrial Development Zones would get a reduced corporate income tax rate of 15 per cent. The new high-tech enterprises in these zones were to be exempted from paying income tax for two years after they started operation.
- Most new businesses in the tertiary industry would be granted income tax exemption or reduction for one to two years. These included new firms engaging in consulting services, transportation or telecommunications services, public utilities, health, storage, tourism, foreign trade, commerce, catering, home service, education, culture, etc. The firms providing agricultural services and institutes or colleges doing technological training and technology transfer, consulting and service, would be exempt from paying income tax.
- Firms in production using recycled materials were to be exempt from income tax for five years.
- Incomes from technology transfer with annual income no more than RMB 300 000 were to be exempt from tax.
- Educational institution workshops, enterprises specially set up for handicapped persons, and service enterprises specially set up for hiring urban unemployed persons were to receive income tax exemption or reduction.
- Township and village enterprises could pay income tax reduced by 10 per cent for community expenses.
- New enterprises in some impoverished areas were to receive tax exemption or reduction for three years.

Most of the above income tax benefits (the first 4) are industry-oriented. The rest are mainly for social welfare or equity purposes.

An important tax policy in the early 1990s was the coordinating tax for direction of fixed capital investment, which was introduced in 1991, to be levied on the amount of fixed capital investment undertaken by indigenous enterprises. A zero tax rate applied to projects 'urgently needed by the state'. These projects included fixed capital investment in agriculture and water conservation, energy, transportation, postal and telecommunications, key raw materials, geological prospecting, certain medical research, certain electronic and machinery investments, pollution control, urban public utilities, some storage facilities, etc. For projects encouraged by the state but constrained by energy supply and transportation facilities, the low 5 per cent tax rate applied. For projects that were of an inefficient scale, employing outmoded technologies, or making products already in excess supply, the state policy was to control strictly their development and therefore the highest rate of 30 per cent was applied.[7] All the other projects were taxed at a rate of 15 per cent.[8]

Another policy instrument that gained greater importance was guidelines for foreign direct investment. Since China opened its door to foreign direct investment in the early 1980s, Beijing has pursued an official policy of encouraging foreign investment in high-tech manufacturing and infrastructure development such as transportation, telecommunications, and energy resources. Export-oriented projects and import-substitution projects have also been preferred.

After China developed its first set of explicit industrial policies in 1989, the government increasingly used the country's vast market potential as leverage to lure foreign investment into areas prioritized by the state industrial policies. At the beginning of 1993 China planned a series of measures to attract foreign investment in the areas of finance, communications, information technology, farm products processing, urban infrastructure and housing renovation.[9]

The official guidelines toward foreign investors remained rather obscure until the State Planning Commission, Economic and Trade Commission and MOFTEC jointly promulgated the first explicit directions/guide for foreign investment in June 1995.[10] In principle, the government divided foreign-funded projects into four categories: namely, projects to be encouraged, projects to be allowed, projects to be restricted, and projects to be forbidden.

Projects to be encouraged included those that:

- involve new agricultural techniques, comprehensive agriculture development, and development of energy, transportation and major raw materials;
- involve new and/or high-tech and thus can help save energy and raw materials, raise the technical level and economic efficiency;
- can meet the demand of the international market and help upgrade products and thus help open up markets and expand exports;

- involve new technology and equipment for the comprehensive use of natural resources, and recycling of resources, and prevention of environmental pollution;
- can provide better use of manpower and natural resources in the central and western parts of the country, and are in accord with the state industrial policies; and
- are encouraged by state regulations or policies.

Projects to be encouraged can enjoy a range of preferential treatment as stipulated by state laws and administrative regulations. In addition, if the projects are connected with the construction and operation of energy and transportation infrastructure (coal, electricity, local railways, roads and ports) that require large investment and have long reimbursement periods, investors can expand their business scope to related areas upon state approval.

Projects to be restricted include those:

- with technologies that have been well developed domestically or already introduced from abroad; or projects that would add to a domestic production capacity that has already well satisfied domestic demand;
- in sectors that are only open for foreign investment on a trial basis or are under state monopoly franchise;
- that involve prospecting and exploiting rare and precious mineral resources;
- that involve industries under the state unified planning; and
- that are restricted by state laws and administrative regulations.

According to the state's industrial policies and needs arising from macroeconomic control, restricted foreign-funded projects are divided into two sub-categories: A and B. Restricted projects are to have a definite term of operation. In the case of a joint venture, the fixed assets put in by the Chinese side should come from the Chinese firm's own capital or assets (without using bank loans or raising funds).

Foreign investment is prohibited for projects that fall into any of the following categories:

- projects that endanger the country's security or social and public interest;
- projects that would cause environmental pollution or bring harm to natural resources and human health;
- projects that would occupy large tracts of farm land, are harmful to environment protection and development of land resources, and/or endanger the security of military facilities and their effective uses;
- projects that would use China's own special craftsmanship or indigenous skills for production;

- other projects that are banned by the state law and administrative regulations.

Projects not belonging to the categories of being encouraged, restricted or forbidden are those in the allowed category. The first catalogue published in June 1995 covered 315 sectors. A more recent catalogue of Major Industries, Products, and Technologies Encouraged for Development in China took effect on 1 January 1998 and covers several hundred products and technologies in 29 industries.

Based on the above principles, the State Planning Commission regularly compiles, updates and promulgates the Guiding Catalogue of Industries for Foreign Investment. Government authorities' evaluation and approval of foreign-funded projects should be made in compliance with the Guiding Catalogue of Industries for Foreign Investment. The Catalogue of Industries for Guiding Overseas Investment (December 1997) provides a more detailed list of projects being encouraged, restricted or forbidden.[11]

INCENTIVE IMPLICATIONS OF INDUSTRIAL POLICY

The incentive implications of industrial policy have been discussed by a number of scholars. Zhang, Zhang and Wan (1998) characterized the features of China's import tariffs as 'high rates, multiple reductions and exemptions, and a narrow base' (pp. 31–34). They also pointed out that the import approval procedure involves high transaction costs and opportunities for rent seeking. Using data for 25 categories of imports, they estimated that trade liberalization could bring in a static gain in consumer surplus equivalent to 19.5 per cent of the sum of domestic production and the landed value of imports before liberalization. Netting out the loss of producer surplus and government tariff revenues, the country could still enjoy a net (static) efficiency gain of US$ 5 billion per year through liberalizing these imports, or 14 per cent of the gain in consumer surplus.

Lu and Tang (1997) examined the change in the composition of GDP by sector from 1980 to 1995 and found that industrial policy had only been partially successful in changing China's industrial structure. The two supposedly prioritized categories, 'transportation, postal and telecommunications services' and 'other tertiary sectors', saw their shares rise in the late 1980s but the trend was reversed in the first half of the 1990s. Within heavy industry, the growth of the extraction and raw material sectors lagged behind the growth of manufacturing in terms of output, sales and fixed assets. This phenomenon did not meet the priorities put forward in the Eighth Five-year Plan. In the manufacturing sector, all three prioritized sub-sectors were outstanding in terms of output growth, asset value and sales.

The view of these mixed effects is shared by some Chinese scholars. Jiang (1996), for instance, pointed out that the state policy to eliminate infrastructure bottlenecks had limited effects in the 1980s. Efforts to restrict additional construction of projects providing over-supplied manufactured goods in the 1980s were a failure. Promotion of textiles and light industries in the late 1970s and early 1980s, however, was very successful.

Taiwan's Chung-Hua Institute for Economic Research published a comprehensive report on China's industrial policy in 1995. The report (CHIER, 1995) found that China's five fastest growing industries from 1991 to 1993 were all related to infrastructure, energy and raw materials. However, of the four efficiency indicators for industrial enterprises, namely the ratio of value-added to output value, the ratio of profit-tax to capital, the ratio of profit-tax to output value, and total labor productivity (the ratio of output value to employment), all but the last one had declined from 1980 through 1993. Finally, the report applied the Data Envelopment Analysis developed by Charnes, Cooper and Rhodes (1978) to work out the rankings of China's industrial sectors from 1987 to 1992. During the period in question, the three pillar manufacturing sectors, namely electronics and telecommunications equipment, raw chemical materials and chemical products, and transport equipment, all ranked very low and did not show much improvement.

Liu, Yao, and Zhang (1999) used a shift-share method to quantify the components of economic growth and structural changes in employment and investment at both the national and regional levels in China from 1986 to 1994. They found that these structural changes followed a clear regional pattern that favored some coastal provinces. Their study, however, only analyzed shifts in employment and investment among agriculture, industry and service sectors.

Guo (1998) estimated an index of barriers to entry for each of the 40 Chinese industries by modeling entry as a function of various incentives to enter relative to the level of barriers to entry. According to his indices, petroleum and natural gas extraction, coal and other minerals mining and processing, tobacco processing, textiles, petroleum processing, engineering, food production, and electric power and steam production and supply had the highest barriers to entry in the period 1990–92.

In the following analysis, we will take some different approaches to measure the incentive implications of industrial policy. We will start with the tax incentives.

Effective Sales-related Tax Rates

The 1994 tax reform unified the nominal corporate income tax rate with some exceptional preferential rates reserved for certain types of foreign investments (see Lu and Tang, 1997 for more details). Most of those preferential rates, however, were gradually phased out in the 1990s. For indigenous firms, the major industry-specific difference in tax burdens arises from the tax on city maintenance and construction, the consumption tax, the resource tax and the extra charge for education, etc. Table 2.3A illustrates these differences across manufacturing sectors by displaying the Effective Sales-related Tax Rate on Added Value (ESTR):

$$ESTR = \frac{\text{Taxes and extra charges on sales of goods}}{(\text{Revenue of sales} - \text{Costs of sales})/(1 + R_{VAT})} \qquad (2.1)$$

where R_{VAT} is value-added tax rate.

Table 2.3A: Effective Sales-related Tax Rate on Added Value (%)

	1991	1995	1998
Light industry	53.6	41.6	42.8
Using farm products as raw material	*60.7*	*47.6*	*51.0*
Using non-farm products as raw material	38.1	29.1	28.1
Heavy industry	45.4	38.4	41.2
Mining and quarrying	58.2	42.2	48.3
Raw materials industry	52.8	49.1	55.6
Manufacturing	*34.1*	*28.3*	*28.4*
Petroleum processing and coke refinery	71.4	60.7	77.3
Raw chemical materials and chemical products	*28.6*	*29.2*	*33.6*
Chemical fiber	*35.9*	*30.8*	43.5
Non-metal mineral products (construction	*42.1*	*35.6*	38.0
Ordinary machinery	53.0	*28.1*	*28.4*
Special purpose equipment	*36.2*	*25.3*	*27.0*
Transport equipment	*24.4*	36.6	36.1
Electronic and telecommunications equipment	*26.0*	*20.2*	*20.1*
Instruments, meters, cultural and office machinery	*30.1*	*25.0*	*22.3*
All industries	49.1	39.7	41.9

Note: Figures in italics are more than 5 percent lower than the rate for all industries

Source: Calculated from *China Statistical Yearbook*, various issues

In Table 2.3A we can observe that, generally, manufacturing industries and light industry using non-farm products as raw materials had tax rates more than five percentage points lower than the rate for all industries. The ranking displayed in Table 2.3B appears to be consistent with official priorities/policies: The sectors of 'electronic and telecommunications equipment', 'instruments, meters, cultural and office machinery' and 'special purpose equipment' were ranked at the top during the period. The 'transport equipment' sector was in number one position in 1991 but dropped to number nine and seven in 1995 and 1998 respectively. In contrast, the 'ordinary machinery' sector notched a gain from tenth in 1991 to fourth in1998.

Table 2.3B: Effective Sales-related Tax Rate Ranking (from low to high tax)

Industrial sector	1991	1995	1998	Mean
Electronic and telecom equipment	2	1	1	1.33
Instruments, meters, cultural and office mach.	4	2	2	2.67
Special purpose equipment	6	3	3	4.00
Raw chemical materials and chemical prod.	3	6	6	5.00
Light industry using non-farm products as raw material	7	5	4	5.33
Transport equipment	1	9	7	5.67
Ordinary machinery	10	4	5	6.33
Chemical fiber	5	7	9	7.00
Non-metal mineral products (construction material)	8	8	8	8.00
Mining and quarrying	11	10	10	10.33
Raw materials industry	9	12	12	11.00
Light industry using farm products as raw material	12	11	11	11.33
Petroleum processing and coke refinery	13	13	13	13.00

Source: Calculated from *China Statistical Yearbook*, various issues.

Effective Trade Protection

It is difficult to evaluate the overall impact of trade protection on business incentives since there are so many tariff and non-tariff barriers to trade. On top of that official intervention towards some domestic prices also has significant incentive impact on business. To capture the combined effects of trade protection and domestic price policy, I compiled a 'Protection Index' based on domestic wholesale and retail statistics:

$$\text{Protection Index} = \frac{\text{exp. (Sales margin)}}{\text{exp. (Import ratio)}} \qquad (2.2)$$

in which:

exp. = the constant 'e' raised to the power of the number in brackets (The constant e = 2.718282, the base of the natural logarithm.)[12]
Sales margin = (Sales revenue – purchase cost)/ purchase cost
Import ratio = Import / purchase cost

Table 2.4: Protection Index in Wholesale Commerce (1998)

Merchandise	Import ratio %	Sales margin %	Protection index
Machinery and electrical equipment	22.0	-5.0	0.76
Natural minerals	29.3	7.2	0.80
Wool, cotton and natural fiber	4.0	-6.1	0.90
Chemical and allied products	12.0	7.0	0.95
Newspapers and books	2.1	-0.2	0.98
Metal products	5.0	5.7	1.01
Farming producer goods	6.6	8.5	1.02
Cars, motorcycles and appliances	0.9	4.1	1.03
Cars	0.9	4.5	1.04
Energy products	5.1	9.7	1.05
Petroleum and products	5.8	8.7	1.03
Coal and products	1.2	17.7	1.18
Recycling industry	0.8	6.3	1.06
Handmade fiber, clothing, shoes, and hats	12.4	18.1	1.06
Building materials	2.9	10.8	1.08
Metals, electric power and chemicals	3.7	11.6	1.08
Artifacts	12.1	22.2	1.11
Daily miscellaneous products	1.7	12.4	1.11
Daily merchandise	4.1	16.1	1.13
Medicines and medical appliances	1.7	14.7	1.14
Food, beverages, tobacco and other households goods	2.7	15.9	1.14
Food, edible oil	10.3	3.9	0.94
Tobacco products	0.3	17.8	1.19
Timber	3.4	16.9	1.14
Products not classified elsewhere	21.6	36.1	1.16
Total	5.5	11.7	1.06

Source: Calculated from *Almanac of China's Domestic Trade*, 1999.

According to Table 2.4, by 1998 some pillar industry products, such as 'machinery and electrical equipment', were not well protected from import competition. The car industry enjoyed effective protection as its import ratio did not exceed 1 per cent, while the wholesalers had a sales margin of 4.5 per cent. This level of protection, however, was much lower than many other types of merchandise. 'Tobacco products' received the most effective protection, followed by 'timber' and 'medicines and medical appliances'. High profit margins and low import ratios indicate huge rents associated with protection. Media reports on smuggling cases seem to be consistent with this indication.

Investment and Trade Structures

Overall, changes in China's economic structure have been largely in line with the industrial policies in the past decade. For instance, in the first half of the 1990s, the three pillar manufacturing sub-sectors, namely 'special purpose equipment', 'electronics and telecommunications', and 'instruments, meters and office equipment' all grew faster than the average in gross output value, fixed assets increment, and sales (Lu and Tang, 1997, pp. 76–77).

Table 2.5: Percentage Composition of Contracted FDI (1988–98)

Shares	1988	1990	1992	1994	1996	1998
Farming, forestry, fishery	3.94	1.85	1.17	1.18	1.55	2.31
Mining and quarrying	0.00	0.00	0.00	0.00	0.00	1.64
Manufacturing	75.92	84.43	56.20	53.10	68.90	59.17
Construction	2.24	2.75	3.16	2.89	2.73	3.36
Prospecting & Water	0.03	0.01	0.00	0.06	0.02	0.00
Transport, storage, telecom	1.72	0.55	2.66	2.46	2.18	4.42
Shares	1988	1990	1992	1994	1996	1998
Commerce & catering	1.21	1.62	2.48	4.74	3.20	2.52
Real estate, utilities & services	10.01	6.86	31.11	28.86	17.54	22.32
Healthcare and social welfare	0.10	0.58	0.68	2.39	0.48	0.27
Shares	1988	1990	1992	1994	1996	1998
Education & culture	0.84	0.08	0.17	0.74	0.23	0.04
Science & technology	0.14	0.48	0.11	0.33	0.24	0.00
Finance & insurance	0.22	0.00	0.01	0.53	0.00	0.00
Other	3.62	0.80	2.25	2.72	2.92	3.66
Total	100	100	100	100	100	100

Sources: Almanac of China's Foreign Economic Relations, various issues

Table 2.5 shows structural changes in foreign direct investment. The share of FDI hosted by the manufacturing sector varied from 45 per cent to 85 per cent over the period. Starting in 1992 the share of investment in 'construction' and 'real estate and public utilities' increased significantly. Another fast growing sector was 'Transportation, storage, post & telecommunications'. These changes are fairly compatible with the industrial policy guidelines.

In terms of creating comparative advantage in certain industries, China's industrial policy has been very successful. The share of exports of goods and services in China's GDP rose from 6 per cent to over 20 per cent during 1980–98. China's merchandise trade balance with the rest of the world moved towards surplus in 1990 and grew to over US$ 43 billion in 1998. The composition of trade shifted drastically from primary products to manufactures, which today account for about 90 per cent of Chinese exports and 80 per cent of imports (Figure 2.1). As one of the world's top ten trading economies, China now contributes roughly one fifth of the US trade deficit, thereby matching another major source of the US trade imbalance, that is, Japan.

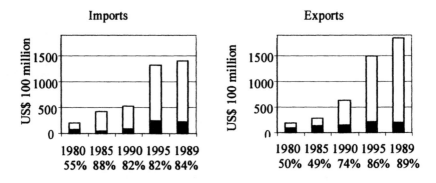

Note: The percentage refers to the share of manufactured goods.

Source: China Statistical Yearbook, various issues.

Figure 2.1: Changes in the Structure of Trade

PROSPECTS AFTER ACCESSION TO WTO

China's industrial policy regime inherited some legacies from the previously centrally planned economy (such as the first, second and third instruments in Table 2.2). As China further restructures its state-owned enterprises and develops its non-state sectors, the relative importance of those instruments associated with administrative measures and central planning is expected to diminish further or to be relevant only to the provision of public goods and services.

With China's accession to the WTO, many of the elements that form the foundation of this industrial policy regime will have to be dismantled or phased out in about five years. Most of the trade barriers are expected to be further lowered or removed. Foreign-funded enterprises will have a better chance to gain 'national treatment'. In its 1999 deal with the US on WTO accession, China committed itself to phase out the remaining import quotas, generally by 2002, but no later than 2005.[13] With lower trade barriers, we can expect that the fifth instrument in Table 2.2, that is, trade protection, will be circumvented significantly.

An indispensable part of China's WTO deals with the European Union and the US is the commitment to open the banking and financial sectors to foreign financial institutions. In particular, foreign banks will be able to conduct local currency business with Chinese enterprises starting two years after accession. From five years after accession, foreign banks will be able to conduct local currency business with Chinese individuals. Foreign banks will have the same rights (national treatment) as Chinese banks within designated geographic areas. Both geographic and customer restrictions will be removed in five years.[14] Competition from the foreign banks in local currency business is set to end the monopoly of the state-owned commercial banks and restrict their role to implementing industrial policy through industry-oriented discriminatory lending. A more developed financial market is also meant to weaken the fourth instrument for industrial policy in Table 2.2, that is, the privileged financing for local governments or state enterprises in pursuing state priority projects.

As for the sixth instrument, accession to the WTO may remove some of the restrictions specified in the existing Guiding Catalogue of Industries for Foreign Investment. For instance, in its 1999 deal with the US on WTO accession, China made commitments to phase out most restrictions in a broad range of service sectors, including distribution, banking, insurance, telecommunications, professional services such as accountancy and legal consulting, business and computer related services, motion pictures and video and sound recording services. It is highly plausible that China will revise rather than abandon these catalogues for guiding foreign investment after its WTO accession.

Those industrial policy instruments which do not directly conflict with the WTO rules may remain. Some of these may become more active and important. For instance, favorable financing for certain projects can still be provided by state-owned policy banks that are virtually funded from the state budget. The preferential tax rates for certain industries and the licensing and approval of investment projects may apply to both indigenous and foreign firms as well. Thus instruments seven and eight will continue to be relevant and important.

However, domestic demand for such preferential policies may not be as strong as before since the WTO's 'national treatment' principle will allow these benefits to be shared by foreign firms and thus will reduce their attractiveness to indigenous companies. In such a context, it will be more difficult to carry out industrial policies specially designed to nurture and protect indigenous firms in industries promoted by state policy.

NOTES

1. *Documents of the Twelfth National Congress of the Communist Party of China*, Beijing: People's Press, 1982
2. *Zhongguo Jingji Nianjian* (Almanac of China's Economy) 1990, pp. I: 55–59.
3. *Renmin Ribao* (People's Daily), Beijing, 23 June 1994.
4. Xinhua News Agency Daily Report, 20 March 1996.
5. *China Economic News*, Beijing, 3 May 1999.
6. Lu and Tang (1997), pp. 72–73.
7. Based on the same principle, the state has also promulgated a list of forbidden projects.
8. State Council, 'The Provisional Regulation on the PRC's Direction-Adjustment Tax on Fixed Capital Investment' (16 April 1991), Zhang and Wu (1994), pp. 584–605.
9. Trade and Development Board, *Trade and Investment Guide: China*, Singapore: Arthur Andersen, 1993, p. 120.
10. *China Economic News*, Beijing, 24 July 1995.
11. *China Economic News*, Beijing, 2 March 1998.
12. The nominator and denominator are made exponential to encompass the possible negative sales margins and near-zero import ratios.
13. US State Department Summary of U.S.–China Bilateral WTO Agreement, 2 February 2000, http://www.chinapntr.gov/bilatsumm.htm.
14. US State Department Summary of U.S.–China Bilateral WTO Agreement, 2 February 2000, http://www.chinapntr.gov/bilatsumm.htm.

REFERENCES

Charnes, A., W. W. Cooper, and E. Rhodes (1978), 'Measuring the efficiency of decision making units'. *European Journal of Operational Research*, 2(5): 429–444.

Chung-Hua Institute for Economic Research (CHIER) (1995), *A Study on the Status of Mainland Industrial Policy and Development* [Research Report 8406-1-185: 0105186(2)]. Taipei: Chung-Hua Institute for Economic Research.

Guo Biao Yang (1998), 'Barriers to entry and industrial performance in China'. *International Review of Applied Economics*, 12(1), 39–51.

Jiang, Xiaojuan (1996), *Industrial Policy in the Transition Period: an Analysis of the Chinese Experience*. Shanghai: San Lian Bookstore.

Johnson, Chalmers (1984), 'Introduction: the idea of industrial policy'. In Johnson C. ed., *The Industrial Policy Debate*. San Francisco: Institute for Contemporary Studies.

Liu, Aying, Shujie Yao, and Zongyi Zhang (1999), 'Economic growth and structural changes in employment and investment in China, 1985–1994'. *Economics of Planning* 32: 171–190.

Lu, Ding and Zhimin Tang (1997), *State Intervention and Business in China: the Role of Preferential Policies*. Cheltenham, UK and Lyme, US: Edward Elgar.

Takahashi, Takuma (1997), 'Industrial policies in developed and developing economies from the perspective of East Asian experience'. In Masuyama, S., Vandenbrink, D. and S. Y. Chia, eds., *Industrial Policies in East Asia.* Tokyo: Club Foundation for Global Studies.

Wade, Robert (1990), *Governing the Market: Economic Theory and the Role of Government in East Asian Industrialization.* Princeton: Princeton University Press.

Zhang, Lianshun and Wu Fang (eds) (1994), *A Practical Guide to New Tax Laws* (in Chinese). Beijing: China Development Publishing House.

Zhang, Shuguang, Zhang Yansheng, and Wan Zhongxin (1998), *Measuring the Costs of Protection in China.* Washington: Institute for International Economics.

Zhang, X. and G. Long (1997), 'China's industrial policies in the process of marketization'. In Masuyama, S., Vandenbrink, D. and S. Y. Chia, eds, *Industrial Policies in East Asia.* Tokyo: Club Foundation for Global Studies.

3. The Future of the Agricultural Sector

D. Gale Johnson

I want to accomplish two major objectives. The first is to evaluate the short-term effects of WTO accession on China's agriculture – the effects over the next five years or so. The second is to address the much more significant economic adjustments that economic growth will impose on agriculture and the rural sector over the coming decades. As I hope to show it is the second that has far more serious implications for the rural sector than joining the WTO. Facilitating the adjustment will require major policy changes and positive support from governmental agencies.

How will Chinese agriculture change if China enters the WTO? There is not a simple answer to that question since China's accession to the World Trade Organization would affect its agriculture in several different ways. If WTO accession leads to more competitive markets for inputs – fertilizers, pesticides, seeds and machinery – and improved access to credit, farm people will benefit directly. Unfortunately entry is unlikely to lead to significant improvements in the markets for labor and land. Restraints on the migration of labor from rural to urban areas could still be maintained and, as long as land is collectively owned, it is uncertain that efficient and competitive markets will emerge for the rental or sale of land use rights or that an effective rural credit system will emerge. Continued imperfections in these factor markets will significantly limit the ability of agriculture to adjust to changes that must occur over the next several decades if rural people are to fully participate in the benefits of economic growth.

Compared to the adjustments required by economic growth, adjustments due to the WTO will be minor. Economic growth requires that employment in agriculture decline – first as a share of national employment, and then absolutely. This decline must occur if rural people are to share in the gains from economic growth. China has already undergone substantial adjustments in its labor force. As of the early 1950s about 85 per cent of its labor force was engaged in agriculture, defined as farming (crop production) and animal husbandry. Currently agriculture accounts for no more than 45 per cent of national employment (Johnson 2000).

Why must agricultural employment decline? There are two primary reasons. First, the income elasticity of demand for farm output is less than one. Since the income elasticity of demand for all products and services of an economy equals one, the income elasticity of demand for non-farm output is greater than one. At the level of per capita income in China it is probable that the income elasticity of demand for non-farm products and services is at least twice that of farm products and this difference will increase as real per capita incomes increase. This means that demand growth due to real per capita income growth will be at least twice as great for non-farm as for farm output. Second, productivity improvement increases agriculture's capacity to increase output. Experience has indicated that productivity improvement in agriculture, either in terms of total factor productivity or labor productivity, has been equal to or greater than in non-agriculture (Johnson 1991). Thus, if there were no decline the share of the nation's labor in agriculture, as well as in the share of total inputs, agricultural output would grow more rapidly than demand, resulting in a decline in real output prices and a fall in the relative return 'to farm labor with a further widening of the income differential between rural and urban workers.

I have projected that agriculture's share of national employment will decline to about 10 per cent by 2030 (Johnson 2000). Much of the labor adjustment that has already occurred has been through the rapid growth of non-farm employment in rural areas. This growth has been encouraged by limitations on rural urban migration and the inefficiencies in urban enterprises that provided a profitable opening for small-scale labor intensive enterprises in rural areas. How much of the transfer will occur through growth of jobs in rural areas or by migration to urban areas will depend to a large extent on national policies.

Can the past rapid growth of rural non-farm employment continue? Cities exist for a reason, namely that they provide for the advantages of agglomeration and specialization in production. If the economy of China becomes more open and competitive, it is unlikely that rural non-farm employment will continue to grow at the rapid rate achieved since 1985 – an annual rate of 14.5 per cent (SSB 1995, 1999). The labor adjustment problem of rural China will not be restricted to agriculture, but will involve the entire rural community. If agriculture's share of national employment is to decline to 10 per cent by 2030, given the prospective growth of China's labor force, the annual creation of 15 million new non-farm jobs between now and 2030 will be required (Johnson 2000). This represents a huge task, but not an impossible one. Since 1978 the estimated annual increase in non-farm employment in China has been 12.5 million, with an average total labor force less than 80 per cent of the current labor force (SSB 1999).

REDUCTION IN TRADE BARRIERS

In its negotiations with the United States and other countries, China has agreed to substantial reductions in tariffs while reducing the role of state trading by permitting some agricultural imports by private traders. Tariff rates on a wide range of farm commodities will be reduced from as much as 100 per cent to a range of 3 to 20 per cent. Under a state trading system stated tariff rates mean little. China has agreed not to use export subsidies, even though many other nations now members of the WTO retain that right, including the United States.

China has adopted an innovation of the Uruguay Round, namely the tariff rate quota (TRQ). Tariff rate quotas are to be applied to soybean oil, wheat, corn and rice. For imports within the quota, the tariff rates are to be very low, no more than 3 per cent for grains and 9 per cent for soybean oil. The tariffs for above quota deliveries will be 65 to 77 per cent. This may sound high, but the rate is modest compared to most of the tariffs applied in similar cases by Canada, the European Union and the United States.[1] The sum of the tariff rate grain quotas for the first year of accession is 14.4 million tons and in the fifth year, 21.8 million; there are specific quota limits for each major grain (wheat, maize and rice); there is no tariff rate quota for barley and the barley tariff will be reduced to 9 per cent. There is a TRQ for soybean oil but not for soybeans and the tariff rate on soybeans was set at 3 per cent. The quota for soybean oil starts at 1.7 million tons and increases to 3.2 million tons. The within quota tariff for soybean oil is 9 per cent.

If these tariffs, tariff rate quotas and procedures for reducing state trading are adhered to, China would have significantly lower barriers to trade for agricultural products than the United States and the European Union.

A SHORT RUN ASSESSMENT

What are likely to be the short run consequences if the above represents China's commitments for agricultural trade? The tariff rate quota system will prevent China from importing large amounts of wheat and/or maize over the next five years and probably longer. China will not be inundated with grain imports.[2] The general expectation, with which I agree, is that China will continue to export rice. Since China is committed not to use export subsidies, the price guarantees, if retained, cannot exceed the import prices for the grains without very adverse consequences. If China produces more of any grain than is needed to meet domestic demand, it must either export the grain or add it to its already burdensome stocks and since it cannot use export subsidies, the domestic price must be reduced to world market levels. If China produces enough grain to meet domestic demand and neither needs to import or export, domestic prices cannot exceed the import prices by more than 3 per cent without resulting in imports up to the tariff quota levels. If the imports were allowed to add to the domestic supply, this would put downward pressure on farm prices.

It appears that the 1999 negotiated price for wheat was approximately the same as the import price in the final months of 1999, while the fixed price was somewhat higher. Maize prices in 1999 were higher than import prices by a margin of about 15 per cent. If the current price guarantees are maintained, China would import up to the limit of the tariff rate quota for maize and possibly for wheat. The world market price for maize, as for wheat, has declined significantly from 1997 and is now at its lowest real level for more than a century.

The government should give serious consideration to abandoning the current price guarantee system and using the savings in government expenditures to make direct payments to farmers. If the annual cost of the program, including the storage costs, equals 50 billion yuan, then it would be possible to make a direct payment to farmers of 30 yuan per mu of land devoted to grain for, say, the average planted area of 1995 to 1999. This would provide an average subsidy of about 200 yuan per farm household, a subsidy acceptable under the WTO subsidy provisions. The subsidy could be higher than this without violating WTO rules. Due to the tariff rate quotas, China's farmers will not face a flood of imports during the first five years. With a tariff on above quota deliveries of 65 to 77 per cent, domestic prices would be significantly above world prices once imports of wheat and maize reached quite modest levels.[3]

Soybean production is likely to be adversely affected. The only protection for soybeans will be a 3 per cent tariff. There is no tariff rate quota for soybeans though there is one for soybean oil. Thus whatever protection will exist for soybeans will go to processors, not to producers. Maize is the primary crop that competes for resources with soybeans and it is protected by the tariff rate quota and its high tariff for all imports in excess of the quota. If maize imports should exceed the tariff quota, soybeans will be at an enormous competitive disadvantage – maize prices could go to 65 or more per cent above the import price and soybeans would be at the import price. These prices would encourage maize production and discourage soybean production. I consider the differential treatment of soybeans and maize a major flaw in the agreement and I assume that the US negotiators exercised enormous pressure on this point.

There is the added problem that the domestic soybean prices in late 1999 were from 15 to 25 per cent above the very low world market prices. Consequently it appears that soybean prices are more distorted than are the grain prices and this will have an added impact on domestic production. Whatever the merits or demerits of protection may be, it is a serious mistake not to give products that directly compete for resources the same level of protection.

While I believe that with existing stocks, if properly managed, domestic supply of grain will equal domestic demand at world market prices for several years (with imports no larger than permitted by TRQs), it is not clear what the situation would be in the longer run. And it is to this point that I now turn.

CHINA'S GRAIN TRADE

China is moving toward liberal trade in farm products, especially the grains, at a very unfortunate time. World market prices for grain, especially wheat and maize, are at historically low real levels. Will there be some recovery over the next five years? My expectation is that there may be some recovery, but not very much. The long run trend is for continuing declines in real international grain prices and there are likely to be only temporary increases in the recent very low prices in international markets.[4]

What is the basis for even a temporary reversal of the trend? Economic recovery in Asia will have some positive effect on grain prices. Perhaps over the next three or four years there will be a world grain crop that falls below the recent relatively high levels. While the current low prices of grain may not result in a decline in world grain production they may delay further output increases. These are very tentative rationalizations of the conclusion that there may be increases in real world grain prices. But, at best, these factors might result in an increase in world grain prices of 10 per cent, meaning that China might still be faced with the need to lower real maize prices by as much as 10 per cent to prevent modest imports over the next five years.

But if real grain prices are at international levels, will China's farmers produce grain in amounts sufficient to meet most or all of domestic demand? Obviously, we can't be sure of the outcome, but it is certain that it must be recognized that there has to be a substantial – no, a huge – increase in the productivity of agricultural resources in the years ahead. The increases must be continuous. The government should undertake actions to ensure that such productivity improvement actually occurs. If such actions are not undertaken, the adverse consequences for rural people will be severe.

PRODUCTIVITY INCREASES FOR LAND AND LABOR

Currently Chinese agriculture is competitive in world markets. The value of exports exceeds the value of imports of agricultural products. But let me be blunt: A major reason why China's agriculture is competitive is because of the very low return to the labor provided by competent and progressive farmers, farmers who have made revolutionary changes in agriculture over the past two decades. Given the current policies and organization of agriculture, its agriculture would not be competitive if the return to farm labor were equal to even half the return to urban labor rather than approximately a third as much. In other words, agriculture can compete because of the numerous policies that have created such a huge differential between the returns for rural and urban workers. Limitations on migration and concentration of public investment in urban areas have created a huge earnings differential.

Research by knowledgeable scholars makes it clear that an important factor in China's ability to produce enough grain to meet most of domestic demand at reasonable prices depends on a significant increase in support for agricultural research (Huang and Chen 1999; Huang, Rozelle, and Rosengrant 1999).[5]

Important as increased investment in agricultural research may be, it is only part of what is required to keep China's agriculture competitive. And it is the easiest part. Both labor and land productivity must be increased rapidly. But contrary to the general perception that limitations in the amount of cropland and difficulties in increasing land productivity will be limiting factors in China's ability to feed itself, the successful integration of agriculture into world markets will be far more dependent on achieving substantial increases in labor productivity. Increases in labor productivity will need to be much greater than in land productivity. Over the next several decades there has to be a very substantial reduction in agricultural employment if farm people are to share in economic growth. Farm employment is likely to decline by at least 60 per cent over the next three decades and, hopefully, even more (Johnson 2000). And that decline, if China is to continue to produce most or all of its grain and other foods, must be accompanied by large increases in labor productivity, increases of the order of 500 per cent or more. This is much greater than the increase in land productivity that will be required to meet demand, which might be of the order of 100 to 150 per cent over the same period of time. The amount of cropland will change very little over the next three decades. During the latter half of the 20th century the increases in labor productivity were much greater than in land productivity in the developed nations undergoing significant economic growth. It is unfortunate that most agricultural research is devoted to increasing land productivity, neglecting labor productivity.

Between 1950 and 1980 farm employment in the United States, Japan and Denmark declined by 65 to 70 per cent while labor productivity increased by 400 to 500 per cent (Hayami and Ruttan 1985). In the same countries land productivity increased by 80 to 135 per cent. So it can be done. But as I will argue, China faces a number of problems that did not exist in these countries and that may require significant changes in the organization of China's agriculture. Research is necessary but not sufficient to serve as the basis for the required productivity improvement, especially for labor. Labor productivity growth depends not only on new knowledge and equipment but also on creating a policy framework that will provide the incentives and possibilities for increasing labor productivity as farm employment declines. If this is not done, most of China's agriculture will not be competitive in world markets.

Labor productivity in China's agriculture has improved significantly in the past 20 years, in large part by jointly increasing the productivity of land and labor through the use of chemical inputs – fertilizer and pesticides – and improved seeds. While there is room for further increases in labor productivity through this route, the large increases required over the next decades will come through finding direct substitutes for labor, primarily with machinery,[6] and by significantly increasing the average years of schooling of the rural labor force. It is clear that over time the increase in labor productivity must be much greater than the increase in land productivity if China is to be approximately self-sufficient in grain and if farmers are to share in economic growth. The yields of grains per hectare are much closer to those in, say, the major grain producers in the industrial countries than is the average output per labor input. China's grain yields range from about 75 per cent (corn) to a quarter higher (wheat) than in the United States, with rice yields being about the same. Compared to Europe the United States does not have a high yield for wheat, though its corn and rice yields are among the highest in the world.

The overwhelming importance of finding substitutes for labor and increasing the productivity of labor is indicated by current labor inputs per ton of grains and soybeans. For rice, wheat and maize the labor input ranges from 52 to 58 days per ton (Huang and Chen 1999). Huang and Chen (1999) estimate that the value of the labor input accounts for 31 per cent of value of a ton of rice.[7] A ton of rice required 59 days of labor, indicating that the value of a day of labor in the production of rice was nine yuan. A similar calculation for the United States, using the hired wage, is approximately $50. This is an enormous difference in the productivity of labor and it is a difference that must be reduced substantially over the next several decades if both urban and rural citizens of China are to share equitably in future economic growth.

SIZE OF FARM OPERATING UNITS

A factor affecting increasing farm labor productivity over the next three decades will be the size of farm operating units. A realistic appraisal indicates that even if farm employment is reduced to 10 per cent of the total labor force by 2030, farms will still be very small. There are two primary reasons. First, most farms will be part time farms. For its real per capita income level China currently has a very large percentage of its rural labor force engaged in rural non-farm employment and a high percentage of part time farms now. This has been the result of restrictions on migration over the past four decades and it will continue to influence the structure of farms for decades to come. Even if all legal restraints on rural to urban migration were removed tomorrow, it would take decades before the rural population could be reduced to a third of the total population.

Second, even when farm employment is 10 per cent of the total, farm employment will be about 100 million. If all farms were full time and employed one worker and there were 130 million hectares of cropland, the average farm would have 1.3 hectares of cropland. But if the majority of farms are part time, there will be many more than 100 million farm units – perhaps not too many less than the 235 million that now exist.

The outcome that I am describing is very similar to what has occurred in East Asia – Japan, South Korea and Taiwan. The number of farms has decreased very little over the past four or five decades; nearly all farms are part time and farm sizes average about a hectare. The size of farm projected for 2030 is much too small to permit the majority of farmers to own the farm machinery required if labor productivity is to increase fivefold over the next three decades. In addition, most farm units, tiny as they are, now consist of several plots of land, which makes low cost mechanization difficult.

It is highly certain that farm sizes will remain very small, perhaps not much larger than they now are, given that population will continue to grow and rural to urban migration of entire households or families will remain at moderate level for a long time.[8] It will be many years before there are many fewer than 235 million farm households.

HOW TO INCREASE LABOR PRODUCTIVITY

The productivity of labor in agriculture (and in the rural sector generally) is very low relative to urban labor in China. This has resulted not only from restrictions on migration over the past four decades but to discriminatory treatment of rural areas in terms of investment in human capital – in the limited access to primary and secondary schools. Much of the public investment in infrastructure has also occurred in urban areas. The urban rural per capita income difference is among the largest in the world and is in excess of three times, approaching four times when all the subsidies given to urban workers and the extra taxes and charges imposed on farmers are counted. The question that must be faced is whether the current organization of farming will facilitate the speedy growth of labor productivity. I fear the answer is in the negative.

Labor productivity is the ratio of output per unit of labor. Labor productivity increases as output per unit of land increases since many of the functions of labor are related to the amount of land involved, rather than to the amount of output per unit of land. Roughly speaking, the amount of labor used for land preparation, seeding, and weeding is a function of area, not yield. So if yield per unit of land doubles, the productivity of labor devoted to these activities will nearly double as well. A large share of the increased labor productivity of the past two decades has been due to higher land yields, which increased by 80 per cent between 1978 and 1998 for grain while cotton, oil bearing crops. and sugar yields increased even more (SSB 1999).

The starting point for any discussion of future gains in agricultural labor productivity is that the average amount of land per farm will remain small; it is unlikely to exceed 1 hectare before mid-century. If prices of farm products are at or near international market prices, this is far too small a farm unit to permit the majority of farmers to own sufficient machinery to increase labor productivity by 400 or 500 per cent in the next three decades. An alternative method of providing machinery services to replace labor services must be found and made available.

An alternative approach does exist and exists in Taiwan. With the rapid economic growth that has occurred since the mid-1960s there has been very little increase in the average size of farms. The large majority of Taiwan's farms are part time and while farm workers have declined from 41 per cent of the total workers in 1968 to 10 per cent in 1997, the number of farms has declined by less than 10 per cent. The average size of farm is now 1.1 hectares, not much larger than in 1967. Taiwan's rural people have adjusted to economic growth, not by large-scale migration to urban areas but by many people remaining in the villages and continuing to operate their farms. This was made possible by the availability of non-farm jobs near their villages and an infrastructure that allowed them to commute to their jobs.

Even though the farms have remained very small, labor productivity has increased significantly since the late 1960s. Between 1967 and 1997, labor productivity increased by 400 per cent, an annual rate of 4.3 per cent.[9] The increased productivity of farm labor has been greatly facilitated by the development of custom farming – a system in which one farmer will undertake most of the field operations for crops for several other farmers, perhaps ten or more. In the early 1990s it was estimated that approximately 98 per cent of all the field work involved in rice production was mechanized and that 80 per cent was by custom work – done by one farmer for several others (Johnson and Hou 1993, p. 26).[10] The labor used per hectare of rice in Taiwan in 1970 was more than 100 days; this was reduced to about 30 days by 1990 and further to 20 days in 1998. In the mid-1990s labor used per hectare of rice was about 300 days on the mainland (Huang and Chen 1999). This difference in labor used is indicative of the magnitude of the task that lies ahead in China's agricultural labor adjustment.

Such a system of custom work could become widespread in the People's Republic and I assume that in many villages it already exists. But the labor use data imply that custom farming or machinery services for hire is still quite limited. Such custom operations would be greatly facilitated, as would any use of machinery, if each farm operating unit consisted of only one plot. The primary reason for the existence of a large number of plots for such small farms was to reduce risks. The risks were of several kinds – poor land quality, a long distance from the village, and sandy soil that would yield poorly in a dry year. Having seven or eight plots reduced such risks. But times have changed since the original allocations or the efforts at plot consolidations in the late 1980s – farmers now have much higher incomes, often including income from non-farm sources not related to the vagaries of farming. Much more is now known about the quality and yield characteristics of the land than was known 20 years ago and there would be more time to adjust the amount of land to the variations in quality than when the original allocations were hurriedly made. If there were a competitive market in land use rights in every village, land consolidation could occur by sales and trades among the farmers.[11] Unfortunately, such markets do not yet exist in more than a few villages, making it difficult for farmers to carry out the consolidations by themselves.

What has been achieved in Taiwan was what was attempted, briefly, in some provinces in China – the provision of socialized services to individual farmers at the same time the effort was made to consolidate the plots in some provinces. But these efforts failed, apparently because of resistance to the compulsion that was involved. But if the machinery services were provided by farmers who are well known to the villagers, the reception is likely to be very different.

Why hasn't such a system arisen in majority of the villages? The provision of the custom services needs to be encouraged by the government, perhaps even with some subsidies in the early years. Credit needs to be readily available to farmers who wish to acquire machinery to provide custom crop services. The current credit system is inadequate, in part because land is not available as collateral for loans. Land use rights could serve as collateral if they were secure for an extended number of years and if there were active markets for buying and selling the rights.

It may well be that an educational effort is required to convince village and township officials that it is in their interest to support the creation of custom services. Without such services it is unlikely that the farms in any area will be able to compete in a global market with a liberal trade regime for agriculture. It must be made clear to everyone that farm employment has to decline at a rapid rate for the next several decades if farm people are to share in economic growth and the villages are to prosper. Extension services should make training available for farmers who wish to undertake custom services, including management advice concerning investments and necessary charges if the services are to be profitable.

CONCLUDING COMMENT

China's agriculture must change rapidly over the next three decades if food output is to continue to grow while the number of farm workers is reduced by 60 per cent or even more. Farmers will need assistance from the other sectors of the economy to achieve these two objectives. The central government has an important role – increase support of agricultural research, carefully examine the policies that may inhibit adjustment and introduce policies to facilitate the substitution of other inputs for labor. Local governments must understand that agriculture must have a diminished role if farmers are to share in economic growth and must be willing to assist in the process rather than impede it. Credit institutions must facilitate the enormous increase in capital that will be required to increase the productivity of workers.

A necessary condition for farmers to fully share in economic growth is the existence of a growing number of non-farm jobs for those who leave farming. These jobs can be either in urban or rural areas but they must exist if the large increase in labor productivity in agriculture is to benefit rural residents. Otherwise the increase in labor productivity will reduce the demand for farm labor, lower its return and farmers will lose from the higher labor productivity. All levels of government need to review their laws and regulations that might inhibit the development of rural non-farm jobs and eliminate or modify those that could adversely effect the creation of such jobs.[12]

NOTES

1. In a summary of the negotiations between China and the United States on agriculture, the US Office of the Trade Representative (USTR) had the temerity to state that in excess of the tariff quotas 'imports above that level quota, for example, was 197 per cent while it was 144 per cent for dairy products' (Ingco 1996). If the Chinese rates are high, what adjective would the USTR apply to those of the United States? The European Union had even higher rates – 297 per cent for sugar and 288 per cent for dairy products – and Canada was not far behind with rates of 226 for poultry and 288 for dairy (Ingco 1996).
2. This conclusion assumes that domestic grain prices are permitted to rise to the level of the import price plus the above quota tariff. This would result in prices much higher in real terms than any recent prices and would significantly reduce consumption and, if maintained, increase production, thus limiting imports. However I see nothing in the agreement that requires China to equate domestic prices with import prices plus the tariff.
3. The tariff rate quotas for wheat range from 7.3 to 9.3 million tons and for maize from 4.5 to 7.2 million tons. Thus if the imports were at the maximum for each, imports would only be 7 per cent of the combined production of the two grains and less than 4 per cent of all grains (SSB 1999). In 1995 China imported 11 million tons of wheat and 5 million tons of maize (SSB 1997).
4. It is not only farmers in China that may face difficulties if their domestic prices reflect import or export prices. Farmers in countries in which domestic prices reflect world market prices are finding it very difficult to produce wheat and maize, and soybeans as well, at the current prices. As indicated, these prices are very low and if they continue for an extended period of

time, China may well find it difficult to produce as much maize and soybeans as it has produced in recent years. But this is likely to be true in other countries as well. The projections of future grain production in China under free trade assumed prices significantly higher than those that now exist. What few people realize is that the inflation adjusted international grain prices, on average, had fallen by 40 per cent between 1960 and 1997 and wheat and maize have declined even further in the past two years.

5. The two studies refer to different time periods – Huang and Chen project trade to 2005, while the other study projects to 2010 and 2020. Neither projects trade as it might be under the terms of China's agreement with the United States but each assumes free trade. Each study assumes a continuation of current policies and compares supply and demand under the current policy framework and free trade. In both the continuation of current policies and free trade it is assumed that world market prices would decline.

   Huang and Chen estimate that in 2005 China would import about 18 million tons of wheat and maize under the continuation of present policies and somewhat more than 60 million tons under free trade (Huang and Chen 1999, p. 39). However, if expenditures on agricultural research were increased significantly, China would be self-sufficient in wheat and maize imports would be reduced significantly. Huang, Rozelle and Rosengrant (1999) project that, with continuation of current policies with free trade, by 2020 China would be expected to import about 40 million tons of grain, principally maize. However, they project that with a high rate of investment in research and irrigation China could be a net exporter of grains by 2020. In both studies it is projected that China will be a net exporter of rice and that it will continue to be a net exporter, in value terms, of all agricultural products under most scenarios.

6. Only a rough approximation of the increase in the average productivity of farm labor for the period since 1978 is possible. The only overall index of agricultural output is the index of the gross output value of farming, forestry, animal husbandry and fishing. This index double-counts the farm produced feed that is used in livestock production. The estimate of real gross domestic product is for primary industry which is not strictly agriculture – at a minimum, it includes forestry and fishing in addition to what is generally considered agriculture. And there are problems with the measurement of employment. I estimate that between 1978 and 1998 the average product of farm labor increased in the range of 130 to 160 per cent, a quite respectable increase. This is a larger increase than occurred in the United States from 1930 to the late 1940s (Hecht and Barton 1950, p. 32).

7. The price of a ton of rice in 1996–1997 was 1504 yuan.

8. Legal restraint on rural to urban migration is not the only factor limiting migration.Other factors limiting migration currently are probably as important – the low level of education of much of the rural population, the limited supply of urban housing for low income workers and their families, and the unwillingness of rural people to break their ties with their villages until the employment they obtain provides social security, access to health care, and high enough wages to permit obtaining housing in urban areas. They also need access to public schools on the same basis as existing urban residents. Thus it is likely that for a long time to come individual household members will constitute the majority of the migrants to cities rather than entire households or families. This is not to say that no families will move, but it will be a long time before they become the majority of migrants. This is an important issue because it will mean that there will be relatively little enlargement of farm operating units unless there is developed a secure and competitive land rental market.

9. For both output and employment, the data refer to agriculture, forestry and fishing.

10. If consolidation were to occur in a market framework, it would require that the property rights in the land use rights be clearly defined and properly recorded, with an appropriate document for each plot of land now existing. In such a market, the function of local authorities would be limited to recording the transactions and issuing appropriate documents verifying the transactions. A market would be greatly inhibited if the local authorities could intervene to prevent transactions from occurring. It would be a daunting task to limit the roles of local officials to this function related to land in the 700 000 villages that exist in China.

11. A recent visit to a village in Hebei Province elicited the comment that the recent land law was designed to limit the transfer of land from agricultural to non-agricultural use. The administration of this law was seriously limiting the availability of land on which to create new non-farm enterprises in the countryside. This law, which was promulgated at a time it was believed China faced grain shortages and had too little land, is now interfering with the necessary transfer of labor out of agriculture. This law, as many others, should be reviewed and changes should be made to facilitate the creation of non-farm jobs rather than to hinder their development.

REFERENCES

Hayami, Yujiro and Vernon W. Ruttan (1985), *Agricultural Development: An International Perspective*. Baltimore: Johns Hopkins University Press.

Hecht, Reuben W. and Glen T. Barton (1950),'Gains in Productivity of Farm Labor', Technical Bulletin No. 1020. Washington: United States Department of Agriculture.

Huang, Jikun and Chunlai Chen (1999), 'Effects of Trade Liberalization on Agriculture in China: Commodity Aspects', Working Paper No. 43. Bogor, Indonesia: CGPRT Centre.

Huang, Jikun, Scott Rozelle and Mark W. Rosegrant (1999), 'China's Food Economy to the Twenty-first Century: Supply, Demand, and Trade', *Economic Development and Cultural Change*, 47(4), 737–766.

Ingco, Merlinda D. (1996), 'Tariffication in the Uruguay Round: How Much Liberalization?'. *The World Economy*, 19(4), 425–446.

Johnson, D. Gale (1991), *World Agriculture in Disarray,* Second edition. London: Macmillan.

—(2000), 'Agricultural Adjustment in China: Problems and Prospects', *Population and Development Review*, 26(02), 319–334.

Johnson, D. Gale and Chi-ming Hou (1993), *Agricultural Policy and US – Taiwan Trade*. Washington, D.C.: AEI Press.

State Statistical Bureau (SSB 1995, 1997, 1999), *China Statistical Yearbook*. Beijing: China Statistics Press.

4. Telecommunications: Moving Towards Competition

Ding Lu

Until recently, China had upheld a policy prohibiting foreign equity investment in the telecommunications service sector. To win accession to the World Trade Organization (WTO), China made crucial commitments at the turn of the century to opening the telecommunications sector to foreign competition and investment in the next few years. These commitments imply drastic changes for an industry that has been nurtured under state protection and various policy supports. To prepare for incoming foreign competition, the Chinese telecommunications sector has been undergoing a series of drastic institutional changes. These changes have far reaching implications for the market structure for this industry after China's WTO accession.

This chapter reviews these changes and analyzes the strategies taken by China's policy makers towards the opening of the telecom market. The next section overviews the contents and implications of China's commitments to opening its telecom market as part of the deals leading up to WTO accession. The section after that discusses the major concerns of China's policy makers over opening the telecom market to foreign investment and competition in the context of the sector being a privileged industry in the country's industrial policy regime. In the section after that we examine the strategic moves by China's Ministry of Information Industry (MII) in beefing up the domestic telecom players to meet the challenges of post-WTO market opening. The concluding section lays out the business prospects for foreign investors in the coming years.

THE WTO DEAL

China's imminent accession to the WTO paves the way for foreign equity investment in this sector. This will mean a change in what has been a long-standing official policy that prohibits foreign involvement in management and equity investment in the telecommunications service sector. A full statement of this official policy can be found in the announcement made by the former Ministry of Post and Telecommunications (MPT) on 25 May 1993: 'no organization, enterprise or individual outside China may engage in the management of China's broadcasting networks, special wire or wireless services, or become a shareholder in a telecommunications business'.[1] As a result of this policy, through the 1990s, China imposed some of the world's tightest restrictions on foreign investment in telecommunications services. Foreign involvement was limited to arm's length agreements, wherein foreign companies discreetly provided investment in exchange for a share of operating revenue (Hsu, 1999). Compared to China's overall policy to attract and encourage foreign direct investment (FDI) in its economy, the draconian restrictions on foreign equity investment in the telecommunications service sector were remarkable.

The Sino-US WTO accord of November 1999 was China's first official commitment to opening its telecommunications sector, both to the scope of services and to direct investment in the telecom business (Table 4.1). Signing the WTO deal binds China to the principles outlined in the WTO Basic Telecom Agreement of 1997, which stipulates that a member country must implement regulations that deter anti-competitive practices. This includes separating the roles of the telecom regulator from the dominant operator, establishing an interconnection right and instituting a telecom law.[2] Specific commitments made by China include:[3]

1. **Regulatory Principles** – China should implement the pro-competitive regulatory principles embodied in the Basic Telecommunications Agreement (including cost-based pricing, interconnection rights and independent regulatory authority) and follow technology-neutral scheduling. This implies that there will be no restrictions on the type of technology in which foreign firms can invest or use, nor will there be any limitations on owned or leased facilities.
2. **Scope of services** – China will phase out all geographic restrictions for paging and value-added services in 2 years, mobile cellular in 3–5 years and fixed line services in 6 years. China's key telecom services corridor in Beijing, Shanghai and Guangzhou, which represents approximately 75 per cent of all domestic traffic, will be opened immediately to value-added services upon accession. Foreigners will also be allowed to own gateways as long as they adhere to the cited geographical and ownership limitations.
3. **Investment** – China will allow up to 49 per cent foreign shareholding in fixed-line and mobile telecommunications businesses and up to 50 per cent in value-added, paging, and Internet service provision businesses.

The Sino-European Union accord on China's WTO entry (signed in May 2000) further accelerated the opening in mobile telephony in the two years after accession. Foreign ownership of up to 25 per cent will be allowed upon accession, 35 per cent after one year, and 49 per cent after three years. Leasing and resale of telecommunications circuits will be allowed for foreign firms in three years.[4]

Table 4.1: China's WTO Agreement Terms with the US

Sector	Maximum % foreign ownership	Geographical limitations
Value-added and Paging Services		
Upon accession	30	Beijing, Shanghai and Guangzhou
1 year after accession	49	Beijing, Shanghai, Guangzhou and 14 other cities – Chengdu, Chongqing, Dalian, Fuzhou, Hangzhou, Nanjing, Ningbo, Qingdao, Shenyang, Shenzhen, Xiamen, Xian, Taiyuan and Wuhan
2 years after accession	50	Nationwide
Mobile Services		
1 year after accession	25	Beijing, Shanghai and Guangzhou
3 years after accession	35	Beijing, Shanghai, Guangzhou and the 14 cities
5 years after accession	49	Nationwide
Fixed Line Services		
3 years after accession	25	Beijing, Shanghai and Guangzhou
5 years after accession	35	Beijing, Shanghai, Guangzhou and the 14 cities
6 years after accession	49	Nationwide
Internet Content Providers (ICP)		
Upon accession	30	Beijing, Shanghai and Guangzhou
1 year after accession	49	Beijing, Shanghai, Guangzhou and the 14 cities
2 years after accession	50	Nationwide
Internet Service Providers (ISP)		
3 years after accession	25	Beijing, Shanghai and Guangzhou
5 years after accession	35	
6 years after accession	49	Beijing, Shanghai, Guangzhou and the 14 cities Nationwide

Source: The Economist Intelligence Unit, *Telecoms & Wireless Asia*, 14 January 2000.

These commitments come as a big shock to China's telecom industry, which has enjoyed the status of a privileged sector that received strong state support. Compared to other sectors in the economy, telecommunications has been one of the most centrally planned and state-controlled industries in terms of market entry, pricing, and business organization.

RELUCTANCE TO OPENING

From the mid-1980s through the 1990s, China's telecom sector developed in
leaps and bounds (Figure 4.1 and Figure 4.2). Riding on strong state support

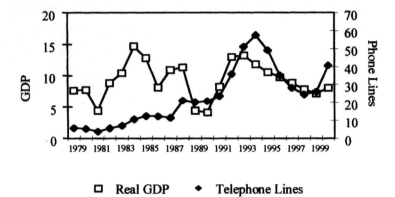

☐   Real GDP   ◆   Telephone Lines

Sources: China Statistical Yearbook and *Yearbook of China Transportation and
Communications*, various issues. Beijing: Ministry of Information Industry web site,
http://www.mii.gov.cn/.

Figure 4.1: Hyper Growth of China's GDP and Telephone Lines

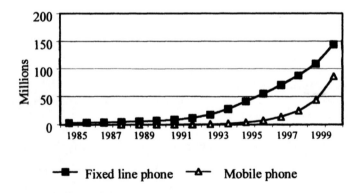

■— Fixed line phone   —△— Mobile phone

Sources: China Statistical Yearbook and Yearbook *of China Transportation and
Communications*, various issues. Beijing. Ministry of Information Industry web site,
http://www.mii.gov.cn/.

Figure 4.2: Fixed Line Phone and Mobile Phone Subscriptions (1985–2000)

and growing demand, China successfully raised its 'teledensity' from 0.6 per cent in 1985 to around 20 per cent by 2000.[5] In 1985, China's telephone network was ranked 17th in the world. Only 12 years later in 1997, it became the second largest, next only to the United States. By 1999, the United States still had the world's largest telephone network, with about 180 million end-user connections compared to 132 million total connections in China in mid-1999. China, however, is adding between 20 and 30 million connections a year, while the US is adding only about 10 million a year. With these trends China is set to surpass the United States in 2002.[6] In the mobile communications market, China is currently adding close to four million mobile-phone users a month. It passed Japan as the world's second largest mobile phone market with about 52 million users in 2000 and is expected to pass the US for the number one spot by mid-2001.[7] By international comparison, China has been remarkably successful in catching up with the rest of the world in raising its teledensity. In 1987 the middle-income country average teledensity was 13 times higher than China's but the gap closed quickly in the following decade: by 1998 the former was only 42 per cent higher than the latter (Figure 4.3).

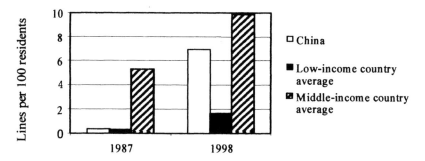

Note: According to the World Bank classification, countries with per capita GNP below US$ 500 in 1987 or with per capita GNP below US$ 760 in 1998 are low-income countries. The per capita GNP range for middle-income countries is US$ 500 to 6000 for the year 1987 while the range is US$ 761 to 9360 for the year 1998.

Sources: Yearbook of China Transportation and Communications 1991 and *ITU Statistical Yearbook* 1995, 1999.

Figure 4.3: Catching Up in Teledensity

All this was achieved under a centrally planned framework without allowing foreign equity investment. Over the past two decades the telecommunications sector has occupied a strategic spot in China's industrial policy regime. In 1979, the State Council made the former MPT the dominant central planner of nation-wide postal and telecom development. In a vertically organized hierarchy, the MPT oversaw some 2000 local postal and telecom enterprises (PTEs) operating with limited financial autonomy in a 'contractual responsibility system' (Mueller and Tan, 1997). In 1988 the MPT set up the Directorate General of Telecommunications (DGT) and the Directorate General of Posts (DGP) to incorporate business enterprise functions. The DGT was later known as China Telecom, which comprised 29 provincial postal and telecommunications authorities (PTAs), all of which offered local and long-distance services through the 1990s. The PTAs in Beijing, Shanghai, and Guangdong provided the gateways to offer international services. China Telecom eventually registered with the government as a corporate group in 1995.[8]

Over the years, the MPT received various financial stimuli from the state. In October 1984, the State Council stipulated a 'six-point instruction' to give priority to postal and telecom development (Gao, 1991). A policy of 'three ninety-percent' was adopted: 90 per cent of the profit was to be retained by the MPT (in other words, the tax rate was 10 per cent, well below the 55 per cent tax rate for other industries); 90 per cent of the foreign exchange (hard currency) earnings were to be retained by the MPT; and 90 per cent of central government investment was not considered to be repayable loans. In addition, PTEs enjoyed favorable interest rates when they borrowed from state banks. The preferential 'three ninety-percent' policy provided favorable conditions for the sector's expansion until 1994 when a major fiscal monetary reform unified corporate tax rates, simplified the tax levy structure, and made Chinese currency convertible for current account transactions.

The 1984 'six-point' instruction also promised to raise gradually the accounting capital depreciation of the postal and telecommunications sector to 7 per cent.[9] From 1980 to 1990, the government adjusted the capital depreciation rate upward three times.[10] A reform of the PTE accounting system in July 1993 again raised the capital depreciation rate.[11] In 1995, the gross fixed capital depreciation rate was as high as 16 per cent. The capital depreciation amounted to RMB 40 billion, accounting for more than 40 per cent of the total fixed capital investment.[12] Thanks to this policy, the weight of technical upgrading and transformation (TUT) investment, which mainly came from depreciation funds, in the postal and telecom fixed capital investment increased from around 35 per cent in the mid-1980s to over 70 per cent in the 1990s, well above the average 20–40 per cent level in the state sector.

Import of telecom equipment has received preferential tariff treatments. In 1985, for instance, the import tariff rate on automatic exchanges and telefax equipment was cut from 12.5 per cent to 9 per cent.[13] For projects involving foreign investment, import tariffs are usually exempted. In comparison, China's average tariff rate was 39.9 per cent before 1994 and this was reduced to 23 per cent by 1996. On top of that domestic producers of electronic and telecom equipment also enjoyed the lowest effective rates for sales-related taxes in the 1990s. As for the 'coordinating tax for directions of fixed capital investment' (introduced in 1991–1998 to levy on indigenous enterprises), the postal and telecommunications sector was taxed at a zero rate, which was meant for projects 'urgently needed by the state'.[14]

Low trade barriers have given rise to a highly competitive telecom equipment market, which in turn has fostered the rapid growth of the telecommunications sector. The introduction of terminal equipment licensing under the MPT in 1989 largely deregulated the terminal equipment used by customers of the network.[15] As a result, telecom service providers can choose among competing domestic and foreign equipment suppliers to minimize their investment costs.

Riding on rapid economic growth, the strong demand for telecom service generated fat profits for the telecom monopoly. In 1984 the MPT system received state permission to adjust its service tariff rates. During the period 1986 to 1990, the MPT made adjustments to a wide range of telecom service rates. Consequently, the rate of capital return in the industry increased from 9 per cent in 1986 to 17 per cent in 1990, much higher than the average rate of capital return for all industries. According to the World Bank, the rate of return in China's telecommunications industry in 1989, adjusted for accounting differentials, was equivalent to 12 per cent by Western business standards (Ma, 1992). The price structure also had a clear cross-subsidizing feature, with the rate of return much lower for local (intra-city) city services and higher for long distance and international services.[16] At the end of 1990, the Ministry adjusted intra-city telephone rates and set a price cap according to local telephone companies' average costs with a mark-up for profit. Local telecommunications companies were authorized to set their own intra-city rates not exceeding the cap, subject to the approval of local government's price control authorities (Sun, 1992).

Under such a pricing framework, the PTEs faced an incentive structure that strongly encouraged business expansion. All revenues from local (intra-city) telephone services were kept by the PTEs. Their share of revenues from inter-regional services was determined by unified national accounting rates and a regional cost coefficient. On top of that, they retained 20 per cent of the increased inter-regional operation revenue over the previous year's basis. For the PTE employees and managers, the effective way to increase their wage fund was to increase the output/revenue of the enterprise and the MPT's national network by generating more telecom traffic. As service prices and tariffs for long distance telecommunications were set by the MPT and local rates and installation charges were capped, revenue maximization was equivalent to output maximization. Therefore the PTEs had strong incentives to increase revenue through expanding the quantity of sales (Lu, 2000).

After 1988, local PTAs were also delegated rights to raise funds for intra-province telecom projects. Given the low teledensity, strong and growing demand, and infrastructure bottlenecks, China's telecommunications market had been supply-constrained before the mid-1990s. To meet the fast-growing demand and overcome fund shortages in telecom infrastructure investment, the central government authorized PTAs to collect installation fees within ranges set by the MPT in 1980. In 1990 the MPT delegated decision-making regarding installation charges to the local level and allowed the charges to be based on line connection costs. In the early 1990s, the installation charges varied from RMB 2000 to RMB 5000 per line (Liu, 1992). In comparison, in 1990, the average annual wage and per capita gross domestic product (GDP) were only RMB 2140 and RMB 1622 respectively. Therefore an average worker had to work 1 to 2.5 years just to pay the installation charge of a new line.

Backed by these policy supports, the telecom sector enjoyed a huge flow

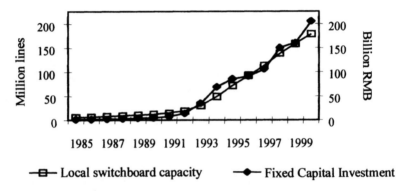

1985 1987 1989 1991 1993 1995 1997 1999

—☐— Local switchboard capacity   —◆— Fixed Capital Investment

Sources: *China Statistical Yearbook* and *Yearbook of China Transportation and Communications*, various issues. Beijing: Ministry of Information Industry web site, http://www.mii.gov.cn/.

Figure 4.4: Growth of Local Switchboard Capacity and Fixed Capital Investment (1985–2000)

of capital investment and explosive capacity growth (Figure 4.4). We can conclude from the above discussion that the telecom sector's spectacular achievements were a result of the growth-oriented incentive structure under the MPT system. This explains China's past reluctance to open its telecom market to foreign equity investors in the 1990s. According to Wu Jichuan, Minister of Information Industry, much work remains to be done to provide more Chinese with access to basic telecommunications services. By 1999, nearly a quarter of all administrative villages still had no access to telephone lines.[17] There is a huge disparity in telecommunications development among different regions. Even areas with the highest telephone penetration rate (such as Shanghai with 30 per cent) still needed to work hard to catch up with the developed countries. To provide universal service in a low-income country with large regional disparities, some degree of cross-subsidization in the tariff structure would be inevitable. This structure, however, is vulnerable to new entrants who are likely to 'cream-skim' the lucrative part of the market. In such a situation, a premature opening of the market to competition would endanger the efforts to provide universal service to residents in rural and underdeveloped regions. The implicit concern is that the various state supports for the telecom sector that have been necessary to promote growth could be taken advantage of by the foreign telecom players once they were given permission to enter. 'For foreign companies investing in telecommunications operations, profits have been to a great extent attributable to preferential policies offered by the state', lamented an MII official in 1998.[18]

For the Chinese policy makers, the pace of opening also hinges on considerations of national security, sovereignty, and protection of strategic industries and indigenous carriers, as well as political stability and ideological control. The Ministry of National Security has always been concerned about the potential threat to communications security and sovereignty once foreign companies are allowed to enter China's telecommunications network. Given China's century-long history of being intimidated and invaded by foreign powers, such a concern is understandable. As part of the efforts to protect national security, China's State Secrets Bureau issued the 'State Secrecy Protection Regulations for Computer Information Systems on the Internet' on 25 January 2000. It stipulated in article 15 that 'National backbone networks, Internet access providers and users shall accept the supervision and inspection conducted by departments in charge of protecting secrets and shall cooperate with them. They shall assist secret-protection departments in investigating illegal actions that divulge state secrets on the Internet.' [19]

MOVING TO A COMPETITIVE ERA

To withstand the anticipated shock brought about by entry into the WTO, the Chinese government has adopted the following strategies: (1) Negotiate for caps and geographic restrictions on foreign ownership and for a longer time period for removing the caps. (2) Beef up domestic competition to pre-empt 'cream-skimming' opportunities for foreign entrants after entry. (3) Nurture the growth of domestic carriers and list them overseas. (4) Prepare a legal framework that ensures state control over the basic network.

The first strategy was actively pursued during the 15-year long negotiation process for China's WTO membership. The second strategy to promote domestic competition emerged during the early 1990s amidst mounting domestic pressure from some non-MPT interests. At that point the MPT was a traditional state-owned and state-controlled monopoly, which combined three functions under its umbrella: policy/regulation, service provision, and equipment manufacturing. All these major functions were challenged by other players in the sector. Over the decades, some non-public networks (vis-à-vis the MPT-managed public network) were established by different government ministries, such as the Ministry of Railways and the Ministry of Electric Power. The capacity of these networks was not inferior to that of the MPT-managed public network (He, 1994), posing a real threat to the latter's monopoly.

The birth of China Unicom in 1993 was a result of high-level 'lobbying' by a political coalition formed by the Ministry of Electronics Industry, the Ministry of Electric Power, and the Ministry of Railways (He, 1994 and Tan, 1994). The State Council adopted the proposal to issue the license to China Unicom while reaffirming the leading role of the MPT in the sector and its functions of network supervision and regulation. As noted by Mueller and Tan (1997), the MPT's primary role in the telecommunications sector was severely circumvented since the new players like China Unicom had a power base outside the MPT that placed them 'almost at the same level in deliberations regarding the sectors future structure'. To resolve the inevitable disagreements among the ministerial stakeholders, in 1994 the State Council created a National Joint Conference on State Economic Informatization (JCSEI), chaired by Zou Jiahua, the then vice premier.

This institutional structure, however, failed to create effective competition in the sector. An original purpose to license China Unicom was to let the new company unite the domestic private networks and use their capacity to compete with China Telecom. China Unicom, however, was not able to meet this expectation largely due to its lack of expertise in telecommunications management and its lack of political clout to 'unite' different stakeholders. In the first four years after the launch of Unicom, the company mainly focused on the mobile communications market, capturing only a 3.5 per cent market share, compared to China Telecom's 96.5 per cent share (Jing, 1999). Meanwhile the temporary 'task force' nature of JCSEI prevented it from performing the role of an effective regulatory authority.

After a few years of tussle for power, at the 9th National People's Congress (NPC) convened in March 1998, the Ministry of Information Industry (MII) was formed through the merger of the former MPT, the former MEI, and the Network Department of the former Ministry of Radio, Film and Television. This was a marriage between odd partners since the MPT and MEI had been rivals all these years. In addition, the new ministry took over information and network administration, handled previously by the former JCSEI and the former State Council's Commission on Radio Frequencies, the former MRFT, China Corporation of Aerospace Industry, and China Corporation of Aviation Industry. Wu Jichuan, the former Minister of Post and Telecommunications, took over the helm of the new ministry. A major objective of this reform was to fulfill the separation of the regulatory and commercial functions in the telecommunication sector so that competition could be developed under the supervision of a single regulatory authority, the MII.[20]

Since its inception, the MII has successfully revamped the former MPT's postal and telecom businesses. By early 1999, almost all assets and employees of the former PTEs under the MPT had been reallocated to the two separate business entities, China Post and China Telecom. After separation from the postal business, China Telecom had about RMB 600 billion worth of assets.[21] The next task for MII was to divest the former monopoly into smaller entities so that effective competition could prevail. At first, some scholars proposed a 'horizontal divestiture' of China Telecom into seven regional 'baby CTs' following the US model in the AT&T divestiture in 1983. With fierce opposition from the MII, the proposal was shot down and the MII won State Council approval for its 'vertical divestiture' plan. Based on this plan, the MII started in December 1999 to divide China Telecom into four separate companies serving different functions, namely, fixed-line, mobile, paging and satellite operations. In fact, before its formal dissolution, China Telecom had already been operating under the framework of four business lines in 1999 (Wu, 2000). These were the China Telecom Group Corp. (with an asset value of about RMB 400 billion), the China Mobile Telecom Group Corp. (with an asset value of RMB 180 billion), the China Paging Telecom Group Corp. (with an asset value of RMB 13 billion) and the China Satellite Telecom Group Corp (with an asset value less than RMB 1 billion).[22]

Meanwhile the MII also tried to position China Unicom as an effective competitor to China Telecom and China Mobile. First, the MII made itself the largest stakeholder of China Unicom by transferring the assets of China Telecom's CDMA Great Wall Network and Guoxin Paging Company paging branch to Unicom in Spring 1999.[23] Second, it revamped the management of China Unicom by replacing its executives with experienced ones from China Telecom. The staff exchange and asset transfer are said to have contributed to an improved business relationship between the two rival carriers.[24] Third, the MII allowed China Unicom to expand into mobile and Internet telephony. In particular, China Mobile is to retain only the GSM (global system for mobile communications) business and the analogue TACS (Total Access Communications System) network while leaving the whole CDMA (code division multiple access) market to Unicom (Li, 2000, p. 17). Last but not least, China Unicom received the MII's blessing to launch an IPO (initial public offering) to raise equity funds. It went 'public' by launching an IPO in the Hong Kong and New York stock exchanges in June 2000 with a plan to raise at least US$ 1 billion, but ended up with a listed market value close to US$ 5 billion.[25] Backed by the MII, in March 2000 China Unicom succeeded in procuring loans of RMB 10 billion and RMB 1.6 billion from the China Development Bank and the Bank of China, respectively to finance its construction of mobile and digital communication networks.[26]

After signing an interconnection agreement with China Telecom in January 2000, China Unicom subsequently unveiled detailed plans to capture more than 30 per cent of the mainland's fast-growing mobile phone and Internet-related services markets over the next five years. It plans to boost the capacity of its CDMA mobile-phone network to 60 million lines by 2005, aiming to attract 45 million subscribers, with the network covering most of the country. It believes that the capacity of its GSM network will by then reach 15 million lines and attract 13 million subscribers, with the network covering the prosperous eastern and middle parts of the country.[27] China Unicom also received a boost in its efforts to compete against China Telecom when it obtained the government's approval to enter the international call market (IDD) in March 2000, thus effectively breaking the China Telecom monopoly in this lucrative market.[28]

The MII's control over the domestic market liberalization process has, however, not been overwhelming. In April 1999, its plan to build a unified broadband network for Shanghai's Pudong area was challenged by the entry of a new operator, China Netcom Corporation (CNC). China Netcom, which has Jiang Mianhong, son of Chinese President Jiang Zemin on its board, is a joint venture among the Chinese Academy of Sciences (with the younger Jiang as its vice dean), the Shanghai Municipal Government, State Administration of Radio, Film and Television and Ministry of Railways. It was created to provide high-speed voice and data service in 15 cities, and to connect with 70 countries.[29] To do so, it planned to build its own broadband network. Following in Netcom's footsteps, Jitong Corp. also announced its plan to develop its own broadband network. The State Administration of Radio, Film and Television (SARFT) vowed to move into the telecom business by setting up 'China Cable Television Networks Corp' and taking advantage of its national cable business networks. Netcom's ambitious project, interestingly enough, was not endorsed by the MII, but by the State Development Planning Commission under the State Council.[30] The political clout of these new players threatens to circumvent the MII's authority over basic network development.

Along with the divestiture of China Telecom and the beefing up of China Unicom, the telecom sector in the late 1990s witnessed a series of reforms that featured opening, tariff readjustment and the formulation and completion of telecom legislation. From 1995 to 1999, the installation fee for a fixed phone line was cut from RMB 300–5000 to below RMB 800. In most rural areas, the fee is below RMB 500. The mobile telephone access charge was reduced by 75 per cent. IDD rates dropped by 60–70 per cent. The Internet access fee decreased by 70–80 per cent (Qian and Zhang, 2000). In June 2000, China Telecommunications (Group) announced a plan to slash its international call charges by as much as 50 per cent in order to strengthen its hold on the telecom market. It also vowed to cancel telephone installation fees and restructure charges for city calls from three-minute blocks to single minutes.[31] Such adjustments in rates are part of the MII strategy to pre-empt the cream-skimming opportunities open to the foreign carriers after China's WTO accession.

Since its inception, the MII has also been the agency authorized to review, approve and grant operation licenses to Internet Service Providers (ISPs). In 1999, the MII and its provincial PTAs approved more than 300 ISPs, among which 53 were approved for nationwide services.[32] With the blessing of the MII, China Telecom launched a nationwide Internet Protocol (IP) telephony trial in May 1999 in partnership with state-owned carriers Jitong Communications and China Unicom. After nearly a year of trial, in April 2000, the MII formally issued four IP telephony licenses to China Telecom, China Unicom, Jitong Communications and China Netcom.[33]

Since early 1999, the MII has openly promoted the development strategy of 'breaking up the monopoly and introducing competition' (*pochu longduan, yinru jingzheng*). The strategy seeks to rely on the market to improve telecommunications services and accelerate technological progress to prepare the sector for global competition.[34] By mid-2000, China's telecom market had been enlivened by competition (Table 4.2). In each category of the telecom businesses, there were at least two players.

Table 4.2: Market Shares in the First Half of 2000

	Telephone user base	Long-distance optical cable	Mobile phone subscription	IP telephony
China Telecom	68.1	86.6		54.4
China Mobile	25.8		81.2	
Unicom	6.0	13.4	18.8	31.2
Jitong				12.3
Netcom				2.1

Source: Zhongguo Jingji Shibao (China Economic Times), 20 October 2000.

After the signing of Sino-US agreement on China's WTO accession in November 1999, the MII accelerated the pace of arranging for the major Chinese carriers to tap into the Hong Kong and other overseas capital markets. In May 2000, the MII arranged for China Mobile Communications (Group) Corp. to become the 100 per cent owner of China Telecom (Hong Kong) Co. by acquiring at no cost the 43 per cent stake in CT(HK) from China Telecom Group Corp. After changing its name to China Mobile (HK) Co., the largest listed company in Hong Kong's stock market started preparations to purchase seven of the mainland's biggest provincial and municipal mobile-phone networks from its state-owned parent, China Mobile Communications Corp. The regions covered are Beijing, Tianjin, Shanghai, Liaoning, Hebei, Shandong and Guangxi.[35] This acquisition was backed by Vodafone, which agreed in October 2000 to invest US$ 2.5 billion to help fund the US$34 billion deal. With this investment, Vodafone would gain a 2.6 per cent stake in China Mobile's current US$ 96 billion market value.[36] The MII's support for China Unicom's launching of a record US$5 billion IPO in Hong Kong and New York in June 2000 was another success of utilizing overseas capital for China's telecommunications development. Following China Unicom, Netcom and Jitong also revealed plans to go public in Hong Kong and other overseas markets. Meanwhile the MII has plans to restructure the local branches of China Telecom in nine coastal cities into independent 'public corporations' for IPO launches in Hong Kong and other overseas stock markets. It also proposed to apply the Build–Operate–Transfer (BOT) model to encourage investment in telecommunications infrastructure in China's inland regions.[37]

A subtle objective of these offshore fund raising efforts is to make it easier for these Chinese state-owned carriers to fulfill China's commitment to allow 49 per cent foreign shareholding upon its entry into the WTO. In China's telecommunications circle, word has it that several more China Telecom subsidiaries at provincial levels are preparing themselves for overseas listing following the China Mobile (HK) model.[38] If every Chinese carrier had a significant portion of its assets owned by the overseas subsidiary of its state-owned parent, little would be left for the real foreign companies to snap up from what is left in the 49 per cent stake allowable for foreign ownership when China enters the WTO. Such a strategy will effectively sustain the state's control over the telecommunications business.

Finally, a legal regulatory framework is being developed to prepare the industry for the post-WTO-accession era. While a Telecommunications Law is still absent, the State Council approved and issued the MII-proposed *Telecommunications Regulations of the People's Republic of China* in September 2000, which standardizes the regulatory framework for the telecom sector and unifies the existing regulations on tariffs, the issue of new licenses, interconnections, network development and private/foreign participation.[39] The document spells out major principles of telecom regulation:

- dividing governmental functions from entrepreneurial/business acts;
- eliminating monopoly, encouraging competition;
- promoting development; and
- being open, fair, and equitable in exercising supervision and administration over the industry.

A remarkable feature of this regulatory framework is opening of the telecom sector to non-state and foreign players. The new rules divide telecom companies into two types: one is the basic telecom business operator who provides public network infrastructure, data and voice transmission services. The other is the value-adding telecom business operator who uses the public network to provide telecommunications and information services. All basic telecom business operators and the value-adding telecom business operators whose service scope covers two or more provincial territories must be licensed from 'the department in charge of the information industry under the State Council' (i.e. the MII). Other value-adding telecom business operators should be licensed by provincial telecom regulatory bodies. A crucial requirement for a basic telecom business operator to be licensed is being a legally established corporation in which the state share or stake is no less than 51 per cent (the controlling stake). As for the value-adding telecom business operators, there is no specific requirement for state control, thus clearing the way for foreign investors (Table 4.3).

To ensure fair access to the public network by the new entrants, the Provisions specify that interconnection between different networks should follow the principles of feasibility, economic rationale, justice, fairness and mutual co-operation. According to the Provisions, a leading telecom operator is obliged to allow interconnection with other telecom operators and specialized (non-public) network units.

The promulgation of the new regulation was also a crucial step to establish the MII as a state regulatory authority. Under the new rules, telecom tariffs consist of market-adjusted prices (set by service providers), government-guided prices (i.e. floating ranges allowed for operators to set their prices/ rates) and government-set prices (for important tariff rates). Pricing is mainly cost-based. The MII is authorized to play a pivotal role in government involvement in telecom tariff setting. The new regulatory framework also reconfirms that 'the State shall foster the system of unified planning, concentrated management, rational allocation and paid use in management of the telecom resources of the country.' These resources refer to radio frequencies, orbit locations of satellites, and codes of the telecommunications network. The operators' possession and usage of such resources will be levied by the state at rates suggested by the MII and the fiscal departments of the State Council. Administrative assignment and public auction are referred to as the two measures to allocate the telecom resources. Meanwhile telecom operators are obliged to fulfill the responsibility of providing universal services, which are enforced through the MII's regulatory specifications or tender clauses. Finally, the Provisions reaffirm the MII's unified planning

Table 4.3: Types of Telecom Operators

Type of operator	Business scope	License authority	Requirement for state equity share
Basic telecom business operator	Provision of public network infrastructure, public data and voice transmission service	MII	The state share or stake is no less than 51 per cent
Value-adding telecom business operator	Using the public network to provide telecommunications and information services	MII for those whose service scope covers two or more provincial territories; provincial telecom regulatory bodies for others	No specific requirement

Source: *Telecommunications Regulations of the People's Republic of China* (September 2000).

authority over the development of public network, specialized (non-public) network and radio/television transmission network Projects involving nationwide networks must be approved by the MII before they can go through the state approval procedure for capital construction projects. Telecom network design, development and operation by any player must meet the requirements and standards of national security and network security. With these rules, the government is set to keep its control over the investment and development of the country's telecommunications infrastructure.

It appears that the recent MII-initiated reforms and the new regulations reflect the following principles.[40]

- emphasis on unified planning and co-ordination in developing the basic network to avoid repeated building up of expensive networks;
- opening the service business to fair competition;
- allowing access to the backbone network, which is to be kept under unified investment and management;
- imposing strict regulation on basic services while having looser regulation on value-added services;
- strengthening the role of dominant state carriers when opening the market to more competition; and
- continuing policies to favor telecommunications network development in rural and underdeveloped areas.

CONCLUSIONS

Recent developments in China's telecommunications sector clearly mark the dawning of a more competitive era featuring an oligopoly market. When China moves to fulfill all of its WTO commitments with regard to opening its telecommunications market in the next few years, we can expect the following.

First, with the rise of new carriers like Unicom, Jitong Communications, and Netcom, the dominance of China Mobile and China Telecom will continue to decline. Competition among the major domestic carriers will intensify, thus dismantling the previous cross-subsidizing tariff structure. This will effectively squeeze the profit margins of these oligopoly carriers and pre-empt the cream-skimming opportunities of foreign entrants.

Second, China's relatively low teledensity and the sector's dynamic growth suggest the enormous potential of its telecommunications market. Although state support for telecom development will continue, it is not realistic to expect infrastructure construction to keep pace with its explosive growth that started in the second half of the 1980s. In particular, given the withering of China Telecom and China Mobile's dominance, their responsibility to provide universal service will have to be compromised with profit drives. New infrastructure investment will tend to be focused on the more 'creamy' part of the market. Basic network construction for the less lucrative underdeveloped regions is likely to be slowed down unless the government intervenes actively or technological progress provides alternatives. No doubt capital will keep flowing into China's telecom sector, but its effect on raising teledensity and the penetration rate of basic services is diminishing. The high end of the market (such as international calls and data transmissions, sophisticated mobile communications, etc. in more developed coastal cities) will be better serviced at the cost of affordability and availability of low-end market services (such as basic telephony) for the local and rural areas.

Because of the above, the MII is likely to remain highly interventionist, given its constant concerns over national security and sovereignty, universal service to the remote and underdeveloped areas, and indigenous carriers' chances of survival in an open market. Its endeavors to oversee infrastructure planning and construction will not fade, despite being challenged by various interest groups. China's industrial policy makers want to promote the information technology (IT) industry as the 'foundation, guide and pillar' of the Chinese economy in the 21st century. The official target is to maintain a 20 per cent annual growth rate for the industry over the next five years (2000–2005), about three times the expected rate of GDP growth. That would double the size of the IT industry to about 5 per cent of GDP.[41] 'Speeding up the informatization of the national economy' is high on the agenda of China's Tenth Five-year Plan (2001–2005). To the Chinese leadership, the possibility of using IT to accelerate China's industrialization is an opportunity in the new century for China to catch up with the West (Zhu, 2000). As the engine and backbone of the IT industry, the telecommunications sector will surely continue to play a strategic role in the government's industrial policy.

Opening to foreign equity investment will be subject to official limits even after China becomes a member of the WTO. Uncertainties remain such as the extent to which the MII would separate itself from the business operations of the divested former China Telecom. Would it restrain itself to be a truly fair umpire rather than a quasi-player in the telecommunications business? By seeking to list Chinese carriers in overseas/Hong Kong stock markets, the government can technically retain its control over the telecom business as before without blatantly violating its commitment to allow 49 per cent foreign ownership upon WTO entry. Since the MII still holds major stakes in the carriers descended from the former China Telecom (and even in China Unicom since April 2000), it is unlikely, if not impossible, for it to adopt a hands-off approach as a passive dominant shareholder if these carriers were to bleed or sink in the post-WTO-entry days. Until the state-owned giant carriers assume their place as pure commercial players and the MII limits itself to being an impartial regulator, a level playing field is unlikely to emerge as foreign investors have hoped. Thus the more successfully the MII beefs up these state-owned carriers to prepare for WTO entry, the less likely or necessary it would be for it to intervene to protect them when the market is fully open for foreign competition.

NOTES

1. *Beijing Review* (Beijing), 14–20 June 1993.
2. The Economist Intelligence Unit (London), *Telecoms & Wireless Asia*, 14 January 2000.
3. *China Daily Business Weekly* (Hong Kong), 21–27 November 1999. For a summary of the Basic Telecommunications Agreement, see Organization for Economic Co-operation and

Development (OECD), July 1999. *Implications of the WTO Agreement on Basic Telecommunications*, Paris: OECD.

4. AFP's report on the EU–China deal, *Straits Times* (Singapore), 20 May 2000.

5. Teledensity is defined as main telephone lines per 100 inhabitants.

6. News report on a speech by Xie Linzhen, vice director of the Department of Electronic Information, MII. *The China Interactive Times Newsletter* (www.shanghai-abc.com), Vol. 2, No. 24, 21 August 2000.

7. *The China Interactive Times Newsletter* (www.shanghai-abc.com), Vol. 2, No. 25, 25 August 2000.

8. *Yearbook of China Transportation and Communications 1996*, p. 234.

9. State Council, 'Instruction to the Postal and Telecommunications Management (12 October 1984)', *Yearbook of China Transportation and Communications 1986*, p. 243.

10. *Yearbook of China Transportation and Communications 1990*, p. 271.

11. The detailed depreciation scale is: 5–7 years for telecommunications equipment, 6–8 years for power equipment, 10–15 years for communications cables, 30–40 years for buildings (*Yearbook of China Transportation and Communications 1994*, p. 235).

12. Wu Jichuan's interview, *Yazhou Seikan* (The International Chinese News Weekly), 19 May 1996, p. 58.

13. *Almanac of China's Foreign Economic Relations 1986*, Beijing: Foreign Trade and Economic Cooperation Press, p. 129.

14. State Council, 'The Provisional Regulation on the PRC's Direction-Adjustment Tax on Fixed Capital Investment' (16 April 1991).

15. *Yearbook of China Transportation and Communications 1996*, p. 232.

16. An MPT source disclosed that in 1993 the profit margin on local service was only 2 to 3 per cent, while the margin on long distance calls was 25 per cent and on international calls, 75 per cent (Mueller and Tan, 1997, p. 41).

17. *China Daily* (Hong Kong), 17 October 1999.

18. Reuters news, *Business Times* (Singapore), 2 December 1998.

19. *China Online News*, 26 January 2000, http://www.chinaonline.com.

20. 'The Plan to Define the Functions, Internal Organizations, and Personnel Quotas of the MII', *Youdian Jingji (P&T Economy)*, 1998 No. 3, Volume 44, pp. 2–4.

21. Interview with officials and scholars of Shanghai Institute of P&T Economy, 20 June 1999.

22. Interview with officials and scholars of Shanghai Institute of P&T Economy, 20 June 1999.

23. *China Online News*, 4 May 1999.

24. Interview with officials and scholars of Shanghai Institute of P&T Economy, 20 June 1999, 8 July 2000.

25. *South China Morning Post* (Hong Kong), 15 April 2000; Lin (2000); and *ChinaOnline News*, 21 June 2000.

26. *China Daily* (Hong Kong), 23 March 2000; *South China Morning Post* (Hong Kong), 1 April 2000.

27. *South China Morning Post* (Hong Kong), 15 December 1999.

28. *South China Morning Post* (Hong Kong), 11 March 2000.

29. *South China Morning Post* (Hong Kong), 15 December 1999.

30. *China Telecom Weekly News* (Boston), 17–21 May 1999.

31. *Zhongguo Xinxi Bao* [China Information News (Beijing)], 2 June 2000.

32. Xinhua News Agency, 16 February 2000, http://www.xinhua.org/chanjing.

33. MII's announcement on the opening of IP telephony market, 24 March 2000 (MII web site news, 30 March 2000, http://www.mii.gov.cn)

34. *Hong Kong Economic Journal* (Hong Kong), 10 December 1999.

35. *China Online News*, 'China Telecom (HK) Changes Name to China Mobile', 22 May 2000, http://www.chinaonline.com.

36. 'Vodafone buys into China Mobile', *Straits Times* (Singapore), 5 October 2000.

37. Interview with officials and scholars of Shanghai Institute of P&T Economy, 8 July 2000.

38. Interview with officials and scholars of Shanghai Institute of P&T Economy, 8 July 2000, 22 October 2000.

39. *The PRC Provisions on Regulation of the Telecommunications Sector* (issued by State Council on 25 September), the Ministry of Information Industry web site, www.mii.cn/news2000/1013_1.htm.
40. Also from interview with officials and scholars of Shanghai Institute of P&T Economy, 8 July 2000.
41. News report on a speech by Lu Xinkui, vice minister at the Ministry of Information Industry, *The China Interactive Times Newsletter* (www.shanghai-abc.com), Vol. 2, No. 25, 25 August 2000.

REFERENCES

China Transportation and Communications Society, *Yearbook of China Transportation and Communication*, various years. Beijing: China Transportation and Communications Society.

Gao Yangzhi (1991) (in Chinese), '*Shanghai dianhua wang de fazhan xianzhuang he fazhan zhanlue* (Shanghai's telephone network: status quo and development strategy)', *Youdian Jingji [P&T Economy* (Shanghai)] 16, 22–28.

He, Fei Chang (1994), 'Lian Tong: A quantum leap in the reform of China's telecommunications', *Telecommunications Policy* 18(3), 206–210.

Hsu, Connie (1999), *Telecoms & Wireless Asia*. London: The Economist Intelligence Unit.

Jing, Xing (1999) (in Chinese), '*Jianchi shishi qiushi, yiqie cong shij chufa – wei jinian gaige kaifa 20 zhounian zuo* (Insist on the principle of pragmatism – on the 20th anniversary of the commencement of reform and opening)', *Youdian Jingji [P&T Economy* (Shanghai)] 46, 1999(1): 2–8.

Li, Jiaju (2000) (in Chinese), '*Waixiang ershiyi shiji de zhongguo liudong dianhua shichang* (China's mobile telephone market towards the 21st century)', *Youdian Jingji [P&T Economy* (Shanghai)] 50, 2000(1): 14–19.

Lin, Sun (2000), 'Exploring new avenues: Unicom's focus on growth', *Asian Communications*, August 14(8), 12.

Liu, Zhaoquan (1992) (in Chinese), '*Youdian fazhan yu chanquan guanli tizhi gaige* (The development of P & T and reform of asset management)', *Youdian Jingji [P&T Economy* (Shanghai)] 18 (1), 2–4.

Lu, Ding (2000), 'China's Telecommunications Infrastructure Buildup: On Its Own Way', in Ito, Takatoshi and Krueger, Anne O. (eds) *Deregulation and Interdependence in the Asia-Pacific Region*. Chicago: University of Chicago Press, pp. 371–414.

Ma, Qiang (1992) (in Chinese), '*Dianxin zifei de pingjia fangfa ji guoji bijiao*(Ways to estimate telecommunications rates and an international comparison of rates)', *Youdian Jingji [P&T Economy* (Shanghai)] 18(1), 27–30.

Mueller, M. and Tan, Z. (1997), *China in the Information Age: Telecommunications and the Dilemma of Reform*. Westport, Connecticut: Praeger Publishers.

Qian, Jinqun and Zhang, Yi (2000), '*Jin nian lai woguo dianxin zifei tiaozheng qingkuang* (Adjustment of telecommunications rates in the recent years)', *Dianxin Ruan Kexue Yuanjiu (Telecom Soft Science Research)* Vol. 3, 28–37.

State Statistics Bureau, *China Statistical Yearbook* (various years), State Statistics Bureau. Beijing: China Statistics Press.

Sun, Yaming (1992) (in Chinese), '*Youdian xin yewu zifei zhengce youguan wenti de tantao* (Issues related to pricing policies regarding P & T new services)', *Youdian Jingji [P&T Economy* (Shanghai)] 18(1), 36–37.

Tan, Zixiang (1994), 'Challenges to the MPT's monopoly', *Telecommunications Policy* 18(3), 174–181.

Wu, Jichuan (1996), 'Carefully study the experience of fulfilling the Eighth Five-year Plan, work hard to fulfil the Ninth Five-year Plan, and strive for making China a country with the most advanced postal and telecommunications sector by the year 2010'. In *Yearbook of China Transportation and Communications 1996*. Beijing: China Transportation and Communications Society, pp. 16–17.

Wu, Jichuan (2000) (in Chinese), 'Interview on reform and opening of the telecommunications sector', *Youdian Jingji [P&T Economy* (Shanghai)] 50, 2000 (1), 2–4.

Yang, Peifang (1991) (in Chinese), '*Lun dianxin hangye de mubiao he xietiao fazhan* (On the goals and ways of a harmonic development of telecommunication)', *Youdian Jingji [P&T Economy* (Shanghai)] 16, 1991(3), 2–4.

Zhu, Rongji (2000), 'On the drawing of the Tenth Five-year Plan', *People's Daily*, 20 October 2000.

5. Telecommunications: Recent Rate Adjustments

Huizhong Zhou

INTRODUCTION

The Chinese telecommunications market is huge and still growing. The industry's strategic importance in the economy offers both opportunities and risks to foreign as well as Chinese investors. No wonder it was one of a few major roadblocks in the negotiations with the US and other major nations over China's membership in the WTO.

Developments in information technologies and changes in policy have been reshaping the telecommunications market in China in the last decade. The central government has taken measures to break state monopolization of telecommunications hoping that competition will improve efficiency. Chapter 4 in this volume provides an excellent account of these developments. This chapter will stress obstacles in opening the telecommunications market. We point out that the industry is still highly regulated and that its enterprises are almost all state owned. With these political and economic constraints, one cannot expect entry or reorganization of a dominant firm to have similar implications for competition as we see in developed market economies. We shall explain that there are major hurdles facing the telecommunications market in China in opening up for competition. Specifically, the Ministry of Information Industry (MII) is a major shareholder of the monopoly incumbent and, hence, a captive regulator in a much stronger sense than what is implied in Stigler (1971). The MII tends to regulate the market in ways that favor the incumbent and impede competition, constrained only by political pressure. The telecommunications market in China has been forced open in recent years only by political pressure or inter-jurisdictional competition. Moreover, state ownership of telecommunications firms severely constrains the MII's ability and interest to promote competition, as competition among state firms may reduce their profitability and hence state revenues from these firms.

In this chapter we shall present a number of less publicized events and arrangements in the telecommunications industry and investigate their anti-competitive implications. We shall see that, while high-profile developments such as new entries may have long-run effects on the structure of the market, detailed arrangements in implementation can sabotage the stated objectives of promoting competition. The rest of the chapter is organized as follows: in the next section we explain how the agency that is responsible for regulating the telecommunications market in China, the MII, identifies its interest with that of the dominant firm. We will further explain that the limited entries that have occurred recently are mainly a result of inter-jurisdictional competition. The section that follows shows that once the market is forced open by political pressure, the MII appears to adopt a policy that confines entrants to specified market segments so as to avoid further competition. Competition is very limited in the so-called basic operations because the MII controls pricing of these operations, while the dominant incumbent controls access to local exchanges, a bottleneck resource. We then introduce recent adjustments in the rate structure and assess the implications of these changes for efficiency, cross-subsidization and competition. The last section concludes.

CAPTIVE REGULATION AND ENTRY AS A RESULT OF INTER-JURISDICTIONAL COMPETITION

To evaluate fully regulatory reforms in the Chinese telecommunications market, one must understand the political and ownership structure of major industries in China. Under the central planning regime from the early 1950s through the early 1980s, industrial ministries were practically the owners of the state enterprises within their respective industries. The ministries were charged with administering the state enterprises within the industries as well as regulating the industries. The political power of ministerial officials and the budget of each ministry were tied to the financial strength of the firms within their jurisdiction. Therefore the ministries not only had substantial control over their firms, but also a financial stake in their performance. The ministry–firm ties in a monopolized industry such as telecommunications were even stronger because the interest of the ministry was associated with a single enterprise. Ministerial regulatory policies and enterprise management decisions were intertwined. In a sense it is difficult to say whether the regulatory function was delegated to or captured by the monopoly firm. Two decades of reform have weakened the ministry–firm relationship in some industries, where there are now many firms owned by diverse governments and non-state firms. As the shares of the firms in these industries owned by the ministries have become smaller, the ministries have had less incentive and less leverage to regulate in ways that favor the firms that they own. Such changes have not taken place in industries that are regarded as critical for national security and political stability, including telecommunications. In fact the ministerial financial stake in the firms in these industries has increased under the reform regime, because reforms rely more heavily on economic incentives as a means of motivation. According to the State Development Planning Commission (SDPC), average wages in monopolized industries have increased faster than in other industries. In 1991 the average wage in the highest-wage industries was 1.24 times that in the lowest-wage industries. In 1997 this ratio reached more than two. The highest-wage industries included financial services and banking, post and telecommunications, electricity and gas, which are all state monopolies (CCTV News, 15 November 2000, www.sina.com).

Given such ministry–firm relationships, industrial ministries, as regulators, are inclined to resist entry. It takes political power to overcome politically charged barriers. Only government agencies can effectively bargain with the central government and can afford to resist the central authorities or ignore regulations. Indeed, first entries into many markets in China in the past two decades were mostly the result of intergovernmental competition. Examples abound, including home appliances and electronics (Liu and Jiang, 1996), tobacco (Zhou, 2000), automobiles (Montinola, Qian and Weingast, 1995), and airlines. The first entry into the telecommunications market, the foundation of the Unicom in 1994, was a result of several years of power struggle between the MPT and a coalition of several government agencies.[1] Following this breakthrough, other telecommunications concerns made their way into the market, for example, the Great Wall, a joint venture between the MPT and the People's Liberation Army, and very recently, the Netcom and the Railcom.

Inter-jurisdictional competition also played a crucial role in the entry into telecommunications by the cable TV network. Cable TV has a very high penetration in China, especially in cities. Many households had cable TV before they had telephones. The State Commission of Radio, Film and Television (SCRFT or *Guang Dian*), which is practically the owner of the TV network, has been planning to offer voice and data services. The MII has vehemently resisted such entries on the grounds that content production must be separate from network operation. However, typical of inter-jurisdictional competition, with strong political allies and the support of officials at the highest level, the SCRFT managed to get a foothold in the telecommunications market. The China Network Communication Corporation (Netcom) was finally founded in April 1999, with the SCRFT, the Chinese Academy of Sciences, the Municipal Government of Shanghai and the Ministry of Railways participating as equal shareholders. The Netcom obtained a license to offer Internet phone (IP) in April 2000. Political wrangling continued, however. In May 2000 the local branch of *Guang Dian* in Zhibo, Shangdong Province, offered broadband access through its TV cables at lower rates, threatening the monopoly position of the local China Telecom. A price war ensued. In reference to that event the Minister of the MII reiterated that currently China prohibited cable TV networks from entering telecommunications businesses, including Internet access, and that a prerequisite for cable TV networks to provide telecommunications services was separation of the network and programming production (NetEase, www.163.com, 27 September 2000).

CONTROLLED COMPETITION AFTER ENTRY

Entry into a monopolized market is a necessary but not a sufficient condition for competition to emerge. Monopolization can continue in a market with multiple firms under certain regulatory or collusive arrangements. The MII's policy appeared to be more concerned with how to divide the market among competing firms rather than to promote competition. From the political bargaining point of view, it seemed that the incumbent conceded a share of the market to the political backers of the entrants. In return, the latter acquiesced in strict regulations by the MII to avoid competition in other arenas, such as price and access. The MII, together with its dominant incumbent, had two powerful instruments to curtail competition. The MII controlled prices of the basic operations, while China Telecom possessed a bottleneck resource, access to local exchange networks. Moreover the common state ownership of telecommunications enterprises and the absence of anti-monopoly laws made it easier for firms to collude.

Price Control

Prices and pricing policy in telecommunications are administered by the MII in consultation with the Price Administration of the SDPC. In the past decade the central administration has loosened its control over rates of telecommunications services and allowed the provincial administrations to make rate adjustments for certain types of services. A combination of directive, indicative and market prices is implemented, with directive prices as the pillar. Directive prices are set by the MII or provincial telecommunications administrations and cannot be changed by the enterprises; while indicative prices are set by the MII or provincial administrations and can be adjusted within a given range by the enterprises. Price control tapers off from what are regarded as important operations to less important ones. Thus pricing of wireline and wireless telephony is under tighter control than that of paging and Internet services. For example, for fixed-line and mobile telephone, monthly subscriptions and all calling rates, local and domestic and international long-distance, are directive prices, while installation and activation charges are currently indicative prices. Lease of lines to ISPs is governed by directive prices, while service fees charged to final users by ISPs are set by ISPs. Over time control of prices for some services has eased up, reflecting changes in policies. For example, installation charges for fixed-line telephones were changed from directive to indicative prices in 1990. Activation charges for mobile phones, being indicative prices, could be adjusted only upward by enterprises by no more than 20 per cent prior to 1998. They can now be adjusted either up or down by no more than 20 per cent. These price regulations clearly reflect a policy that attempts to keep the basic operations centralized, while introducing competition in value-enhanced operations.

Stiff price control for basic operations prevents more efficient entrants from setting lower prices and expanding their market shares. Even though Unicom is allowed to set the rates of all its services 10 per cent below those of China Telecom, lower rates do not necessarily give Unicom advantages to expand, because it has a much smaller network than China Telecom and relies on the latter for access. In fact the 10 per cent discount serves as a lower limit on the entrant's prices. Thus official prices not only allow the incumbent to maintain its high profit margin and market share, but may also facilitate collusion among competitors.

Competition fares better in less controlled open operations, where rates are largely in the category of indicative and market prices. For example, there were more than two thousand providers in paging and messaging as of 1997, including 17 that operated nation-wide. China Telecom's market share declined from over 70 per cent in 1996 to 63 per cent in 1997. Monthly subscriptions for paging were reduced from Y25 in 1996 to Y10–15 in 1997; for messaging, from Y50 in 1996 to around Y30 in 1997. While prices tend to decline in paging and messaging, competition is constrained by price floors set by governments. Specifically, fees and rates are subject to approval by the provincial telecommunications administrations (PTAs) and provincial price administrations (PPAs). The governments, fearing of loss of revenues from state enterprises, tend to maintain price floors when competition threatens the profitability of state enterprises, which occurs in other industries as well. These price regulations, however, do protect the incumbent from aggressive competition and facilitate price-fixing by the incumbent.

Access to the Local Exchange Network

One of the thorniest issues in opening the telecommunications market for competition is access to the local exchange network owned by the dominant incumbent (Vogelsang and Mitchell, 1997). Without proper regulations, the incumbent can squeeze an entrant out of the market by raising the entrant's access costs (Economides, 1998). China Telecom controls practically all local networks in China. Without access to the local network, Unicom and other entrants could hardly operate their long-distance and mobile businesses. The MII has adopted a policy toward interconnection on the basis of private negotiations. According to the 'Temporary Regulations for Inter-Network Operations in Telecommunications' promulgated by the MII in 1999 and 'Telecommunications Regulations of the People's Republic of China' by the

State Council in September 2000, interconnection between networks should be arranged through agreement. If the involved parties cannot reach an interconnection agreement, either one may request interventions by the MII. The dissatisfied party may make two requests for co-ordination. The administration may propose a solution during the co-ordination and, if both parties fail to accept the proposal, either one may request an arbitration. During arbitration the administration must hold public hearings before making an administrative decision. If both parties do not accept the administrative decision, either one may choose to bring the dispute to court. It is indeed unusual for the MII to rely on private negotiations to resolve such important structural matters, since it has rarely hesitated to exercise tight control. Moreover the MII does not have a default plan in case an interconnection agreement cannot be reached. As there are neither telecommunications laws nor anti-competition laws, the option for legal resolution of disputes is practically not available. The policy clearly leaves entrants at the mercy of the incumbent for access and interconnection and puts the MII in charge of determining where an entrant can operate.

Take Unicom as an example. Although it has been granted a license to operate in long-distance wireline telephony, the service is available only in 25 cities where access to China Telecom's local exchange network has been ordered by the MII. Because of limited accessibility, Unicom does not even advertise and few customers know that its rates are lower than those of China Telecom. Unicom fears that advertising rates may lead people to dial numbers outside the 25 cities and misinterpret failures to connect as evidence of inferior quality (Interview with Shanghai Telecom). The control of access by China Telecom has also impeded the growth of Unicom's mobile phone business. Unicom adopted the GSM system ahead of China Telecom in 1995. However during an entire year from July 1995 through July 1996, Unicom's GSM network could not be linked to China Telecom's network. Thus, while Unicom initially had a 15.7 per cent share in the digital mobile phone market, its share declined to 5.3 per cent in 1996 and 5.9 per cent at the end of 1997 (Chen, 1999).

The following event is a manifestation of market power that the incumbent enjoys when it controls access. On 2 August 2000, 260 000 thousand users of mobile phones in the City of Lanzhou were blocked from access to the local fixed line network. The interconnection was restored on 3 August evening, with the intervention by government agencies. It was reported that Lanzhou Telecom and Lanzhou Mobile had failed to reach an agreement on interconnection. Lanzhou Telecom chose to block access of mobile phones to its fixed-line network, resulting disruptions of communications on a large scale.

Common State Ownership and Monopoly Leveraging

Common state ownership facilitates controlled competition and collusion. Although telecommunications enterprises are controlled by different government agencies, they are in principle all state enterprises and these controlling agencies are all subordinate to the central government. The central government, while believing in competition as a means of improving efficiency, is also concerned about its revenues from state enterprises when competition threatens their profits. Therefore it tends to endorse co-operation among state enterprises. The MII and the incumbent firms are taking advantage of this political inclination. The China Telecommunications Group and the China Mobile Communication Group signed a co-operation agreement on 29 April 2000, less than ten days after the latter was formally spun off from China Telecom as a result of reorganization. This agreement was clearly endorsed by the MII, for the minister and deputy ministers of the MII attended the signing ceremony (MII web site, 8 May 2000). As the details of these agreements have not been published, it is hard to judge to what extent these agreements are collusive. An officer of Shanghai China Telecom revealed that China Telecom has given China Mobile preferential treatment in interconnection, and that these arrangements do not require the approval of the MII because of the special relationship between the two companies (Interview with Shanghai China Telecom, August 2000).

The lack of anti-monopoly laws enables the incumbent to extend its monopoly power to other markets. There are no anti-monopoly laws so far in China, although such laws have been contemplated for years. Delays in passing these laws are understandable because the monopolized industries are all owned by the state. Anti-monopoly considerations are so weak that some monopolistic practices, such as price-fixing, are tolerated by governments, while others, such as monopoly leveraging, have not even received attention from consumers and the general public. In addition to the aforementioned agreements, China Telecom is leveraging its monopoly power into other markets. For example, China Telecom also provides Internet services. By controlling access, it enjoys great advantages over other ISPs in terms of access costs. It also has advantages in using its monopoly position to obtain contents. Recently China Telecom signed an intent to co-operate in Internet news services with seven national news agencies, including the Xinhua News Agency, People's Daily and the Central Television Station. It was reported that China Telecom would offer technical assistance to Internet services offered by the seven news agencies and a 50 per cent discount on leases and network usage fees. In return the news agencies would provide guidance to China Telecom's own news web sites (*ShengJiang Dao Bao*, 31 July 2000).

THE NEW RATE STRUCTURE AND ITS IMPLICATIONS

Recent Adjustments in Telecommunications Rates

In December 2000, the MII, the SDPC and the Ministry of Finance (MF) jointly announced structural adjustments in telecommunications rates. Later on 1 July 2001, the MF and MII announced that telephone installation fees and surcharges on telecommunications would be eliminated, taking effect on the day of the announcement. The adjustments announced in late 2000 are summarized as follows:

1. Domestic long-distance telephone rates are to be simplified from four rates (Y0.50, 0.60, 0.80 and 1.00 per minute) to one rate. The new rate is Y0.07 per 6 seconds. Operators may determine discount rates for night, weekend and holiday calls, which should be filed with the MII and SDPC before they are put into effect. International telephone rates are to be simplified to one rate, regardless of the nations or regions in which a call terminates. Calls to Hong Kong, Macao and Taiwan are to be simplified to one rate, regardless of the region from which a call originates. The new rate for international calls is Y0.80 per 6 seconds; for calls to Hong Kong, Macao and Taiwan, Y0.20 per 6 seconds.

2. Rates for lines leased to domestic users are to be simplified from five rates, Intra-LNOA (local network operation area), Inter-LNOA, Intra-provincial, Inter-provincial, less than 800 km and Inter-provincial, greater than 800 km, to three rates, Intra-LNOA, Inter-LNOA and long distance. The rates of leased lines for domestic users and foreign and Hong Kong, Macao and Taiwan users are to be lowered dramatically.

   Carriers that are licensed to operate in domestic and international long-distance telephony and line leases, except China Telecom, are allowed to propose their own rates. These rates are to take effect after approval by the MII, and should also be filed with the SDPC.

3. Adjustments for fixed-line local telephone: monthly subscriptions are no longer to be based on the switch capacities of the LNOAs. They are classified into four categories: provincial capitals, regional cities and counties, rural areas and offices. In each category there are to be two or three different rates from which the PTAs and PPAs choose one, subject to ratification by the provincial government. The rate for local subscriber lines is to be set at Y100 per month, regardless of the switch capacity of the LNOA and the use for telecommunications or non-telecommunications businesses.

   An LNOA is to be extended to cover at least an administrative county (including county-level cities). Thus calls between rural and urban areas within the same county are to be charged the same intra-LNOA rate.

Calling rates within an LNOA are to be set at Y0.18, 0.20 or 0.22 for the first three minutes, and Y0.09, 0.10 or 0.11 each minute thereafter. The PTA and PPA are to determine the rates from these three options, subject to ratification by the provincial government.

4. The rate of digital subscriber lines for Internet access is to be reduced from Y4500 to Y2000 per month. Internet access through dialing is to be reduced to Y0.02 per minute, from currently half of the local telephone rate. ISPs are to be encouraged to experiment with monthly rates. Experimental rates are to take effect after the approval of the MII. ISPs are also to be encouraged to offer optional service packages. Cross-provincial operators are to be directed to file these rates with the MII and SDPC, while local operators file with the PTAs and PPAs. China Telecom, owing to its dominance in local exchanges, is to obtain approvals from the MII before offering programs for its own Internet service.

   The rates between ISPs and telecommunications enterprises will be set separately by the MII.

5. All surcharges on telecommunications services are to be abolished.

6. Prices for the following four operations will be set by operators on the precondition that government monitoring shall be strengthened.

   a. Paging services: network owners are to be prohibited from engaging in unfair competition practices such as caller pay principle.

   b. Internet phone (IP), except international calls.

   c. Management of customer servers.

   d. Other value-enhanced services: call forwarding and transfer, caller ID, messaging and others. Items included in this category will be published separately by the MII and SDPC. Enterprises are to be prohibited from charging for free services that are specified by the MII.

   All of the above market rates are to be filed with the MII and SDPC or PTAs and PPAs. These authorities may reject proposals if rates are regarded as inconsistent with costs or the rate structure.

7. Experimenting with leases of fiber-optic cables, pipes and other unbundled network elements (UBNEs). Rates are to be proposed by operators on the basis of construction costs and implemented for one year, subject to the approval of the MII. The MII will set official rates after one year of experimentation.

8. The settlement between the long-distance and local telephone networks will be adjusted accordingly. The new rates will be set separately by the MII.

These adjustments were to take effect on 1 January 2001. However, considering the large amount of work involved, enterprises were given the option to postpone implementation until 1 March 2001, subject to the approval of the MII. As the adjustments affect China Telecom most, China Telecom was given permission to postpone rate adjustments for a small number of operations until 1 June 2001, subject to the approval of the MII.

Assessment of the New Rate Structure

The new rates and accompanying policies attempt to address three pressing tasks facing the industry: the need for rate rebalancing, emerging competition and readiness for accession to the WTO.

The reduction of domestic and international long-distance call rates and the increase in local rates is an effort to reduce cross-subsidization from the former to the latter. While this move is inevitable, considering increasing competition in the long-distance market, it is an important step toward overcoming political obstacles in balancing the telecommunications rate structure. Very few households in China make domestic long-distance calls, let alone international calls. Therefore they will benefit little from rate reduction in long-distance calls, at least in the short run, while paying more for local calls. In addressing cross-subsidization between the long-distance and local operations, the adjustments do not seem to consider efficiency pricing. For example, the changes in local rates mainly involve a significant increase in calling rates, while subscriptions on average do not change much. A more efficient way of increasing revenues from the local telephone operation is to increase subscriptions while reducing calling rates. However this can be an even tougher sale politically. Many Chinese households make only a small number of calls. For these households a high subscription charge will be a big hurdle, especially for those at the margin.

Rural customers will enjoy substantial savings as a result of the extension of an LNOA to cover at least the administrative county. Prior to the adjustments, many rural areas had not established LNOAs. Thus they are outside of the nearest LNOA, which is centered in the capital of a county, and calls from a rural area to its county capital are regarded as local inter-LNOA, with rates ranging between Y0.30 and Y0.50 per minute.[2] It has been estimated that 40 per cent of inter-LNOA calls were within counties. Therefore the extension of an LNOA to a county will reduce phone bills substantially in rural areas. The measure is an effort to achieve universal service and facilitate communication between rural and urban areas. However it is likely to increase further cross-subsidization from urban to rural areas. Subsidization to rural areas is inevitable in order to achieve universal service in telecommunications. However the adjustments fail to make an effort to make subsidization transparent and competition-neutral. In particular lower revenue prospects in rural areas will make it more difficult for competitive carriers to expand their networks there. The adjustments reflect the MII's policy of relying on the incumbent to carry out universal service.

Line leases, both to domestic and foreign users, will see the most dramatic reductions in rates. Reductions in most types of leased lines will exceed 50 per cent. Rates for foreign users are to be reduced by 72 per cent, on average, according to the MII. These changes will further facilitate the development of information technologies and the new economy in China. Dramatic reductions in rates to foreign users are also a response to potential foreign competition and an effort to compel domestic operators to move ahead with preparations for China's entry into the WTO.

Finally, let us assess the implications of the rate adjustments for competition. Price control is eased for rates for domestic long-distance calls during nights and weekends and ISPs are encouraged to offer optional plans to target different users. Price liberalization for operations listed in item 6 though, is less significant than it looks. Rates for some operations specified there are already determined by operators, such as paging and messaging; while for others, such as IP, rates are already very competitive. Moreover the condition of strengthening government monitoring is ominous in terms of possible hidden regulations. Two measures, however, deserve special attention. First, the adjustments will allow rates for leased lines to be proposed by carriers, except China Telecom, rather than determined by the MII. This measure is not likely to have much impact on competition, since competitive carriers do not have meaningful capacities and must obtain approvals from the MII before implementing their rates. Nevertheless it is a breakthrough because line leases are in the category of basic telecommunications operations, which have been under tight price and other controls. Another breakthrough is that leasing of UBNEs is officially mentioned for the first time. However the document was not clear whether cost-based pricing was meant to be forward looking or backward looking. The vagueness of this important concept led one to believe that there were unsettled disputes between the incumbent and the entrants.

Implications of the Elimination of Installation Charges

Revenues from wireline installation and mobile phone activation charges have been a major financial source for the rapid growth of the telecommunications industry in the 1990s. Investment in fixed capital in the industry was mainly financed by the enterprises themselves from 1990, when the central government adopted a fiscal decentralization policy and cut its investment in telecommunications. Funds raised by the industry itself, so-called self-raised funds, accounted for over 78 per cent of the total investment on average from 1991 through 1997. Moreover, of the self-raised funds, about 90 per cent came from the enterprises themselves (PTE, 1999). One of the major sources of self-financing was revenues from installation charges. For lack of data, estimates for the share of revenues from installation in the total investment vary, ranging from 40 to 50 per cent.[3] The difficulty in calculating the total revenues from installation stemmed from the fact that charges varied across regions and over time. In March 1999, the MII reduced the installation charges to Y500–1000 for fixed line phones and Y500–1500 for mobile phones. The revenues from installation were estimated at around 10–14 per cent of the total investment in that year, still a significant sum (Zhou, 2001).

The telecommunications firms will lose substantial revenues as a result of the elimination of installation charges. However, the impacts will be different on the incumbent and the entrants. China Telecom currently owns an overwhelming 99.9 per cent of the local exchange capacities, while its miniscule competitor, Unicom, is so far offering local telephony service only in three cities. The dominant incumbent can transfer increased revenues from its large installed base to finance installations for new subscribers, as the calling rates are now higher. The entrants, however, have no such revenue bases to recover installation costs if they cannot collect installation fees. It is therefore much more costly for entrants to expand their network capacities.

A competitor could offer a more efficient rate structure to attract new subscribers, if there were no price control. For example, Unicom could charge an installation fee coupled with lower calling rates. As the marginal cost of making a call is typically lower than the ongoing rate, such a change is a Pareto improvement and should attract new customers. However as calling rates and monthly fees for wireline and wireless telephony are currently in the category of directive pricing, exchange carriers are prohibited to set their own rates that are different from the official ones. This further hampers the entrants in competing with the incumbent in the local exchange market.

On the whole the adjustments have not promised much in curtailing the market power of the incumbent and encouraging competition. Prominent in the adjustments is a fundamental proposition that access and interconnection, including settlement between ISPs and network operators, are still to be highly centralized with the public kept in the dark. Access and interconnection are most critical for entry and competition in telecommunications. Entries alone may not improve competition if access and interconnection are not properly arranged. The opaqueness of access and interconnection arrangements between the incumbent and its competitors would generally benefit the incumbent.

CONCLUSIONS

This chapter tries to provide a balanced picture of competition and restructuring in the telecommunications market in China by adding less known inefficient regulations and arrangements to a backdrop of well-publicized, ostensibly pro-competitive changes in the industry. We emphasize that major entries in telecommunications have so far been a result of inter-jurisdictional competition. The industry is still tightly controlled by a captive regulator and a dominant incumbent. With the regulator controlling pricing of basic operations and the incumbent controlling access, it is difficult for competition to emerge. Furthermore common state ownership of telecommunications enterprises plays a role in facilitating collusion.

Inter-jurisdictional competition does, however, have important market implications, especially in the long run. Under certain conditions, diverse interests of different governments may dilute or offset political influences and the market may take its own course. The home appliance and electronics industries, for example, have become very competitive after the entry of many competitors backed by their local governments. The conditions that are present in the home appliance and electronics industries may not emerge in the near future in the telecommunications market because of the dominance of the incumbent and network externalities. However the entry of a few has broken the ice and set competition into motion. Actually the recent adjustments of the rate structure could not have happened without the pressure of entry or potential entry. For example the downward adjustment of long-distance phone rates was simply a matter of formality, because IP providers had already charged much lower rates, which had pressured the incumbent to offer discounts in various ways. Recently China Telecom and Unicom started to offer fake IP long-distance telephony, in response to aggressively low rates charged by Netcom. These calls are in fact circuit switched, with rates as low as 30 per cent of the official long-distance rates. It is our assessment that politically forced entries have ended state monopolization of telecommunications and will eventually improve competition in the long run. However common state ownership will be a major obstacle to competition, especially when competition threatens state revenues from the industry. The opening up of the telecommunications market, especially in local exchanges, will be long and hard, because of state ownership of the industry and network externalities.

NOTES

1. For a detailed account of the emergence of the Unicom, see Zhang (1996).
2. There was a benchmark rate at Y0.40 per minute. PTAs were allowed to adjust by no more than 25 per cent.

3. Zhang (1996) mentions that the revenues from installation charges accounted for 40–50 per cent of total investment in 1985–1990, while Lu (2000) puts the figure at 40 per cent. They do not give details for their figures.

REFERENCES

Chen, Xiaohong (1999), 'A Preliminary Investigation of the Chinese Telecommunications Industry', mimeo, State Council Research Centre for Development, Economics Research Division.

Economides, Nicholas (1998), 'The Incentives for Non-price Discrimination by an Input Monopolist', *International Journal of Industrial Organization*, 16, 271–284.

Liu, Shijin and Jiang, Xiaojuan (1996), 'Industrial Policy and Growth: A Study of Refrigerator Industry', in Zhang, Shu-guang (ed.), *Case Studies in China's Institutional Change*, Shanghai, China: Shanghai People's Publisher.

Lu, Ding, (2000), 'China's Telecommunications Market at the Doorstep of the WTO', mimeo.

MII web site, http://www.mii.gov.cn, the Ministry of Information Industry.

Montinola, Gabriella, Qian, Yingyi and Weingast, Barry R. (1995), 'Federalism, Chinese Style – The Political Basis for Economic Success in China', *World Politics*, 48 (1), 50–81.

PTE (1999), *Post and Telecommunications Economy*, Shanghai Institute of Post and Telecommunications Economy, No. 46.

Stigler, George J. (1971), 'The Theory of Economic Regulation', *Bell Journal of Economics*, 2, 3–21.

Vogelsang, Ingo and Mitchell, Bridger M. (1997*), Telecommunications Competition: The Last Ten Miles*, Cambridge, MA: The MIT Press and Washington, DC: The AEI Press.

Zhang, Yuyan (1996), 'Deregulation: A Case Study of the China United Communications Corporation', in Zhang Shuguang (ed.), *Case Studies in China's Institutional Changes*, Shanghai: Shanghai People's Publisher.

Zhou, Huizhong (2000), 'Fiscal Decentralization and the Development of the Tobacco Industry in China', *China Economic Review*, 11, 114–133.

Zhou, Huizhong (2001), 'An Assessment of Recent Rate Adjustments in Telecommunications in China', working paper, Western Michigan University.

6. Automobile and Fuel Industries

Jason Z. Yin and David F. Gates

INTRODUCTION

Looking at the prospects for economic growth in China over the next 20 years, it is impossible to ignore the potential for strong growth in cars and car fuel. Despite China's economic accomplishments since reform began, the number of passenger cars today is still less than five per 1000 people, a rate that is lower than most other emerging economies. It is also lower than almost any other major country's historical level, that is, when other countries were at a comparable level of economic development. Given the limited number of cars in China, it is not surprising that the volume of car fuel per capita is also far lower than most other countries. However the number of cars and the volume of car fuel are expected to grow more rapidly in the future and this growth is likely to continue for years to come. This potential growth in cars and car fuel has important implications for the future development of the Chinese economy, including activity levels, mobility and employment. It also has important implications for foreign investment.

After a brief review of recent developments, this chapter projects the growth rate of cars and car fuel in China and then analyzes the constraints on the growth of these industries including fragmentation, 'special treatment' and local protection, the limited road network, and growing concern for the environment. It next considers the impact of China's entry into the WTO and the potential contribution of foreign direct investment. It concludes with several policy suggestions for the Chinese government as it seeks to meet the challenge of strong demand for cars and car fuel and the consequences of its anticipated entry into the WTO.

RECENT DEVELOPMENTS

Despite its obvious promise China's car market is relatively small and has been slow to develop. According to *The China Yearbook 2000* the number of privately owned vehicles was 5 339 000 by the end of 1999, about 4.1 cars per 1000 people. This compares with about 400 cars per 1000 people in South Korea and more than 700 cars per 1000 in the US. Moreover China's car production capacity is very low and highly fragmented. There were 122 auto manufacturers with a combined capacity of about 1.5 million units, which collectively produced 571 000 cars and 425 000 buses in 1999.[1] Together the top 13 domestic auto producers produced roughly 92 per cent of national output in 1998. The top three auto manufacturers – the First Automobile Works (Group) Corp. (FAW), the Tianjing Automobile Industrial Group Co. and the Shanghai Automobile Manufacturing Corp. (SAM) – account for about 80 per cent of the domestic market. Furthermore China's road and highway system has often been described as inadequate to support the expansion of traffic that private car ownership will bring. Many cities simply cannot afford more cars on their already jammed roads.

For years the Chinese government has expressed its intention to restructure its auto sector by inviting foreign investment. But it has been reluctant to allow foreign auto companies to dominate such a major industry, especially in the case of passenger cars. In this regard the government has limited the role of foreign players by requiring foreign auto makers to enter China only through joint ventures, by setting limits on production volumes and prices and by dictating what types of vehicles they could produce and the share of components that must be made locally. To date it has put tight restrictions on passenger car projects. For instance GM was required to share its latest technology and to use locally made components for 60 per cent of the value of locally produced vehicles. The intent was to reserve the mass market for indigenous manufacturers and to protect them from competition. The government expected that these restrictions on foreign investment would help China's auto manufacturers eventually become competitive in global markets.

Unfortunately these Chinese government policies, which have been in effect for the last 40 years, have not been successful in producing a world class and globally competitive auto industry. Instead the market is still splintered with more than a hundred companies that on average utilize only about 60 per cent of their capacity. Few would have the scale or quality to compete against imported cars if the Chinese government were to carry out its promise to slash trade barriers after its accession to the WTO.

In July 1999 the Chinese central government announced its intent to accelerate the restructuring of its auto sector and the State Machine–Building Industry Bureau was assigned responsibility for formulating the necessary plans to achieve the necessary consolidation. The plan initially aimed to close small township and village enterprises that receive funding from local governments, operate under poor manufacturing conditions and produce substandard vehicles and parts. To date however this policy has achieved little success because the local governments that view auto manufacturing as an important source of tax revenue and employment have hindered the central government's efforts to consolidate this scattered and inefficient industry.

The Chinese government views its entry into the WTO as an opportunity for many sectors, but recognizes that it presents a major challenge for Chinese automakers. Motivated by concerns over the impact of WTO accession on an auto industry that is ill prepared for global competition, the

Chinese central government is eager to formulate and implement a new strategy to vitalize its auto industry. To be successful such a strategy will clearly require a realistic projection of the likely demand for cars and car fuel over the next ten to 15 years.

PROJECTING POTENTIAL GROWTH

In developing a long–term outlook for the car and car fuel industries in China, it is helpful to begin with an objective projection of how large these industries might become. Most experts believe that cars and car fuel in China are in the beginning stages of what is likely to be an extended period of rapid growth. As a basis for policy making it is important to have an appreciation and a quantitative estimate of how rapid that growth might be and how large these industries might become.

Among many possible approaches to this type of projection, we chose an approach that compares the cars per capita in China with that in other countries. We then developed projections by assuming that China would respond in more or less the same way as other countries to likely future changes in income and other factors. The forecast of cars per 1000 people that was the basis for the quantitative comments in this assessment was developed using a multiple regression approach, which was a combination of time series and cross section analysis.

A total of 413 observations from 19 countries over a period of 26 years were used in the analysis. Since not all years were available for all countries, the number of observations was necessarily limited to those available. The countries in the sample included Australia, Indonesia, South Korea, Austria, Ireland, Spain, Belgium, Italy, Taiwan, Canada, Japan, Thailand, China, Malaysia, the UK, France, Pakistan, the US and India. Note that in all cases the countries included are from East, South and Southeast Asia, North America and Europe. The reason for this is that these countries appeared to be the most plausible models for the type of car population growth that we would expect to see in China. Other regions and countries do not show the type of consistent positive relationship between income growth and numbers of vehicles that we would expect to see in China and thus were excluded from the analysis.

Figure 6.1 illustrates one of the basic building blocks for this approach. The chart shows cars per 1000 people for the sample counties, including China, plotted against their Purchasing Power Parity (PPP) GDPs expressed in real dollars per capita. The data on numbers of cars are from the country level surveys that until recently were compiled by the American Automobile Manufacturers Association (AAMA, 1999). The data on PPP GDP per capita are from the World Bank. Note that a foreign exchange rate based measure of

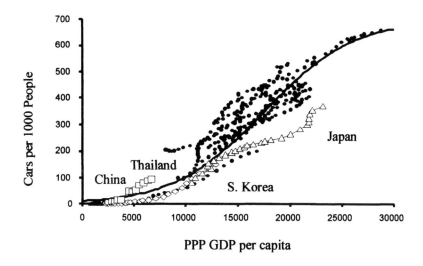

Figure 6.1: Cars per 1000 People versus PPP GDP per Capita

GDP per capita could have been used but the PPP approach offers some slight advantages in making comparisons. The graph in Figure 6.1 shows the 'S' shape relationship between cars/1000 people and PPP GDP using the coefficients generated in the regression analysis and holding all variables other than PPP GDP constant. Historical data for several countries have been highlighted, specifically, Thailand, South Korea and Japan in addition to China, which is buried in the collection of data points at the lower left. As mentioned China had less than five cars per 1000 people and its PPP GDP was about $3500 per capita in 1998.

The full set of independent variables included PPP GDP per capita, population density, calculated as each country's population divided by its geographic area, and the ratio of IMF debt to GDP. PPP GDP per capita is the most important causal factor and was expected to be positively related to the demand for cars. The second variable, population density, was expected to be negatively related to car demand because countries with fewer people per square kilometer, like Australia, tend to have more driving and more cars per capita. The third variable, the ratio of IMF debt to GDP, is a rough but not unreasonable measure of IMF involvement. The idea here is that countries that are in serious enough difficulty to require IMF involvement and loans, especially over an extended period of time, generally have fewer cars per 1000 people than other countries with similar incomes and population densities but no IMF involvement. IMF involvement is not a factor in China but this variable is helpful to take account of variations in cars per 1000 people in countries that have had extended periods of economic difficulty that required IMF assistance.

Also included in the regression were a limited number of dummy variables that were designed to take account of major changes in government policy that are expected to impact the car and car fuel industries, that is, Korea in the early 1980s and China, before 1983 and between 1983 and 1994. The thinking here is that the changes in policy in both these countries were sufficiently profound that dummy variables were appropriate to capture these critically important factors in the historical evolution of these countries' car fleets. In this regard Korea appears to have eased up on its traditional government constraints on car ownership in about 1983 and there was an immediate inflection in the trend in cars per thousand people. Policy changes in China were more general and less specific to cars. Even so the shift in the reform program from agriculture to industry in and after 1983 and the further shift toward structural reform in and after 1994 were sufficiently dramatic that it is reasonable to expect that each would contribute to a shift in the trend demand for cars. A further reason for using dummy variables for China is a practical consideration in that estimating the equation without dummy variables would have resulted in an estimate/forecast that was much higher than the recent actuals. This problem could have been dealt with by using a convergence equation to bridge between the last actual observation for China and the equation based trend. Both approaches, that is, use of dummy variables or use of a convergence formula, are somewhat arbitrary but the convergence approach seemed somewhat more arbitrary and also would have implied a larger number of cars per 1000 for China in 2010 and 2015.[2]

A matrix of simple correlation coefficients is shown in Table 6.1 and the Statistical results for the regression are shown in Table 6.2. The signs of the correlation coefficients are consistent with expectations and the magnitudes are such as to imply minimal problems with multicolinearity. Regarding the

Table 6.1: Matrix of Correlation Coefficients

	PPP GDP	Density	IMF debt /GDP	Korea	China 1	China 2	China 3
PPP GDP	1						
Density	−0.21	1					
IMF debt / GDP	−0.47	−0.01	1				
Korea	−0.24	0.25	.00	1			
China 1	−0.26	−0.07	−0.02	−0.03	1		
China 2	−0.25	−0.08	−0.02	−0.03	−0.02	1	
China 3	−0.12	−0.04	−0.03	−0.01	−0.01	−0.01	1

Table 6.2: Summary Regression Results

	Coefficients	Std. Error	t stat
Intercept	−3.99	0.10	−40.9
PPP GDP	0.25	0.01	47.5
Density	−1.48	0.19	−7.8
IMF debt/	−0.05	0.01	−10.0
Korea	−5.51	0.17	−31.7
China 1	−8.19	0.18	−46.3
China 2	−6.84	0.17	−40.6
China 3	−5.90	0.31	−19.4
Multiple R		0.98	
R-square		0.95	
Adjusted R-square		0.95	
Standard error		0.53	
Observations		413	

regression results all of the standard statistical measures: R-square, t-values, etc., are satisfactory, as are the signs and magnitudes of the coefficients, which are consistent with our hypotheses. Indeed the only coefficients that warrant comment are those for the dummy variables. The coefficients for the Korea dummy and for the three China dummies can best be interpreted in comparison with the intercept for the whole sample, which was estimated as '1' for all years and all countries except Korea before 1983 and China, which were entered as '0'. '1's were entered for Korea before 1984 (with '0's for Korea after 1983 and for all other countries and years), for China before 1984 (with '0's for China after 1983 and all other countries and years), from 1984–93 (with '0's for China before 1984 and after 1993 all other countries and years) and for 1994 forward (with '0's for China before 1994 and all other countries and years). Given this construct the intercept for the overall sample does not apply to Korea before 1983 or for China in any of the years. Rather the coefficients for the dummy variables perform this function. The intercept for the overall sample is −3.99. The coefficient for the dummy variable for Korea before 1983 is −5.5 and the coefficients for China are −8.2 before 1984, −6.8 from 1984 to 1993 and −5.9 after 1994. The coefficients for all of the dummy variables are lower (more negative) than for the overall sample, suggesting that numbers of cars per 1000 people were consistently lower than for the overall sample during those periods. After the 1984 policy change the number of cars per 1000 in Korea shifted upward toward the sample average. China showed a similar pattern, starting off well below the sample average with a dummy variable coefficient of −8.2 that shifted up to −6.8 with the first set of policy changes in 1984 and then shifted up once again to –5.9 with the next set of policy changes in 1994. In other words, consistent with our hypothesis, the policy changes in Korea and in China all contributed to upward shifts in the number of cars per 1000 people. The last China dummy was kept in place for the forecast even though a case could be made that at some point during the forecast period China could reach the point in which cars per 1000 people will be on the same trajectory as the sample average. Making this adjustment would result in a somewhat higher forecast than that shown here but since the forecast is already high enough to imply tremendous increases in activity, it seemed prudent to continue with what can reasonably be characterized as a conservative forecast.

Once the equation had been derived, preparing the projection of possible future cars per 1000 people in China was simply a matter of combining the coefficients from the equation with actual and forecast values for China for the various independent variables. The resulting forecast was then combined with a standard depreciation formula to derive an estimate of likely retirements by year and by difference, a possible profile of future growth in sales of new cars. This in turn was compared with government and automobile manufacturers forecasts of future production capacity to provide a further check on the reasonableness of the overall fleet and sales profile. Such a projection can also be broken down into implied numbers of new car sales and retirements – an exercise that can serve as a useful check for overall feasibility and reasonableness. Finally the projected car fleet can be combined with estimates and forecasts of miles driven per car and estimates and forecasts of average fuel efficiency, for example, miles per gallon (mpg) or liters per kilometer (l/km), to arrive at estimates and forecasts of car fuel.

Figure 6.2 shows the results of the statistical analysis for China's cars per

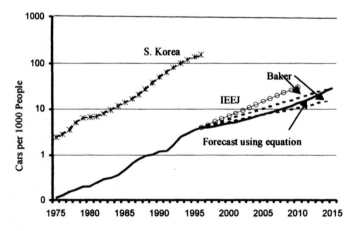

Figure 6.2: Projections of Cars per 1000 People in China

1000 people as projected though 2010 – the solid line with the blank box markings – in comparison with the results of some other published projections. These other projections are one by the Institute for Energy Economics – Japan, the line labeled IEEJ, that was done in the mid-1990s (Tanaka, 1997) and two by economists at the Baker Institute at Rice University that were done in the late 1990s (Medlock and Soligo, 1999). Similar results were derived by economists for the World Bank in the mid 1990s but are not shown on the chart (Stares and Liu, 1997). Note that the actuals and the projections are shown on a log scale. This makes it easier to make comparisons with other countries but it tends to make differences in the forecasts for China look smaller than they actually are. For 2010 the projections for China range from 30 cars per 1000 people in the Institute for Energy Economics – Japan study and 25 cars per 1000 in the World Bank High Case, down to about 13 cars per 1000 in our calculation. Thirteen is just slightly higher than the level that would be implied by the Low Case prepared by the economists at the Baker Institute.

Since all of the projections for China imply substantial increases in the number of cars and, by extension, the volume of car fuel, between now and 2010, it is not worth arguing over which projection is more correct. Some of the other forecasts assume higher real GDP growth (8 per cent or so versus 7 per cent) and the forecasts of the Institute for Energy Economics and the World Bank were done before the Chinese economy began to grow more slowly as it did during 1998 and 1999. But for various reasons we think a number closer to 13 cars per 1000 is somewhat more likely than a number that is much higher than 13.

Thirteen cars per 1000 in 2010 would imply that it will have taken about 10 years from the present time for the number of cars in China to have slightly more than doubled. An increase of this magnitude looks fairly impressive. However if we compare it with what happened historically in Korea, we need to question whether a forecast of 13 or so for China in 2010 might be too conservative. As shown here it took Korea in the order of 16 years to go from where China is today in terms of cars per 1000 to 100 cars per 1000, an increase of more than 20 times. Twenty is, of course, many times the increase we show for China over roughly the same number of years. Though not shown, it took Japan only about 12 years, starting in the mid-1950s, to achieve an increase in the number of cars per 1000 that was similar to that for Korea.

The bottom line is that an increase to 13 cars per 1000 or so by 2010 is possible and the increase could be even higher if we look at the results of other forecasts or the experience of other countries such as Korea and Japan. Moreover assuming that other key determinants such as the average distance each car is driven and average fuel efficiency (mpg or l/km) will not change dramatically over the next ten years, car fuel per capita is also likely to increase by a similar factor. Thus it is reasonable to conclude that the potential for cars and car fuel is very large. But whether this potential is realized or not will depend on a number of other constraints including the characteristics of China's car and car fuel industries, government development strategy, and increased concerns for air pollution, which are the focus of the rest of this chapter.

CONSTRAINTS ON GROWTH

As projected above there is great growth potential for both the car and car fuel industries and this presents considerable investment opportunities for foreign capital and multinationals. However this potential growth could be constrained by many factors. The following four aspects may warrant particular policy attention.

Problems of Small Scale and Fragmentation

Both the car and car fuel manufacturing industries are characterized by large numbers of relatively small manufacturing plants that are spread across the country with little or no consideration to the location of current or potential demand. At present China's car manufacturing industry reportedly consists of more than 120 firms, some of which have annual production volumes as low as a few thousand units. Since China is a large country 120 car manufacturers may not seem to be a large number. But it is large when compared with the US, Europe or Japan, which are also large countries/regions and yet, by our rough count, have only about ten car manufacturers or so each. It is generally recognized that economies of scale are fundamental to car manufacturing everywhere in the world and that trying to maintain and operate more car manufacturers than are needed is likely to mean that costs will be higher and the growth in the number of cars slower than if production were to be concentrated in a smaller number of larger more efficient facilities.

Similar to the car industry China's oil refining industry is also fragmented and geographically dispersed. Until very recently China had roughly 200 oil refineries with a total capacity of about 4.3 million barrels per day. But included in this total were 160 facilities with an average capacity of less than 5000 barrels a day. By comparison China's largest refineries have capacities in the range of 160 000 to 200 000 barrels per day, which is more in line with what we see in the rest of the world. The same points about economies of scale apply to refining as they do in car manufacturing.

'Special Treatment' and Regional Protection

For many years both the car and car fuel industries have been singled out for 'special treatment' by all levels of government – central, provincial and municipal. At the central government level industries singled out for special treatment fall in three categories: 'pillar industries', 'bottleneck industries' and 'infrastructure industries'. From a practical standpoint the official reason for the designation is less important than the designation itself, which can differ from one level of government to the next and which can apparently be changed relatively easily, at least at the lower levels. Special treatment has traditionally taken the form of favorable financing, for example, open ended, low or no interest loans, favorable regulations, assistance in restructuring and restrictions on foreign participation. From the standpoint of this chapter, however, the most important aspect of the special treatment approach is that by focusing on individual industries, there is a risk that it will be difficult for the government and for the industries themselves to recognize the interrelationships between cars and car fuel that can be critical to growth and to the protection of the environment.

Though less codified than the 'pillar', 'bottleneck' and 'infrastructure' designations, the problems inherent in a special treatment approach are compounded by regional protectionism, a related practice, which involves special treatment for particular firms rather than particular industries. Basically regional protectionism is a series of practices that provincial and municipal governments use to limit the inflow of potentially competing products or otherwise protect the interests of local companies. Reasons for regional protectionism range from maintaining local employment to protecting the interests of local investors, who in some cases are the same local officials that are responsible for the policies. Moreover the range of practices encompassed by the term 'regional protectionism' is essentially unlimited, in effect, anything that the local officials can devise that will accomplish their objectives. At the present time none of China's car or car fuel manufacturers has a national market. Several have large regional markets but most markets are regional in scope or smaller.[3] Given the current size of most manufacturers this is not surprising. But the problem is that as long as regional protectionism persists, none of China's car or car fuel manufacturers can expect to progress beyond regional market status.

Concerns over Air Pollution

The emergence of environmental protection and especially air quality as a priority introduces another layer of complexity to the issue of restructuring and growth. Both the car and car fuel industries will be greatly affected by the emerging concern for the environment and especially urban air quality.

While international comparisons have long shown major Chinese cities to be among the worst in the world in terms of standard measures of air quality, stationary sources, that is, factories, home heating and cooking, rather than mobile sources, that is, trucks and cars, were correctly viewed to be the principal causes. In this context poor air quality was seen as largely a consequence of China's reliance on old, inefficient furnaces, heaters and stoves and its heavy reliance on coal. Trucks and the limited number of cars were seen as no more than marginal contributors to urban air quality problems. Over the past several years interest in improving the environment has increased dramatically especially in urban areas. Moreover, for a number of reasons, including progress in dealing with stationary sources, the focus of interest in urban pollution control has gradually shifted more towards trucks and cars. Steps to deal with the problem of vehicle pollution generally take the same form as in other countries and include restrictions on driving and efforts to bring about cleaner combustion, through cleaner engines, cleaner fuel or both.

At the present time central government regulations and standards in this area seem to be primarily the responsibility of the national environmental protection agency, although a number of other agencies are also involved. Whatever the arrangements at the central government level, however, the combination of the pillar industry approach, which tends to view industries in isolation, plus the ability of provincial and lower level governments to establish and enforce their own regulations and standards, seems to make this whole process an order of magnitude more complex and less effective than it could be.

The purpose of this chapter is not to pass judgment on the reasonableness of any actions taken by any Chinese government agencies in trying to bring about improvements in urban air quality by controlling vehicle traffic or by tightening standards on vehicle emissions and fuel quality. But an objective assessment of recent actions has to conclude that prospects for long term progress in this area would be better if more consideration were given to more comprehensive approaches. At the least it has to be recognized that vehicle emissions and fuel quality are closely interrelated and that prospects for technological solutions to vehicle related air quality problems will be much better if remedial actions are based on an objective understanding of the current and near term future capabilities of each industry, including the individual enterprises that make up each industry.

What is required is a greater understanding of the interactions and the dynamics between cars and car fuel, engineering, technology and air quality. No country has yet done an adequate job in developing this understanding. China clearly has a chance to do this but if it does not, the unique features of China's situation are likely to result in a situation in which at least some of the central government's objectives, economic growth, employment and air quality for three, will not be met. Before giving policy suggestions let us first examine the question of whether foreign direct investment might have something to contribute.

THE IMPACT OF WTO ACCESSION AND FDI

Besides the potential constraints on the growth of the car and car fuel industries discussed above, both car and car fuel manufacturers could be greatly affected by China's joining the World Trade Organization (WTO). As envisaged by the Americans and Europeans, China's entry into the WTO will have dramatic implications both for China and for its trading partners. Effects on car manufacturing, car parts manufacturing and sales are likely to be greater than the effects on fuel manufacturing but even fuel manufacturing will be affected by lower tariffs and the potential for greater exposure to foreign competition. The US–China WTO accession agreement signed in November 1999 requires China to reduce tariffs on cars from 80 to 100 per cent at present to 25 per cent by 1 July 2006; import quotas are to be phased out by 2005; and non bank foreign financial institutions will be allowed to provide auto financing upon accession. The EU–China Agreement also focused on trade barriers affecting entry into the Chinese auto market (Mastel, 2000). To date, after completion of all bilateral negotiations, China is negotiating generic provisions in the final multilateral accession protocol. Although the substance of some of these provisions was already negotiated through bilateral agreement, concerns such as measures to provide oversight with respect to the implementation process and safeguard provisions are likely to delay China's WTO accession into 2002. Whether China will be able to comply with its promises covering market access for foreign cars is one of those concerns. However it is quite certain that China's WTO entry will result in lower tariffs that will make imported cars cheaper for consumers. Meanwhile, with multinational automakers' active participation, the degree of competition in the Chinese auto market will be further intensified.

As with any far-reaching trade agreement the early stages of this process will likely be disruptive. But we are less confident that this will quickly lead to the type of dramatic changes that many of China's trading partners currently envision. The level of China's commitment to actually implementing the agreement will likely be contingent on the speed of China's economic reform and the degree to which the Chinese economy can absorb the disruption and pain of its entry into the WTO. One scenario, which clearly worries the Chinese government, is the possibility that there could be a flood of foreign cars into the Chinese market that could cause a large number of bankruptcies among Chinese auto companies and the loss of employment for millions of workers. Concern over this possibility may force the government to slow its compliance with the WTO accession agreements. But this scenario is less likely to happen if the Chinese government can be more aggressive in attracting foreign direct investment into China's car and car fuel industries and in creating new job opportunities to replace those likely to be lost.

Another possible scenario is that given the pervasiveness of local protectionism, we may be in for many years of something like the experience with other countries in this region in which central governments have signed market opening agreements but then local governments and firms have been successful in frustrating serious efforts to gain entry for foreign goods. Given the later poor performance of the countries that have tried this approach, we would hope that China would focus on the potential opportunities rather than the potential short–term disruptions. Indeed, in the case of cars and car fuels, we would think that entry into WTO could be extremely helpful in addressing some of the issues discussed above. Indications that the prospect of early entry into the WTO was a factor in the formation of a number of new joint venture automobile manufacturers, for example, GM and VW with Shanghai Automotive etc., provide important support for this view.

One of the most import impacts of WTO entry is that a more open market will provide opportunities for more foreign direct investment which should help integrate China's car and car fuel industries into world markets. Many analysts and policy makers in China, the multinational agencies, the Western governments and many Western companies have tended to view foreign direct investment primarily as a source of technology, finance and in some cases, operational management techniques, basically, information on how to run a factory more efficiently. But in situations such as those facing China's car and car fuel industries, this view of FDI is perhaps too narrow. In addition to their technical and financial needs what China's car and car fuel manufacturers really need is help with investment management, that is, knowing what technologies and equipment to invest in and when and how to modify those investments such that the venture is in the best possible position to cope with and take advantage of ongoing changes in the business environment. Car and car fuel manufacturing are both highly capital intensive. Knowing what to build to begin with is important but the modifications that are made over time are also critical to success. What is confronting China's car and car fuel industries today is in many respects unique, that is, fragmentation of production and markets, the inherent complexity of regional protectionism, the development of road networks and stepped up efforts to protect the environment. But it also has a great deal in common with what is confronting these industries elsewhere in the world, that is, the ongoing effort to work out sensible, cost effective, combinations of engine technology and fuels. The track record in the rest of the world in this area is far from perfect and there is no guidebook that China can pick up from an international agency that will provide all of the answers. But the experience of the international car and car fuel manufacturers in understanding the critical interactions is something that China can clearly use. Moreover the recent approvals of major joint ventures such as those involving many of the main automobile manufacturers in car manufacturing and Exxon Mobil and Shell in oil refining suggest that the Chinese are prepared to at least experiment with these approaches. These joint ventures will not solve all of China's problems. Sensible government polices are essential. But these could help.

Assuming that the question of business structure can be taken care of the next step will be to create an internal environment in which the investment management capabilities of foreign investors can best be combined with the knowledge and experience of the local investors. What is needed is a better understanding on both sides of what they are trying to accomplish together and what each of them is in the best position to contribute. To the extent that these things can be established, the prospects for any investments will be better. Prospects for the venture itself will also be better since what we are talking about is a process that can better utilize the specialized knowledge of each participant, that is, not a piece of equipment or a technology that either side can take away or copy or that will have value outside of the venture.

RECOMMENDATIONS AND CONCLUSIONS

To seize the opportunity provided by likely strong demand for cars and car fuel in the coming decades and to meet the challenge of open market competition after China's WTO accession, we would suggest that the Chinese government consider the following points.

First, China should further realize that along with the globalization of world economy, the world auto industry has itself gradually been globalized and a strategy of protecting its auto industry from global market competition will not be a viable option for achieving its objectives with respect to the development of China's auto industry. The better strategy would be to partner and collaborate with multinational car and car fuel manufacturers to integrate its auto industry into the global market, including adapting to the WTO framework. In this regard China should recognize the potential contribution of FDI in achieving its objectives for growth in the car and car fuel industries while protecting its environment. As indicated above the problems that China faces in trying to grow its car and car fuel industries while protecting and improving the environment and especially the air quality in its major cities are unique primarily in degree. Since foreign investors are facing similar problems in other countries, it is not unreasonable to assume that they should have something to contribute to China's efforts to maximize its growth while minimizing the costs of that growth. New technologies will certainly be a part of the eventual solution. But these new technologies must be introduced as part of a well formulated investment strategy if they are to lead to the types of cost effective outcomes that China clearly needs. Planning, implementing and updating these investments are where FDI can make its most important contribution in both these industries.

Second, China should formulate new policies to accelerate the consolidation of the auto sectors to improve economies of scale and efficiency. This consolidation should be achieved through open market processes rather than through administrative planning and intervention. Worldwide experience with car and car fuel manufacturing has consistently demonstrated the overwhelming importance of economies of scale. The central government of China clearly recognizes that it has too many small car manufacturers and too many small refineries and has been taking steps that should lead to reductions. But regional protectionism has been a continuing roadblock to full scale restructuring. In the past the central government tried to eliminate duplicate investment and spur consolidation by asking provincial authorities to identify enterprises operating under poor manufacturing conditions and violating intellectual property rights and to force them to close. However the local governments that view auto manufacturing as an important source of tax revenue and employment have hindered the central government efforts. The new strategy we would suggest is to facilitate mergers and acquisitions across provincial boundaries. The targets of such policies should include town and village manufacturers and small joint venture players that have already developed market niches. Currently the three largest automakers in Shanghai, Changchun and Tianjing may play a leading role in this industrial consolidation. The government should also allow foreign automakers to play a more active role in this process, especially in the passenger car segment.

Third, attention should be given to the development of related industries, including road construction and oil refining and distribution. China should speed up the construction of its road networks that are currently inadequate to support the necessary increase in mobility in cities and between cities. Road construction and modernization should be one of the most important building blocks for the continued growth of the Chinese economy. By the end of 1999 there were only roughly 14 million kilometers of highways and 11 600 kilometers of expressways and these numbers will be increased to 16 million kilometers and 25 000 kilometers by 2005, according to China's Tenth Five-year Economic Plan (*People's Daily*, 17 March 2001). Obviously slow growth in the number and quality of roads will be a major constraint on the growth of the auto industry. Designing and constructing the necessary refining and product distribution facilities are a similar concern if China is to be successful in satisfying the double–digit growth of cars and car fuel currently projected.

Lastly, to keep the growth of the auto industry in balance with other sectors, China should pay even greater attention to institutional reform. Despite its unorthodox methods – unorthodox in terms of Western economic theory – China's accomplishments in building and reforming its economy over the past 20 years must be viewed as one of the outstanding successes in the history of modern economic development. The clear priority at the moment is to continue these efforts until the reform of China's economy is complete. From our perspective this effort must include the continued modernization of key institutions, that is, political and legal as well as economic, progress on social security reform, continued modernization of markets and renewed commitment to market determined pricing, reducing and hopefully eliminating regional protectionism, and reinforcing intellectual property protection. Nothing in economic development is ever guaranteed, but the judgment of most economists is that if China persists in these efforts as it has for the past 20 years, its economy should continue to grow reasonably rapidly with important positive implications for the welfare of its people and its neighbors. Moreover unless this can be accomplished, the clear implication is that the car and car fuel industries will not grow as rapidly as they could and China will almost certainly not have the resources that it needs to deal with the problem of environmental protection.

In conclusion, China's car and car fuel industries have the potential to grow rapidly and to be important contributors to economic growth, employment and protection of the environment. However prospects for realizing this potential will be substantially greater if China will recognize the interrelationships between cars, car fuel, and the environment and government development strategies and policies. As argued above there would seem to be a case for re-examining the strengths and weaknesses of China's current approach and especially the limitations of its pillar industry policies, including the excessively narrow focus on individual industries, and the set of policies encompassed by the term regional protectionism. Beyond this we would hope that any re-examination would also include the possibility of a more active and constructive role of foreign investment which as we see it could make an important contribution to achieving what we anticipate will be an extremely bright future for China's car and car fuel industries and for the economy as well.

NOTES

1. The auto manufacturers also collectively produced 840 000 trucks in 1999 in addition to cars and buses, 19 per cent growth from previous year.
2. The key independent variable was per capita income, specifically real PPP GDP per capita, which was expected to be a positive determinant of cars per 1000 people. Other measures of income such as a simple foreign exchange based real GDP per capita could have been used

but PPP GDP, as published by the World Bank had the advantage of at least attempting to compensate rigorously for differences in purchasing power across different counties.

3. Two major National Oil Companies (CNPC/Petrochina and Sinopec) each have responsibility for roughly half of the downstream oil business including oil refining – CNPC/Petrochina in the north and west and Sinopec in the south and east. However, the operations of the individual refineries, distribution systems and retail networks remain fragmented.

BIBLIOGRAPHY

American Automobile Manufacturers Association (1999), *World Motor Vehicle Data*, Washington, DC.

Ingram, Gregory K. and Zhi Liu (1998a), 'Vehicles, Road and Road Use: Alternative Empirical Specifications', *World Bank Policy Research Paper*, Washington, DC: The World Bank.

Ingram, Gregory K. and Zhi Liu (1998b), 'Motorization and the Provision of Roads in Countries and Cities', *World Bank Policy Research Paper 1842*, Washington, DC: The World Bank.

Mastel, Greg (2000), 'China and the World Trade Organization: Moving Forward without Sliding Backward', *Law and Policy in International Business*, Washington, DC.

Medlock III, Kenneth B. and Ronald Soligo (1999), 'Automobile Ownership and Economic Development: Forecasting Passenger Vehicle Demand to the Year 2015', James A. Baker III Institute for Public Policy, Preliminary Version (October).

Stares, Stephen and Zhi Liu (1997), 'Motorization in Chinese Cities: Issues and Actions', in *China's Urban Transport Development Strategy*, The World Bank Discussion Paper No. 352, Washington, DC: The World Bank.

Tanaka, Yasuhiro (1997), 'Motorization in China: Status Quo and Future Subjects', *Energy in Japan*, 143 (January), pp. 1–10.

U.S.–China Business Council (2000), 'The Bilateral Agreement and the United States', *The China Business Review*, www.uschina.org.

U.S. Department of State (1999), 'China – Vehicle Emissions Control Technology Market', *U.S. Department of State Documents* (January).

Walsh, Michael (1999), 'Motor Vehicle Pollution Control in China – A Strategy for Progress', *China Environment*, www.chinaenvironment.net.

Wayne, W. J. King (1999), 'Shifting Gears: With ambitious government plans to make an impact, the auto sector is facing a major restructuring', *The China Business Review*, www.uschina.org.

Woodrow Wilson International Center for Scholars (1997a), 'The Environment in China: An Overview', *China Environment Series 1*, Woodrow Wilson International Center for Scholars, Environmental Change and Security Project.

Woodrow Wilson International Center for Scholars (1997b), 'Transportation Options and Trends in China', *China Environment Series 1*, Woodrow Wilson International Center for Scholars, Environmental Change and Security Project.

Woodrow Wilson International Center for Scholars (1997c), 'The Chinese Political Economy and Central–Local Government Dynamics/Urban, Township and Village Air Pollution', *China Environment Series 1*, Woodrow Wilson International Center for Scholars, Environmental Change and Security Project.

Appendix 6.1: Output of Motor Vehicles in China (1000 units)

	Vehicles	Trucks	Cars	Buses
1952–70	361.7	87.5		
1971	111.0			
1972	108.2			
1973	116.2			
1974	104.8			
1975	139.8	77.6		
1976	135.2			
1977	125.4			
1978	149.1	96.1		
1979	185.7			
1980	222.3	135.5		
1981	175.6			
1982	196.3	121.8		
1983	239.8	137.1		
1984	316.4	181.8		
1985	437.2	269.0		
1986	369.8	22.9		
1987	471.8	298.4		
1988	644.7	403.3		
1989	583.5	363.4		
1990	514.0	289.7		
1991	71.4	38.3		
1992	1066.7	47.7		
1993	1298.5	59.8		
1994	1366.9	663.0		
1995	1452.7	596.0	337.0	216.0
1996	1475.2	625.1	382.9	189.5
1997	1582.5	547.0	486.0	265.6
1998	1630.0	734.0	507.1	321.1
1999	1832.0	839.6	571.0	424.9

Sources: China Statistical Yearbook, 1996–99 and 'Automotive Resources Asia', New York Times, 24 October2000, p. w1.

PART 2

Social Implications

7. Reconfiguration of the Labor Market

Haizheng Li and Guifang (Lynn) Yang

INTRODUCTION

China's accession to the World Trade Organization (WTO) would inevitably affect the fundamentals of its economy. In the heated debate over China's accession, a particular concern is how entry would affect domestic employment. WTO accession will formally commit China to reduce dramatically its tariff and non-tariff barriers on imports of foreign-made goods and services. As inexpensive foreign-made goods fill Chinese markets, domestic products will face much greater competition. If the demand for domestic goods shifts to imports, total domestic employment is likely to decline.

Moreover the state-owned sector still employs about one half of China's urban employees. The inefficiency of state-owned enterprises (SOEs) has been a problem for many years and 30–40 per cent of SOEs are loss making. China's WTO accession will certainly engender competition in domestic markets. Many SOEs will not be able to survive and possible bankruptcies and massive layoffs from state-owned sectors could aggravate the country's unemployment problem.

In the last several years millions of workers in SOEs have been laid off during the restructuring of state-owned industry. As China's social safety net is still under construction, large-scale unemployment can create many problems and risks to social stability. In this context the impact of WTO accession on China's unemployment has been a primary concern for policy makers. Some are even concerned that rising unemployment would cause a conservative backlash that could derail further progress in ongoing market reforms and subsequent economic growth.

While the dominant trade effect associated with China's accession to the WTO seems to be a boost in imports, WTO membership may also increase exports, especially for labor-intensive textile and apparel products. WTO membership will require China to open more than half of its service sectors and will also help China to attract more foreign direct investment (FDI). These factors will generally increase the demand for labor and employment. Therefore the net WTO effect on employment is largely unknown.

There are many existing studies on the impact of WTO accession on the Chinese economy. Most of them focus on trade and social welfare (for example, Wang, 1997, 1999; Bach, Martin, and Stevens, 1996; Yang, 1996).

However a quantitative study on unemployment caused by WTO accession is still lacking. Changes in unemployment are generally difficult to estimate and empirical methods can hardly be applied. Usually the potential trade effects and welfare effects are estimated using computable general equilibrium (CGE) models as in the studies mentioned above. A traditional CGE model, however, is based on the assumption of an efficient labor market, that is, it assumes full employment in the economy. Thus the traditional CGE modeling approach cannot be applied to investigate changes in unemployment.

This study attempts to estimate the impact of WTO accession on unemployment using a modified CGE model. More specifically, following Balistreri (2000), we formulate equilibrium unemployment based on job matching models (Pissarides, 1990). Unlike a traditional CGE model that assumes full employment, this model divides labor into three parts based on employment status: employed, unemployed, and out of the labor force. A job matching process is incorporated with externalities in the labor market. A job match or search is costly in terms of the possibility of not matching a job and thus, one's job search behavior will impose externalities on other individuals. By introducing a special 'technology' that transforms the labor supply into employed labor, unemployment can be introduced into the CGE framework. As a result labor can move among employment, unemployment and labor force withdrawal in response to shocks such as WTO accession. Therefore WTO-induced trade effects may cause labor distribution changes within these three states.

Based on the modified CGE model with equilibrium unemployment, we simulate the effects of WTO on the Chinese economy. Using 1995 as a base year, we develop a dynamic multi-region and multi-sector trade model. Several policy scenarios associated with WTO accession are simulated and analyzed. Ten sectors are included in the model, which are aggregated based on their openness before joining the WTO and their factor intensity. Clearly WTO accession will mostly affect the semi-opened and closed sectors. The simulation captures tariff changes for these sectors. Non-tariff barriers such as quotas in textiles and wearing apparel in developed countries are incorporated as well.

By comparing these different scenarios, we can evaluate the impact of WTO accession on China's total employment, unemployment rate, and employment shifts among sectors, as well as the trade effects. To arrive at our main findings, the scenario without China and Taiwan's accession was compared to a benchmark policy scenario with China and Taiwan's accession.

The main findings are as follows. First, WTO accession will increase China's total imports by 29 per cent and 25 per cent and will increase its total exports by 17 per cent and 22 per cent in 2005 and 2010, respectively. The largest increase in imports will occur in the motor vehicle and agriculture sectors and the largest increase in exports will be in wearing apparel and textiles. Second, joining the WTO will lower China's unemployment rate by about one percentage point primarily because the increase in exports will be concentrated mainly in labor-intensive sectors such as textiles and wearing apparel. Moreover our estimates of possible effects on the unemployment rate are conservative because this model does not take into account the impact of WTO-induced increases in FDI and the opening of service sectors to foreigners. Third, total employment will increase about 1.7 per cent in 2005 and employment will shift quite dramatically among sectors. Because of the simplifications in our model, the results should be interpreted with caution and should be taken as indicative rather than as precise forecasts.

In the next section, we discuss the possible effects of China's WTO accession on its labor market. The section that follows explains the modified CGE model with unemployment. Simulation designs are discussed in the next section and the section after that concludes.

THE WTO AND CHINESE LABOR MARKETS

China's entry into the WTO will require further substantial liberalization of its economy. The required trade liberalization will include reducing or otherwise modifying tariffs on approximately 6500 industrial and agricultural products from 16.9 per cent to a final average of 10.2 per cent by 2008; eliminating non-tariff restrictions such as quotas and licensing on 361 products by 2005 and providing varying degrees of access to nine of its 12 service sectors (United States General Accounting Office, March 2000). The most dramatic tariff reductions will be directed at some specific items, such as automobiles (from 80–100 per cent to 25 per cent by 2005) and agricultural goods (from 20–40 per cent to 10–12 per cent) (Frazier, 1999).

Several studies have estimated the potential impact on China's imports resulting from this trade liberalization. Rosen (1999), using a partial equilibrium model, estimates that the induced increase in world exports of goods and services to China will be $21.3 billion, with an immediate increase in US exports to China of $3.1 billion (13 per cent of its 1998 level). Another study, published by Goldman Sachs, estimates that WTO entry would boost China's total annual imports by $105 to $115 billion (Hu, 1999). The United States International Trade Commission (1999) estimates that China's membership of the WTO would result in an increase of 9.0–10.1 per cent in US exports to China.

The current import component of China's economy is 14 per cent of GDP. The increase of imports induced by WTO accession will divert some demand for domestic goods and thus reduce total labor demand. WTO membership, however, will also increase China's exports. In particular China will ultimately be freed from the quota restrictions imposed under the Multi-Fiber Arrangement, which is being phased out as part of the WTO agreement on clothing and textiles. This phaseout will enable China to compete freely in the textile and apparel markets and it is thus expected that employment in these labor-intensive industries will increase. Increases in foreign direct investment and market access to the service sectors by foreign investors will also increase the demand for labor.

The net effect of WTO accession on unemployment will have important implications for the Chinese economy. The official unemployment rate in China is quite low: 2.9 per cent for 1995 and 3.0 per cent for 1996. Because the official number is calculated based on the number of unemployed who register with the government, however, it likely underestimates actual unemployment, since some unemployed workers simply do not register with the government. The unemployment rate based on survey data is considerably higher. Using survey data, Li and Zax (2000) estimate the actual rates to be 4.3 per cent and 4.6 per cent for 1995 and 1996, respectively. These numbers, however, still underestimate unemployment because many would-be unemployed workers are technically employed by SOEs. This is the so-called hidden unemployment represented by the large number of redundant workers in SOEs. If a large number of SOEs go bankrupt because of WTO accession, the unemployment problem will be magnified.

Since 1994 massive layoffs have occurred in urban China during the restructuring of state-owned industries. The total number of layoffs was 8.9 million in 1996, 7.45 million in 1997, and 7.10 million in 1998. The effects of these massive layoffs are twofold. On the one hand, because a large number of redundant workers have been laid off, the WTO shock should be smaller. On the other hand, additional layoffs caused by WTO accession will increase the financial burden on the government and magnify the problems within the social security system.

Besides possible changes in unemployment, employment will also shift among sectors because the demand for goods will shift after China joins the WTO. It is likely that employment will shift out of previously protected sectors (semi-closed or closed) and into sectors benefiting from WTO membership. Such re-allocations of labor resources also have important policy implications.

It is generally difficult to estimate the quantitative effect of WTO entry on a country's unemployment. One possible solution is to estimate trade effects using a traditional CGE model and then estimate employment changes caused by the trade effects. This approach, however, treats unemployment as exogenous in estimating trade effects. Because a change in unemployment is endogenous in an economy, it is desirable to incorporate it directly into the CGE model as an endogenous variable.

This study uses a modified dynamic CGE model in which unemployment is treated as endogenous to estimate the effects of WTO membership on unemployment and employment shifts in China. To incorporate unemployment into a traditional CGE model, several labor market indicators or measures are needed. We will briefly introduce the magnitudes and trends of these variables for the Chinese labor market. For other regions, we simply use the published number or take a close estimate (using a simple average or a representative number).

The first of these measures is the labor force participation rate (LFPR). In our CGE model with equilibrium unemployment the LFPR is used to measure the leisure rate, that is, $s = 1 - \text{LFPR}$. The leisure rate indicates the percentage of a country's total labor endowment that is used for leisure. Those who could be in the labor force choose to stay out of it (choose to consume leisure) because the market wage is below their reservation wage and/or because job search costs are too high. Generally LFPR measures the percentage of those in the labor force relative to those age 16 and above. In China the LFPR is very high. An estimate indicates that the overall LFPR was 81.6 per cent in urban China in 1996 and that it is declining during the economic transition (the LFPR was 85 per cent in 1989) (Li and Zax, 2000).

Another measure is the annual job turnover rate. This measures the proportion of current employees who will go through the job search or matching process to find a new job next year. This proportion is important in calculating the dynamics of the CGE model with labor search or matching costs. In China the annual job turnover rate is rarely available. Based on estimates from Li and Zax (2000), for those with 1 to 5 years of work experience, the turnover rate is 6.9 per cent; and for those with 6–10 years, it is 21.7 per cent. Thus we approximate the annual job turnover rate in China as 2 per cent.

CGE MODELING AND UNEMPLOYMENT

A traditional CGE model usually incorporates an efficient labor market with assumed full employment. In the model production sectors maximize profits, individuals maximize welfare and all product and input markets clear in equilibrium. By choosing appropriate functional forms for production and utility and for baseline parameters, the model can be solved. The model becomes dynamic upon inclusion of inter-temporal decisions concerning consumption and investment.

Because China is undergoing a transition to a market economy, some assumptions related to a market economy underlying a CGE model, such as perfect competition, may not be applicable. Moreover for China's SOEs, it is even questionable to apply any profit-maximizing conditions. It is difficult to relax these assumptions in the CGE framework and our model is therefore only an approximation of the Chinese economy.

To study the effect of WTO on unemployment, the traditional CGE model has to be modified to accommodate unemployed labor. This can be done by introducing search costs in job matching and by introducing an important externality (Pissarides, 1990, and Balistreri, 2000). For any region individuals are either in the labor force or out of the labor force. For those in the labor force, individuals are either employed or unemployed. Thus a region's total labor endowment can be divided into three parts: leisure (for those who are not in the labor force), unemployed labor and employed labor.

Given an exogenously specified labor endowment, the representative agent first chooses between leisure and labor supply. An individual will enter the labor force if the market wage is higher than his or her reservation wage. In this case the individual will supply labor. The existence of unemployment, however, will discourage the individual from entering the labor force because of the risk of being unemployed. This probability can be incorporated by including search or matching costs, that is, if an individual decides to enter the labor market, there is a chance that he or she may not secure a job match and thus will become unemployed. Therefore for a representative agent, as a result of unemployment, only part of the labor supply can be shifted into employed labor.

This is one feature of the job-matching model presented by Pissarides (1990), that is, supplying labor is costly in terms of the foregone reservation wage and the chance of not being matched to a job. The second feature of the matching model is the existence of an externality. The risk of an individual not being matched to a job is affected by the aggregate behavior of other agents. If the labor market gets very congested, as it may if too many individuals enter the labor force, search costs will increase. An individual, however, takes the cost of the labor supply as given and does not consider the effect of his or her labor supply decision on the costs faced by others. Similarly, each firm will hire workers until the marginal product of labor equals the wage and does not consider the effect of its hiring behavior on aggregate employment. Based on these two features, unemployment can be modeled as a natural feature of equilibrium. Related techniques can be found in Pissarides (1990) and Balistreri (2000).

SIMULATION DESIGN

The model used to study the effect of WTO membership is a dynamic, multi-region general equilibrium model. Conceptually, it is a modified conventional neoclassical general equilibrium model based on relative prices and optimizing behavior without a monetary sector. A new formulation of equilibrium unemployment is incorporated into the model for studying the labor market.[1]

The global economy is represented by nine regions. These regions are: (1) the United States, (2) Japan, (3) the European Union (EU, 15 member countries), (4) other OECD countries (including Australia, New Zealand and Canada), (5) China, (6) Taiwan, (7) South Asia (including Korea, Indonesia, Hong Kong, Malaysia, Philippines, Singapore, Thailand), (8) other Asian countries and (9) rest of the world. In each region there is one competitive firm in each sector, which only produces one good. In this model we include ten aggregated sectors: (1) textiles, (2) wearing apparel, (3) agriculture sector I (including rice, wheat, other grains, plant-based fibers, other non-grain crops, and processed food), (4) agriculture sector II (including livestock products, meat and milk products, fishery, and forestry), (5) motor vehicles and parts, (6) electronic equipment, (7) other light manufacturing, (8) mining, (9) machinery and intermediate manufacturing and (10) utilities, housing, construction and services.

The model is benchmarked to the Global Trade Analysis Project (GTAP4) data set (Hertel, 1997), which provides a social accounting matrix for each region and reports bilateral trade flows, an import tariff rate and an export tax rate across countries for different industries. Our model solves in five-year intervals spanning the horizon from 2000 to 2030.[2]

Different scenarios are simulated to study the impact of WTO accession on China's unemployment, employment shift among sectors and trade. Scenario I simulates the Uruguay Round without China and Taiwan's WTO accession. Scenario II is similar to Scenario I in exogenous assumptions, but includes China and Taiwan's accession. In this case China and Taiwan liberalize their trade and enjoy the accelerated growth rate of the Multi-Fiber Agreement (MFA) quotas in exports of textiles and clothing. Scenario II is the benchmark policy scenario we use to present our main results. Under this scenario it is assumed that China implements half of the reductions in tariff rates before 2005 and implements full reductions in 2005 after its WTO accession. In addition MFA quotas will phase out in 2005 as specified in the Uruguay Round agreement. Table 7.1 presents detailed summary descriptions of the different scenarios.

Appendix 7.1 summarizes the major assumptions about baseline GDP growth, the unemployment rate and the labor force growth rate. The leisure value share is assumed to be 20 per cent for each region. Similar to Wang (1999), two scenarios are compared to study the impact of China's WTO accession.[3] Scenario I simulates the Uruguay Round case, where WTO members liberalize their trade but without the accession of China and Taiwan. In this case we use detailed data concerning bilateral tariff cuts under the Uruguay Round agreement in seven regions (without China and Taiwan's participation) on their imports from the other eight regions. It is a seven by nine matrix for each of the ten sectors.

Table 7.1: Description of Scenarios

	China and Taiwan Accession	Reductions in tariff rates for China and Taiwan after accession	MFA quota growth rate	MFA quota system phase out schedule
Scenario I	No		Accelerated for other developing countries; constant for China and Taiwan	2005 for other developing countries; no phase out for China and Taiwan
Scenario II	Yes	Half before 2005 and full in 2005	Accelerated for all WTO members including China and Taiwan	2005 for all WTO members including China and Taiwan

Appendix 7.2 presents the average reduction in tariff rates in each region (reductions in tariff for China and Taiwan are used only in Scenario II). Each region's average tariff reduction by sector is calculated as the weighted average of the tariff reductions on imports in that sector from all other regions. This calculation uses bilateral import data from the GTAP4 data set as weights, aggregating over the more than 40 sectors included in that data. In the simulation we also apply an average 20 per cent reduction in domestic agriculture support for developed countries (16.8 per cent for the EU), and an average 13.3 per cent reduction for developing countries. For agriculture export subsidies, an average 36 per cent reduction is applied to developed countries and a 24 per cent reduction for developing countries, following Wang (1999). We assume that for developed countries the full reduction has been implemented before 2005, but for developing countries, half of these reductions are implemented before 2005 and the full reductions are assumed to be implemented in 2005.

Scenario II simulates China and Taiwan's WTO accession. All the assumptions are the same as in Scenario I but with China and Taiwan joining the WTO and liberalizing trade. Appendix 7.2 gives the average reduction in tariff rates if they join the WTO. We similarly assume that half of the implementation happens before 2005 and that the full reductions will be implemented in year 2005. Since the base year data are from 1995 data in GTAP4, an average 50 per cent tariff cut is incorporated in the baseline to represent China's tariff cut after 1995.

Another important difference between Scenario I and Scenario II is in the MFA quota growth rates. In Scenario I, since China and Taiwan are not WTO members, it is assumed that their exports of textiles and apparel are subject to a constant growth in MFA quotas. For other developing countries, however, the growth rates in MFA quotas are accelerating and the quota system will terminate in 2005. The base quota growth and the accelerated quota growth under the Uruguay Round are from Wang (1999). Specifically, for WTO members, the accelerated annual quota growth is 16 per cent higher than the growth rate established for the previous MFA restrictions for the period 1995–1997 (stage one). For 1998–2001 (stage two), it is 25 per cent higher than the stage one growth rates; and for 2002–2004 (stage three), it is 27 per cent higher than the stage two growth. The quantity restriction terminates in 2005. In contrast, in Scenario II, since China and Taiwan become WTO members, their exports in textiles and apparel enjoy the same accelerated growth rates in MFA quotas and the MFA quota will phase out in 2005.

MODEL RESULTS

This section provides results for the two scenarios: the benchmark policy scenario with China and Taiwan joining the WTO (Scenario II) or not joining (Scenario I). The model runs to year 2030. Theoretically it would be ideal to run an infinite horizon model but such a model is not practical computationally. Due to the constraint of terminal capital imposed by the model, we only report the results for 2005 and 2010. The actual finite time horizon used in computation may cause inaccuracy in the results when close to the endpoint.

Our main purpose in this chapter is to incorporate equilibrium unemployment in CGE modeling. Since China has not finalized the terms of its WTO concessions, we make some simplified assumptions about the size of its trade concessions and the time schedule of implementation. Therefore the actual numbers reported in this chapter should be interpreted with caution and should be taken as indicative but not as precise forecasts.

The overall WTO effects on trade are summarized in Table 7.2. For the years 2005 and 2010, if China joins the WTO, its total value of imports will increase by 28.8 per cent and 25.2 per cent, respectively. Imports into the agriculture sector II, previously fairly closed, will increase by 18.2 per cent and 14.3 per cent. Imports into the motor vehicles and parts sector will increase 67.2 per cent and 60.4 per cent in value in these two years. Imports from the United States will increase in value 7.6 per cent in 2005 and 4.4 per

Table 7.2: Trade Impacts of China's WTO Accession (Percentage Change)

	2005	2010
China's total imports	28.8	25.2
China's total exports	16.8	22.1
China's imports in motor vehicles	67.2	60.4
China's imports in agriculture II	18.2	14.3
China's exports in textiles	38.1	39.0
China's exports in wearing apparel	47.8	46.2
China's imports from USA	7.6	4.4
China's imports from EU 15	24.1	19.9
China's exports to USA	17.6	22.5
China's exports to EU 15	23.0	27.6

cent in 2010, estimates that are lower than the United States Trade Commission estimates of 9 – 10 per cent. The imports from the US for motor vehicles will increase by 138.5 per cent and 129.2 per cent, and for agriculture sector II, 13.3 per cent and 9.4 per cent in these two years. China's imports from the European Union will increase 24.1 per cent and 19.9 per cent in 2005 and 2010, respectively.

Since China will also enjoy benefits from WTO membership, its total value of exports will increase by 16.8 per cent in 2005 and 22.1 per cent in 2010. For industries in which China has a comparative advantage, the increase in exports is substantial. For example, for 2005 and 2010, exports of textiles will increase by 38.1 per cent and 39 per cent; while exports of wearing apparel will increase by 47.8 per cent and 46.2 per cent. China's exports to the US will increase by 17.6 per cent in 2005 and 22.5 per cent in 2010, increases that are larger than the increases in imports from the US. For textiles the increase in exports to the US will be 107.8 per cent in 2005 and 83 per cent in 2010. For wearing apparel the increase in exports to the US will be 107.3 per cent in 2005 and 82.7 per cent in 2010. China's total value of exports to the European Union will also increase by about 23 per cent in 2005 and 27.6 per cent in 2010.

As indicated above the possible effect of WTO accession on China's unemployment is one of the most important concerns for policy makers. If imports surge after China joins the WTO, domestic industries will face massive layoffs. Our simulation results, however, show that the WTO effect on unemployment actually will be favorable for China. In 2005, WTO membership would reduce China's unemployment rate from 4.37 per cent to 3.27 per cent and in 2010, from 4.36 per cent to 3.54 per cent.

WTO-induced increases in exports clearly help employment. Moreover employment shifts among sectors may also contribute to the predicted lower unemployment rate. Although the WTO-induced increase in the value of imports is higher than that of exports in percentage terms, the employment structure is different for these sectors. The increase in labor demand derived from the increase in exports for labor-intensive industries such as textiles and wearing apparel may exceed the decrease in labor demand in some capital-intensive industries like motor vehicles. We also find that WTO accession will reduce the total number of unemployed by 24.8 per cent in 2005 and by 18.3 per cent in 2010. In 2005, China's total unemployment will decrease from 42.03 million to 31.59 million and in 2010; it will decrease from 47.13 million to 38.5 million.

The results for unemployment only provide a lower bound for the WTO effect on the unemployment rate because our model does not include FDI and the opening of the service industries. FDI will generally increase demand for domestic labor and so will the opening of the service industries. For example, it is expected that foreign insurance companies and banks will recruit most of their employees in China. If these effects are taken into account in the model, as they will be in future research, the reduction in unemployment for China should be even larger.

China's total employment will increase by 1.73 per cent and 1.44 per cent in 2005 and 2010, respectively. The number of workers will increase from 919.3 million to 935.1 million and from 1035 million to 1049.9 million for these two years, respectively. The results also show a very minor reduction in total employment in the United States, that is, about 0.01 per cent.

WTO accession will also cause shifts in employment among sectors in China. Table 7.3 provides details of sectoral shifts in employment. As expected the largest increase in employment occurs in the wearing apparel industry, followed by electronics, light manufacturing and textiles. The employment increase in wearing apparel will be 36.3 per cent and 34.1 per cent in 2005 and 2010, respectively. Since these industries are mainly labor-intensive, this will contribute to the increase in total employment and the lower unemployment rate. In 2005 the total number of workers employed in wearing apparel, electronics, light manufacturing, and textiles will increase from 12.45 to 16.97 million, from 10.19 to 10.96 million, 40.87 to 42.52 million, and from 17.89 to 18.27 million, respectively. The largest decrease in employment will be in the motor vehicle sector with a magnitude of about 30 per cent. The total number of workers employed in the motor vehicle sector will decrease from 3.08 million to 2.16 million in 2005. Employment in the agricultural sector will also decrease especially for the agriculture sector I; while for the agriculture sector II, the effect will be very small. Employment in agriculture I will decrease from 155.25 to 150.58 million in 2005.

Table 7.3: Employment shifts in Different Sectors with China and Taiwan's WTO Accession (Percentage Change)

Sector	2005	2010
Textile	2.1	2.3
Wearing apparel	36.3	34.1
Agriculture I	−3.1	−2.5
Agriculture II	−0.5	−0.4
Motor vehicles and parts	−29.7	−30.5
Electronics	7.6	11.5
Light manufacturing	4.0	6.9
Mining	0.9	1.7
Machinery and intermediate manufacturing	0.5	2.0
Utility and service	2.3	1.6

The WTO-induced employment shifts among sectors raise new policy issues for the Chinese government. To minimize transaction costs, the government should help facilitate and smooth the shifts. In particular, the government can help in job searches, and especially by offering job training to those who need to find jobs in different industries.

CONCLUSIONS

This chapter attempts to assess the potential impact of China's WTO accession on its unemployment rate, employment shifts among sectors, and trade. To evaluate the overall change in the unemployment rate, we adopt a modified CGE model with endogenous equilibrium unemployment. Unemployment is incorporated into a traditional CGE framework by adopting a job search or match model.

Based on our simulations the WTO-induced increase in imports is larger than that in WTO-induced exports. China's overall unemployment rate, however, will be about one percentage point lower after joining the WTO. The reduction in the unemployment rate is likely to be caused by structural differences in the import and export sectors. In particular the increase in exports mainly occurs in labor-intensive sectors, while the increase in imports occurs in capital intensive sectors. Therefore the increases in labor demand due to larger exports will exceed the decrease in employment because of higher competition in import sectors. Our estimates may just provide a lower bound for the reduction in the unemployment rate because we do not include FDI in the model. In addition the WTO will require China to open most of its service sectors. Both FDI and the opening of the service sectors will likely increase total employment.

On the other hand employment shifts among sectors as a result of WTO accession are quite dramatic, especially for the wearing apparel and automobile industries. The Chinese government should pay close attention to employment shifts among sectors. It is important for the government to smooth such shifts and to reduce the associated transaction costs, for example, by providing job training for workers.

Due to the complicated structure of dynamic CGE modeling with unemployment and the unfinalized terms of China's joining the WTO, our model inevitably involves some simplified assumptions. Thus, the exact number should be interpreted with caution. Future research needs to separate skilled and unskilled labor, as well as incorporate more accurate terms on China's WTO agreement. More importantly, although very difficult, it is desirable to include FDI and other non-tariff barriers in the model to have a more accurate simulation.

NOTES

1. Due to the limitation on chapter length, the techniques of the model are not presented here and can be provided on request
2. The software we use to solve the model is GAMS and MPSGE (Rutherford, 1999).
3. We would like to thank Wang Zhi for providing data on tariff rates with and without the Uruguay round.

REFERENCES

Bach, Christian F., Will Martin, and Jennifer A. Stevens (1996), 'China and the WTO: Tariff Offers, Exemptions, and Welfare Implications', *Weltwirtschaftliches*, 132 (3).

Balistreri, Edward J. (2000), 'Operationalizing Equilibrium Unemployment: A General Equilibrium External Economies Approach', *Journal of Economic Dynamics and Control*, forthcoming.

Frazier, Mark W. (1999), 'Coming to Terms with the "WTO" effect on U.S.–China Trade and China's Economic Growth', The National Bureau of Asian Research, *NBR Briefing*, September 1999.

Hertel, T.W. (ed.) (1997), *Global Trade Analysis: Modeling and Applications*, Cambridge: Cambridge Univ. Press.

Hu, Fred (1999), 'WTO Membership: What This Means for Greater China', *Global Economics*, Paper No. 14.

Li, Haizheng and Jeffrey Zax (2000), 'Economic Transition and the Evolving Labor Market in China', working paper, School of Economics, Georgia Tech.

Pissarides, C. A. (1990), *Equilibrium Unemployment Theory*, Cambridge: Basil Blackwell.

Rosen, Daniel H. (1999), 'China and the World Trade Organization: An Economic Balance Sheet', *International Economics Policy Briefs*, Institute for International Economics.

Rutherford, Thomas F. (1999), 'Applied General Equilibrium Modeling with MPSGE as a GAMS Subsystem: An Overview of the Modeling Framework and Syntax', *Computational Economics*, 14, pp. 1–46.

State Statistical Bureau (1998), *China Statistical Yearbook*, China Statistical Publishing House.

United States General Accounting Office (2000), 'World Trade Organization – China's Membership Status and Normal Trade Relations Issues', Report to Congressional Committees, March 2000.

United States International Trade Commission (1999), 'Assessment of the Economic Effects on the United States of China's Accession to the WTO', Executive Summary, Publication 3228, August 1999, pp. 11–12.

Wang Zhi (1997), 'China and Taiwan Access to the World Trade Organization: Implications of the U.S. Agriculture and Trade', Agriculture Economics, 17, 239–264.

—(1999), 'The Impact of China's WTO Entry on the World Labor-intensive Export market: A Recursive Dynamic CGE Analysis', *World Economy*, 22, 379–405.

Yang, Y. Z. (1996), 'China's WTO Membership: What's at Stake?', *The World Economy*, 19 (6), 661–682.

Appendix 1: Baseline Assumptions for GDP Growth, Labor Force Growth and Unemployment (Percent)

	US	Japan	Europe	Other OECD	China	Taiwan	SE Asia	Oth Asia	ROW
GDP Growth	2.4	1.5	2.4	2.7	6.6	4.7	4.0	4.9	3.6
LF Growth	1.1	0.6	0.5	1.4	1.1	0.9	2.4	2.4	2.1
Unemployment	5.0	3.4	10.0	9.0	4.3	2.6	2.6	2.6	5.0

Source: Wang Zhi (1999)

Appendix 2: Assumptions on Reductions in Tariff Rates

	Textile	Apparel	Agr I	Agr II	Motor Veh	Elec	Light Mfg	Mining	Mach & Interm Mfg	Utility & Service
US	21.1	0.0	82.9	1.7	0.0	4.3	13.0	40.6	51.3	0.0
Japan	9.3	7.5	58.5	15.8	100.0	88.7	16.9	7.2	33.8	100.0
EU 15	7.5	2.1	58.9	42.8	0.6	4.4	35.2	11.4	36.8	100.0
Oth OECD	32.8	17.6	20.0	11.5	4.2	1.2	23.9	73.9	28.5	0.0
China	72.7	74.6	44.5	49.2	57.8	67.2	70.8	64.3	62.9	0.3
Taiwan	42.0	42.0	33.0	19.6	42.0	42.0	42.0	42.0	42.0	0.0
SE Asia	0.5	5.6	51.2	26.2	4.6	17.9	8.7	6.7	15.9	0.0
Oth Asia	30.3	35.0	42.4	25.2	53.5	38.9	47.2	29.9	50.9	0.0
ROW	12.0	8.2	22.1	38.1	7.5	7.5	10.4	24.6	8.3	42.4

Source: Wang Zhi (1999).

8. Regional Inequality

Xiaobo Zhang and Kevin Honglin Zhang

INTRODUCTION

Globalization in developing countries has held forth two promises: promoting economic growth and greater convergence across countries and regions. This may be best seen from the role of international trade and foreign direct investment (FDI), the two primary driving forces behind globalization, in economic development. Many studies in the literature have suggested that trade liberalization could contribute to economic growth by (a) increasing specialization and expanding the efficiency raising benefits of comparative advantage, (b) offering greater economies of scale due to an enlargement of effective market size, (c) affording greater capacity utilization and (d) inducing more rapid technological change (Pack, 1988; Bliss, 1989; Evans, 1989; and Rodrik, 1995).

Under the standard Hecksher–Ohlin theorem, with the assumption of integrated factor markets, opening up trade will stimulate the relative demand for unskilled labor in the developing countries and thus make developing countries more egalitarian (Deardoff and Stern, 1994; Wood, 1997).

In a similar way FDI may foster economic growth in a host country through increasing capital formation, augmenting employment, expanding exports and transferring technology (Krugman, 1995). Since FDI is theoretically driven by a host country's location advantages such as lower labor costs, the gains from FDI may be expected to be larger in those regions with lower incomes (Zhang and Markusen, 1999), leading to convergence in a less developed economy.

Much of the literature on the relationship between globalization and inequality has focused on developed countries, especially the case of the United States (Edwards, 1993; Richardson, 1995; Feenstra and Hanson 1996; Borenstein et al., 1998). However the empirical evidence for the impact of globalization on income distribution in developing countries has been limited and the findings of existing studies are at best, mixed. The existing work for developing countries has been limited to the effects of trade liberalization on wage inequality (for example, Wood, 1997; Robbins, 1996; Hanson and Harrison, 1999), shedding little light on how international trade and FDI affect regional inequality in developing countries.

Considering the increasing trend of globalization, it is important to assess empirically the link between globalization and regional inequality in developing countries. In this study we attempt to tackle this issue using China as an example. China has clearly become a major participant in the process of globalization. It is virtually certain to become even more important in the future because of its size, dynamic economic growth and continuing policy reforms, especially its entry into the World Trade Organization in the near future. Yet there is relatively little understanding of many of the fundamental elements of China's emergence, such as the impact of foreign trade and FDI on regional inequality. This study aims to assess how important foreign trade and FDI have been to China's regional inequality. In particular we develop a framework to quantify empirically the effects of globalization and test whether trade liberalization has reduced regional inequality in China as theoretically predicted.

The rest of the chapter is organized as follows. The next section describes recent trends in foreign trade, FDI, economic growth and regional inequality over the past two decades. The section after that develops the conceptual framework. The section that follows provides our estimates of the production functions needed to decompose the sources of regional inequality. The last section highlights our conclusions and policy implications.

FOREIGN TRADE, FDI AND REGIONAL INEQUALITY

In recent years few developments in economic globalization have been more important than the sudden emergence of China as a trading nation and major host for FDI (Lardy, 1995). For the two decades since economic reform was initiated in the late 1970s, the role of the foreign sector in the Chinese economy has burgeoned in ways that no one anticipated (Wei, 1995; Zhang, 2000).

China's economic reforms and its opening to the outside world have resulted in phenomenal growth in international trade and inward FDI flows. Between 1984 and 1997 the value of exports grew 19 per cent annually, while manufactured exports grew 24 per cent per year. By 1994 China exported manufactured goods worth more than $100 billion and was the eighth largest such exporter in the world. Changes in FDI flows into China are even more astonishing. From an almost isolated economy in the late 1970s, China has become the largest recipient of FDI among the developing countries and globally, the second only to the US since 1993. FDI flows into China in 1997 totaled $46 billion, which constitutes 40 per cent of total FDI in all developing countries. By 1997 the total FDI received in China reached as much as $226 billion (UNCTAD, 1998).

Table 8.1: Openness, FDI and Regional Inequality

Year	Openness	FDI/GDP	Gini
1978	0.05	0.00	0.22
1979	0.06	0.01	0.20
1980	0.07	0.04	0.20
1981	0.08	0.07	0.19
1982	0.08	0.07	0.19
1983	0.08	0.09	0.19
1984	0.09	0.22	0.19
1985	0.11	0.31	0.19
1986	0.12	0.41	0.19
1987	0.18	0.45	0.20
1988	0.18	0.70	0.20
1989	0.19	0.72	0.20
1990	0.23	0.85	0.20
1991	0.27	1.10	0.21
1992	0.29	2.55	0.22
1993	0.29	4.54	0.24
1994	0.39	6.56	0.24
1995	0.35	5.49	0.23
1996	0.32	5.08	0.24
1997	0.32	5.00	0.24
1998	0.30	4.43	0.26
Annual growth (%)			
1978–84	3.57		−1.04
1985–98	3.86	11.80	0.63
1978–98	3.77		0.34

Note: The Gini coefficient is calculated by the author using labor productivity (GDP/labor) with total labor force as weights at the provincial level. The openness variable is defined as the ratio of total trade relative to total GDP. FDI / GDP are in percentages.

With the rapid increase in foreign trade and FDI, China's economy has become increasingly integrated with the world economy. As shown in Table 8.1, the share of FDI in total GDP reached 4.4 percent by 1998. The ratio of total trade (the sum of exports and imports) to total GDP increased fivefold, from 0.05 to 0.3, during this period. China's boom in foreign trade and inward FDI has been accompanied by fast economic growth. GDP grew annually at nearly 10 per cent during the period 1978–98. The role of foreign trade and FDI in the Chinese economy has become increasingly important. The success in the promotion of manufactured exports provides China with a powerful mechanism for technological upgrading and thus a source of rapid productivity growth in the domestic economy. Inward FDI flows in 1995 constituted 26 per cent of gross fixed capital formation. Foreign funded firms employed 18 million Chinese by the end of 1996, constituting 18 per cent of the total non-agricultural labor force. In 1997 19 per cent of total gross industrial output was produced by foreign affiliates (UNCTAD, 1998). However the gains in economic growth and trade liberalization have not been evenly distributed across regions. Table 8.2 details the foreign trade and FDI for six selected provinces from 1986 to 1998. In 1998 the three coastal provinces, Guangdong, Jiangsu and Shanghai, rank as the top three; while the three inland provinces, Guizhou, Inner Mongolia and Jilin, are the bottom three in terms of attracting FDI. The above three coastal provinces alone contributed more than 60 per cent of total foreign trade in 1998. It seems that the coastal provinces have attracted far more foreign direct investment and generated more trade volume than the inland provinces during the liberalization process.

In order to further investigate this issue, we divide China into two zones: the coastal zone, which includes Beijing, Liaoning, Tianjin, Hebei, Shandong, Jiangsu, Shanghai, Zhejiang, Fujian, Guangdong and Guangxi and the inland zone, comprising all the remaining provinces. Hainan is included in Guangdong Province. We calculate the mean ratios of GDP, domestic capital, FDI, education levels and economic openness along the coastal and inland divide in Table 8.3.

Two features are discernable from these mean ratios. First there indeed exist significant disparities between the coastal and inland areas. GDP in the coastal region is more than 40 per cent higher than that in the inland region in 1998. Both the levels of domestic capital and FDI per unit of labor in the coastal region are much higher than those in the inland region In particular more than 80 percent of FDI has been concentrated in the coastal provinces. The average years of schooling in the inland provinces has been more than 25 percent less than that in the coastal provinces. The share of trade in total GDP in the coastal region has been at least two times higher than in the inland region. It seems that the higher labor productivity in the in the coastal areas is accompanied by more capital input, better education and a higher degree of openness.

Table 8.2: Foreign Trade and FDI in Six Provinces ($ US million current prices)

Year	Coast			Inland		
	Shanghai	Jiangsu	Guang-dong	Inner Mongolia	Jilan	Guizhou
			Trade			
1986	5204	2412	6809	7	1	1
1987	5996	2873	21329	0	0	1
1988	7245	3458	31684	3	6	4
1989	7848	3843	36674	0	3	7
1990	7431	4139	42835	0	17	5
1991	8044	5310	53870	0	18	7
1992	9759	6962	67443	5	66	20
1993	12832	9129	80913	30	238	43
1994	15867	11759	99360	40	318	64
1995	19025	16278	106239	52	399	57
1996	22263	20688	112246	72	452	31
1997	24764	23621	132068	73	403	50
1998	26046	26426	131707	91	409	45

Year	Coast			Inland		
	Shanghai	Jiangsu	Guang-dong	Inner Mongolia	Jilan	Guizhou
			FDI			
1986	98	18	675	7	1	1
1987	212	50	603	0	0	1
1988	364	103	1033	3	6	4
1989	422	95	1264	0	3	7
1990	177	141	1560	0	17	5
1991	175	233	1999	0	18	7
1992	1259	1403	4003	5	66	20
1993	2318	3002	8546	30	238	43
1994	3231	4177	10271	40	318	64
1995	3250	4781	11235	52	399	57
1996	3941	5210	12543	72	452	31
1997	4255	5435	13340	73	403	50
1998	3602	6632	12737	91	409	45

Sources: Foreign trade figures are from *Comprehensive Statistical Data* and *Materials on 50 Years of New China*. Realized Foreign Direct data are from various issues of *China Statistical Yearbooks*.

Table 8.3 Coast–Inland comparisons

Year	GDP	Capital	FDI	Education	Openness
1985	1.12	1.20	13.23	1.27	4.68
1986	1.13	1.24	7.35	1.26	3.37
1987	1.15	1.26	8.69	1.26	4.92
1988	1.18	1.30	7.42	1.25	5.19
1989	1.20	1.34	11.83	1.26	5.26
1990	1.16	1.27	16.04	1.28	5.93
1991	1.22	1.35	16.38	1.29	5.50
1992	1.28	1.48	9.35	1.33	4.90
1993	1.36	1.61	6.81	1.32	4.70
1994	1.41	1.64	7.15	1.27	4.91
1995	1.39	1.67	7.03	1.24	4.86
1996	1.38	1.69	7.36	1.29	5.45
1997	1.38	1.56	6.21	1.32	6.14
1998	1.45	1.52	6.82	1.35	5.90
Growth (%)	29	26	−48	6	26

Notes:
a. Author's calculation. GDP, capital formation(K), and foreign direct investment (FDI are from various issues of *China Statistical Yearbooks*. The schooling variable is the average years of education, derived by the authors based on the proportions of the population with primary, secondary and above levels of education. Openness is defined as the ratio of total trade (imports plus exports) relative to total GDP.
b. The coast zone includes the following provinces: Beijing, Liaoning, Tianjin, Hebei, Shandong, Jaingsu, Shanghai, Zhejiang, Fujian, Guandong and Guangxi. Remaining provinces are classified as west zone. Tibet is excluded due to the lack of data. Hainan is included in Guandong Province.

Second the coastal inland gap has increased sharply throughout the period. The GDP gap between the two regions rose by 29 per cent between 1985 and 1998. The difference in the growth rates between the coastal and inland regions has been as high as three percentage points during the past two decades. Domestic capital investment has become increasingly concentrated in the coastal region with a rise in 26 per cent during the period. The difference in economic openness also has increased by 26 per cent. The average years of schooling between the two regions has widened by 6 per cent. Due to severe year to year fluctuations, the ratio of FDI has not exhibited a clear trend. It appears that the increased disparity in output levels among regions might have been caused in large part by differences input levels. The question is which factors have contributed more to the overall increase in inequality?

It is legitimate to speculate that the changing comparative advantage associated with globalization might be an important factor behind the changes in regional inequality. Figure 8.1 plots the relationship between regional inequality and openness; while Figure 8.2 graphs the correlation between FDI and regional inequality. The two figures suggest a positive

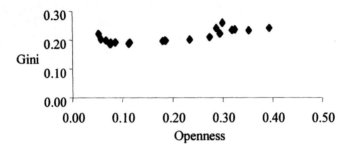

Figure 8.1: Openness and Regional Inequality

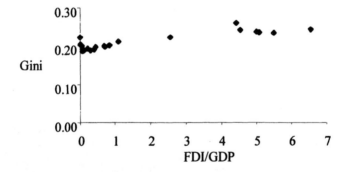

Figure 8.2: FDI and Regional Inequality

relationship between openness and FDI and inequality. However we cannot simply infer causation from these two figures. There are possibly many other factors affecting regional inequality as well during this period. A more systematic framework is needed to quantify the contributions of various components to overall regional disparity. While there is a considerable literature on the causes of China's regional inequality (Lyons, 1991; Tsui, 1991; Fleisher and Chen, 1997; Kanbur and Zhang, 1999; Yang, 1999), previous studies have not systematically examined the role of globalization in regional inequality.

One constraint on assessing the distributional impact of FDI and other production factors is the lack of a suitable analytical framework to decompose the contributions of production factors, such as FDI, on regional inequality. In the literature inequality is decomposed based on either exogenous population groups or income sources (Shorrocks, 1982, 1984). The distributional effect of production factors cannot be directly analyzed with these existing frameworks. Moreover because the returns to FDI have not been documented in the official GDP statistics, it is hard to evaluate directly the impact of FDI on inequality. In this chapter we develop an indirect approach based on Shorrocks' method to quantify the impact of FDI and economic openness on both growth and regional inequality using a panel data set at the provincial level.

CONCEPTUAL FRAMEWORK

We assume that each region has the same production functions at a given time but that they lie at different points on the production surfaces. Following standard procedures in the literature, we assume that the aggregate production functions are of Cobb–Douglas form as follows:

$$Y = AL^{\beta_1} K_D^{\beta_2} K_F^{\beta_3} E^{\beta_4} OP^{\beta_5} \tag{8.1}$$

where Y = total GDP,
A = intercept,
L = labor input,
K_D = domestic capital stocks,
K_F = foreign direct investment,
E = education level,
OP = openness,
β_i = parameters to be estimated.

Since each region varies in size, it does not make sense to calculate regional inequality using total GDP. Therefore we use labor productivity to compare regional differences. Both output and conventional inputs (excluding education and openness) in (8.1) are divided by the number of laborers L, to yield:

$$\frac{Y}{L} = AL^{\delta-1} \left(\frac{L}{L}\right)^{\beta_1} \left(\frac{K_D}{L}\right)^{\beta_2} \left(\frac{K_F}{L}\right)^{\beta_3} E^{\beta_4} OP^{\beta_5} \tag{8.2}$$

where $\delta = \sum_{i=1}^{3} \beta_i$ Notably, labor still appears on the right-hand side of equation (8.2) unless an assumption of constant returns to scale is imposed on the production function so that $\delta = 1$. In this chapter, following the standard practice in the literature, we assume constant returns to scale.

The Logarithm form of equation (8.2) is given by:

$$y = a + \beta_2 k_D + \beta_3 k_F + \beta_4 e \quad , \qquad (8.3)$$

where lower cases indicate logarithms. An error term ε is added to represent the stochastic shocks to output and is assumed to be unrelated to the other variables.

Following Shorrocks (1982), the variance of y in equation (8.3) can be decomposed as:

$$\sigma^2(y) = \text{cov}(y, \beta_2 k_D) + \text{cov}(y, \beta_3 k_F) + \text{cov}(y, \beta_4 e) + \text{cov}(y, \beta_5 op) + \text{cov}(y, \varepsilon) \qquad (8.4)$$
$$= \beta_2 \text{cov}(y, k_D) + \beta_3 \text{cov}(y, k_F) + \beta_4 \text{cov}(y, e) + \beta_5 \text{cov}(y, op) + \sigma^2(\varepsilon),$$

where $\sigma^2(y)$ is the variance of y and cov(y, •) represents the covariance of y with other variables. Since all the right-hand side variables in equation (8.3) are not correlated with the error term, the covariance of y and ε is equal to the variance of ε. Considering that y is already in logarithmic form, $\sigma^2(y$ is a standard inequality measure known as the logarithmic variance (Cowell, 1995). It has the property of invariance to scale. According to Shorrocks (1982), the covariance terms on the right-hand side of (8.4) can be regarded as the contributions of the factor components to total inequality.

Under the above framework we need first to estimate a labor productivity function (8.3) and then to decompose inequality into the components of production factors following (8.4).

DATA AND EMPIRICAL RESULTS

A panel data set including 28 provinces over the period 1986–1998 was constructed from various issues of the *China Statistical Yearbook*. Tibet is excluded from the analysis due to the lack of consistent GDP data. Hainan Province is included in Guangdong Province because data are not available until 1988 when it became a separate province. Both nominal GDP and annual growth rates of GDP for each province are published in the *China Statistical Yearbook*. We assume that prices were the same for all provinces in the initial year of 1986 and that the nominal GDPs are equivalent to the real GDPs. Under this assumption real GDP estimates for the whole period from 1986 to 1998, which is the latest available year, can be derived from nominal GDP data for 1986 and the published annual growth rates in real GDP.

The capital accumulation reported in the national accounts is used as a proxy for the domestic capital stock. This variable is further deflated by the fixed asset price index (1986 = 100). FDI data are adjusted using a three-year moving average to overcome the year to year fluctuations at the province level. Similar to domestic capital, FDI is converted to constant values using a deflator for US dollars. The total trade volume data are from *Comprehensive Statistical Data and Materials on 50 Years of New China*. China State Statistics Bureau publishes the proportions of population with primary, secondary, high school and college levels of education in *China Population Statistics*. Assuming that the years of schooling for the above categories are five, eight, ten and 14, respectively, we are able to calculate the average years of schooling for the total population in each province.

Labor productivity functions for inland and coastal regions were estimated respectively based on equation (8.3). A regime dummy was included to capture the policy shift toward a more open system beginning from 1992. To reduce the endogeneity problems inherent in the FDI and openness variables, we use a one year lag for these two variables in the estimation. Table 8.4 reports the estimation results. The adjusted R^2s for the labor productivity functions are 0.90 and 0.94, respectively, implying good fit.

Because we assume constant returns to scale, the labor elasticities for the two regions can be calculated by subtracting the elasticities for domestic capital and FDI from 1. The labor elasticities in inland and coastal regions are 0.436 and 0.300, respectively. Among the production factors and shift variables considered in the estimation, capital has the largest impact on labor productivity. The elasticities with respect to domestic capital, FDI and openness are higher in the coastal region than in the inland region. Both regions have greater capital elasticities than labor elasticities. The elasticity of schooling in the inland region is larger than in the coastal region. The results indicate that inland and coastal regions indeed have different production frontiers. As a result FDI and openness have different effects on labor productivity growth for the two regions.

Given the estimated coefficients for the labor productivity functions, we can now apply the inequality decomposition method outlined in equation (8.4) to quantify the contributions of the production factors, human capital and openness to total regional inequality in labor productivity. Table 8.5 presents the overall inequality and the contributions from these factors to total inequality.

Table 8.4: Estimation results for Labor Productivity

Variables	Inland	Coast
Intercept	1.148**	1.322**
	(0.167)	(0.281)
Domestic capital	0.533**	0.673**
	(0.021)	(0.026)
FDI	0.011**	0.027**
	(0.006)	(0.012)
Schooling	0.533**	0.325**
	(0.063)	(0.162)
Openness	0.050*	0.077**
	(0.027)	(0.024)
Regime dummy	0.119**	0.108**
(1992–98)	(0.023)	(0.034)
Adjusted R2	0.900	0.940

Notes: All variables are in logarithms. GDP, domestic capital and foreign direct investment (FDI) are in constant prices (1986=100). The dependent variable is GDP per unit of labor. Domestic capital is measured as capital accumulation deflated by fixed asset prices. FDI is adjusted using the official deflator for US dollars and it is smoothed through a three year moving average to overcome extreme year to year fluctuations. FDI and openness have a one year lag. Because FDI data are not systemically available until 1985, the decomposition is conducted for only the years after 1985. One and two asterisks indicate statistical significance at the 10% and 5% levels respectively. Figures in parentheses are standard errors.

Source: Various issues of *China Statistical Yearbooks.*

The inequality index, measured as the log variance, in the second column in Table 8.5 has increased by 52.5 per cent from 0.198 in 1986 to 0.301 in 1998, indicating a widening gap in labor productivity over the period. The distributions of domestic capital, schooling, FDI and openness account for −48.2 per cent, −22.1 per cent, 9.4 per cent and 3.3 per cent, respectively, of the total increases in regional inequality. The uneven distribution of domestic capital has been a dominant factor behind the increase in regional inequality. Schooling has been the only equalizing factor, which contributed -42.2 per cent to the increase in total inequality. The uneven distribution of FDI and difference in openness across provinces have contributed 17.9 per cent and 3.3 per cent, respectively. Putting these two together, economic liberalization has explained 21.2 per cent of the increase in total regional inequality. In short, after controlling for many other factors, economic liberalization is still a rather important force behind the widening regional disparity. This finding is contrary to the standard theoretical prediction that economic liberalization has an inequality reducing effect in developing countries.

In this chapter we argue that the implicit assumption of integrated factor markets underlying the standard analysis does not hold in China. Segregated

Table 8.5: Inequality Decomposition by Factors

Year	In-equality	Domestic Capital	Schooling	FDI	Openness	Other factors
1986	0.198	0.175	−0.017	−0.001	0.009	0.032
1987	0.206	0.182	−0.020	−0.001	0.009	0.035
1988	0.213	0.192	−0.024	0.008	0.009	0.028
1989	0.213	0.198	−0.025	0.010	0.010	0.021
1990	0.220	0.194	−0.028	0.011	0.011	0.033
1991	0.226	0.193	−0.034	0.012	0.011	0.044
1992	0.238	0.213	−0.038	0.012	0.011	0.040
1993	0.254	0.233	−0.046	0.013	0.011	0.043
1994	0.259	0.250	−0.049	0.013	0.011	0.033
1995	0.274	0.261	−0.054	0.015	0.012	0.039
1996	0.284	0.266	−0.058	0.016	0.013	0.047
1997	0.293	0.267	−0.060	0.017	0.014	0.054
1998	0.301	0.270	−0.061	0.018	0.015	0.059
Growth (%)	52.5	48.2	−22.1	9.4	3.3	13.7
Contribution	100.0	91.9	−42.2	17.9	6.4	26.1

Notes:
a. The decomposition method is based on the formula outlined in equation (8.4).
b. The second column refers to the measure of inequality (log variance). Columns (3)–(6) are the shares of contributions to the overall inequality by the domestic capital, schooling, FDI, openness and province-specific effects.

factor markets can aggravate the distributional impact of changes in regional comparative advantages associated with globalization. In a closed economy with agriculture as the predominant mode of production, the comparative advantage is mainly determined by the difference in land/labor ratios across regions within a country. When the economy opens its door to the outside world, a region's comparative advantage is evaluated in a broader global context. In this context regions adjacent to more developed countries may enjoy a far better location advantage for trade and development than landlocked regions, and therefore may have a faster growth.

For instance, in 1978, labor productivity in Guangdong Province ranked 14th, which was almost the same as the inland Sichuan Province. In a closed economy Guangdong did not enjoy any obvious better resource endowments than inland provinces. However after China opened its door to the world, Guangdong has become the most favored place for foreign direct investment and international trade in large part due to its proximity to Hong Kong. Meanwhile labor productivity in Sichuan has declined from 15th in 1978 to 23rd in 1998. Clearly the relative comparative advantages between the two provinces have changed significantly as economic liberalization has proceeded.

In the ideal case, with fully integrated factor markets, changes in comparative advantages will not affect regional disparity. With free movement of labor and capital regional differences in returns to labor and capital can in large part be mitigated. However because of geographical and institutional barriers, there exist strong segmentations and distortions in China's factor markets as shown in Kanbur and Zhang (1999) and Yang (1999). Restrictions on rural–urban and regional migrations have been identified as the major factor contributing to labor market inefficiency.

In addition to segmentations in the labor market, there exist large distortions in China's capital market as well. Over the past two decades China has implemented a coast biased development policy in utilizing the location advantages of the coastal region since the early 1980s. For instance, until the early 1990s, almost all the economic zones had been established in the coastal provinces, which enjoyed far more favorable polices regarding attracting FDI than the inland region. As a result the capital/labor ratio between the coastal and inland regions has increased significantly. Fan, Zhang and Robinson (1999) show an increasing variation in marginal returns to capital since 1985, implying the existence of distortions in the capital market.

In summary, globalization has led to changes in regional comparative advantages, which, in turn, have negatively affected regional inequality due to the existence of segmentations in labor and capital markets.

CONCLUSIONS

This chapter provides a method for examining the effect of globalization on regional inequality in developing countries and applies the method to China. Using a provincial level data set for the period 1986 to 1998, a model was estimated that enables the impacts of FDI and openness on regional inequality to be quantified.

The increasing trend of regional disparity can be in large explained by the uneven distribution of production factors and variations in openness among regions. Both domestic and foreign capital investments have been concentrated in the more developed coastal regions, leading to faster growth in these areas. Even after controlling for many other factors, we still find FDI and openness have played important roles in contributing to changes in overall regional inequality. This finding is in contrast to theoretical predictions by the standard trade model that implicitly assumes integrated factor markets. Our empirical finding can be explained by the fact that China's factor markets have been rather segmented. Because of the segmentation most gains as a result of globalization have just reached part of the country, leading to widening regional disparities.

With China joining the WTO the economy will become more liberalized, likely resulting in more dramatic changes in regional comparative advantages. If the government continues to favor the coastal region in its investment strategy, then regional disparity will widen further. Further liberalizing the economy in the inland region is an important development strategy for the government to both promote economic growth and reduce regional inequality. In general removing distortions in factor markets will help mitigate the negative distributional effects of the globalization process.

REFERENCES

Bliss, C. (1989), 'Trade and development', in H. Chenery and T. N. Srinivasan (eds), *Handbook of Development Economics, II*, Oxford: Elsevier Science B. V.

Borenstein, E., J. De Gregorio and J.W. Lee (1998), 'How does foreign direct investment affect economic growth?', *Journal of International Economics*, 45, pp. 115–135.

China State Statistics Bureau (SSB) (1998), *China Development Report*, Beijing: China Statistical Press.

China State Statistics Bureau (SSB), *China Fixed Assets and Investment Statistics*, China State Statistics Bureau (SSB), *China Statistical Yearbook*, various issues, Beijing: China Statistical Press.

China State Statistics Bureau (SSB), *China Population Statistics*, various issues, Beijing: China Statistical Press.

China State Statistics Bureau (SSB) (1999), *Comprehensive Statistical Data and Materials on 50 Years of New China*, Beijing: China Statistical Press.

Cowell, F. (1995), *Measuring Inequality*, 2nd edn, London, New York: Prentice Hall/Harvester Wheatsheaf.

Deardorff, A. and R. Stern (eds) (1994), *The Stolper–Samuelson Theorem: A Golden Jubilee*, Ann Arbor: University of Michigan Press.

Edwards, W. (1993), 'Openness, trade liberalization, and growth in developing countries', *Journal of Economic Literature*, 31 (3), pp. 1358–1393.

Evans, D. (1989), 'Alternative perspectives on trade and development', in H. Cheery and T. N. Srinivasan (eds), *Handbook of Development Economics, II*, Oxford: Elsevier Science B. V.

Fan, S., X. Zhang, and S. Robinson (1999), *Past and Future Sources of Growth for China*, EPTD Discussion Paper No. 53, Washington, DC: International Food Policy Research Institute.

Feenstra, R. and G. Hanson (1996), 'Foreign investment, outsourcing and relative wages', in R. Feenstra and D. Irwin (eds), *The Political Economy of Trade: Papers in Honor of Jagdish Bhagwati*, Cambridge, MA: MIT Press.

Fleisher, B. M. and J. Chen (1997), 'The coast–non-coast income gap, productivity, and economic policy in China', *Journal of Comparative Economics*, 25(2), pp. 220–236.

Hanson, G. and A. Harrison (1999), 'Trade liberalization and wage inequality in Mexico', *Industrial and Labor Relations Review*, 52, pp. 271–288.

Kanbur, R. and X. Zhang (1999), 'Which regional inequality? The evolution of rural–urban and inland–coastal inequality in China, 1983–1995', *Journal of Comparative Economics*, 27: pp. 686–701.

Krugman, P. (1995), 'Increasing returns, imperfect competition and the positive theory of international trade', in G. Grossman and K. Rogogff (eds) *Handbook of International Economics, III*, Amsterdam: Elsevier Science B. V.

Lardy, N. R. (1995), *China in the World Economy*, Washington, DC: Institute for International Economics.

Lyons, T. P. (1991), 'Interprovincial disparities in China: output and consumption, 1952–1987', *Economic Development and Cultural Change*, 39(3), pp. 471–506.

Pack, H. (1988), 'Industrialization and trade', in H. Chenery and T. N. Srinivasan (eds), *Handbook of Development Economics*, I, Amsterdam: Elsevier Science B. V.

Richardson, J. (1995), 'Income inequality and trade: how to think, what to conclude', *Journal of Economic Perspectives*, 9, pp. 33–55.

Robbins, D. (1996), *HOS Hits Facts: Facts Win; Evidence on Trade and Wages in the Developing World*, Developing Discussion Paper No. 557, Harvard Institute for International Development.

Rodrik, D. (1995), 'Trade and industrial policy reform', in J. Behrman and T. N. Srinivasan (eds), *Handbook of Development Economics, III*, Amsterdam: Elsevier Science B. V.

Shorrocks, A. F. (1982), 'Inequality decomposition by factor components', *Econometrica*, 50(1), pp. 193–211.

Shorrocks, A. F. (1984), 'Inequality decomposition by population subgroups', *Econometrica*, 52(6), pp. 1369–1385.

Tsui, K. (1991), 'China's regional inequality, 1952–1985', *Journal of Comparative Economics*, 15 (1), pp. 1–21.

United Nations Conference on Trade and Development (UNCTAD) (1998), *World Investment Report 1998*, New York: United Nations.

Wei, S. (1995), 'The open door policy and China's rapid growth: Evidence from city-level data', in T. Ito and A. O. Krueger (eds), *Growth Theories in Light of the East Asian Experience*, Chicago: The University of Chicago Press.

Wood, A. (1997), 'Openness and wage inequality in developing countries: the Latin American challenge to East Asian conventional wisdom', *World Bank Economic Review*, 11, pp. 33–57.

Yang, D. (1999), 'Urban-biased policies and rising income inequality in China', *American Economic Review* (Paper and Proceedings), 89 (2), pp. 306–310.

Zhang, K. H. (2000), 'Roads to prosperity: assessing the impact of FDI on economic growth in China', *Economia Internazionale*, forthcoming.

Zhang, K. H. and J. R. Markusen (1999), 'Vertical multinationals and host-country characteristics', *Journal of Development Economics*, 59, pp. 233–252.

9. Urbanization and Population Relocation

Guanzhong James Wen

INTRODUCTION

Accession to the WTO will have a number of fundamental effects on China's society. In the short term its state-owned sectors, including its banking and finance sectors and heavy industries, will feel most of the impact. However in the long run, China will have a rare opportunity to greatly accelerate its societal transformation from basically a nation of agriculture to a nation that is based on the modern economy. This transformation process has already taken more than a century but so far, has suffered numerous setbacks and enormous pain.

Industrialization goes hand in hand with urbanization in most countries. In some countries, where grain can be imported and the population is small, urbanization moves even faster than industrialization. In general, the level of urbanization is determined by the availability of domestic grain surplus when trade in grain is unavailable. China has had trouble producing surpluses because of its limited arable land. For centuries China faced the formidable task of using its limited arable land to feed its huge population. From 1840 when China started to participate in the early rounds of globalization, China saw a significant acceleration in its urbanization because of the availability of imported grain. Along its coastline and the Yangtze River valley, there emerged a number of modern cities.

However after 1949 the isolationist policy adopted by the Chinese government worsened China's chances of urbanizing its society. Although the government pushed industrialization vigorously, China made slow progress in urbanization in the first 30 years largely because of the fact that the limited grain surplus that it produced could hardly sustain rapid urbanization. In addition the Great Leap Famine further deepened a sense of grain crisis within the Chinese government. In response the government tightly controlled the growth of all types of cities after the early 1960s by prohibiting migration from rural areas to urban areas and sending millions of urban residents to rural areas.

Since the late 1970s China has started gradually to reform its social-economic system and to open up its economy. The government has relaxed its restrictions on population mobility. As a result around one hundred million rural residents have left the farming sector to work in township and village enterprises (TVEs) (*The Statistical Yearbook of China* or SSB 1999). Another one hundred million rural residents have become part of the floating population, seeking jobs in urban areas (SSB 1999). In other countries these two groups of people would have become the natural source of the urban population. However not knowing how to deal with urbanization, the Chinese government, at various levels, either discouraged them from settling down in urban areas or discouraged TVEs from being relocated. Without such restrictive policies, China could have achieved even faster urbanization. Since urbanization is an important basis for a society to gain allocation and production efficiencies, it is obvious that China suffers a significant amount of efficiency losses from these policies.

Currently China claims to have about one third of its total population living in cities or towns. This amounts to about four hundred million.[1] According to Zhang (1996), half of these people are living in towns and small cities. By the middle of this century, China's population is expected to reach 1.6 billion or more (Sun 1994). If 80 per cent of its rural population leave agriculture, as some experts predict (Johnson 2000), then more than eight hundred million of China's rural population will need to be absorbed by non-agricultural sectors within a period of a little longer than two generations. To accomplish this China will see large-scale migration within its own borders of a magnitude that has never been seen before. It is easy to imagine that during this process, everyone's life will be either fundamentally changed or deeply affected.

China's current official urbanization policy encourages the growth of towns and small cities at the same time that it controls the growth of large cities (*Renmin Ribao* 19 March 2001). This new policy focusing on the growth of small cities and towns represents a breakthrough in China. Recently the Chinese government has also decided to reform the household registration system. The new policy aims to encourage TVEs to move closer to towns and small cities and to allow the floating population and TVE workers to settle down there. While the new policy moves in the right direction, it still has limitations, as I will discuss below.

In the decades to come China must make difficult decisions on its urbanization policies. In particular it must decide whether or not it is willing to let market mechanisms determine the speed and magnitude of urbanization and the distribution of city size.

Accession to the WTO will allow China to reorganize its production based on its dynamic comparative advantages. The traditional constraints that made China's quest for modernization so difficult can be eliminated or at least relaxed, when it has full access to world resources and products, including grain, under the free trade arrangement. However whether China can wisely utilize this opportunity or not depends on its urbanization policies.

The organization of this chapter is as follows. The next section discusses why urbanization is one important source of growth. The section that follows reviews the unique pattern of urbanization that China has been following since 1949. The section following that discusses the main constraint that has caused the conspicuously low urbanization rate in China. The section that follows argues that accession to the WTO can remove this constraint. However whether China can utilize this opportunity or not depends on how thoroughly China will reform its economic system and change its urbanization policies. The final section presents the conclusion.

URBANIZATION – AN IMPORTANT SOURCE OF GROWTH

Theoretically, there are ultimately only three sources of economic growth: an increase in conventional inputs; technical progress; and institutional innovation. The latter two are more important sources of growth because even a country as large as China has limitations on its resources. Decreasing returns to scale occur when one or more inputs can not be increased. For example, a fixed amount of land leads to diminishing returns to labor. However there is unlimited potential for technical progress and institutional innovation. Technical progress pushes the production possibilities frontier outward and institutional innovation pushes an economy to move from the interior to the frontier. Urbanization can be viewed as part of institutional innovation. By relocating firms and population into an urban setting, for the same amount of conventional inputs and the same level of technologies, an economy can produce more or can produce the same amounts at lower costs.

It is not by accident that most people choose to live in close vicinity to other people once they can make a living outside the farming sector. The non-agricultural populations tend to locate themselves in proximity to each other for the following two economic reasons: economies of localization, and economies of urbanization (Cheshire and Mills 1999). The logic of economies of localization is that when increasing returns to scale exist, that is, as long as they have not been exhausted, a firm will be induced to expand its scale to reap the benefits made possible from a falling average cost. In doing so a firm hires more and more employees. Most likely the latter will choose to live near the firm to cut their commuting costs. As population concentrates, the service industry will emerge to cater to the various needs of the local people. Thus economies of localization explain how this type of town emerges.

The logic of economies of urbanization explains the emergence of cities. Firms often find that by moving close to each other, each of them can reduce their production costs through sharing some inputs, such as the same labor pool, public capital, city infrastructure, business information and new developments in technology. Because of non-excludability and non-rivalry, one firm's use of these public or quasi-public inputs will not affect others' use. Therefore by clustering together, they significantly reduce their production cost. As a result cities emerge when different types of firms move together seeking efficiency gains.

The combined effects of economies of localization and economies of urbanization are usually called economies of agglomeration. Firms with increasing returns to scale may not choose to cluster together. However as long as each of them has incentives to grow larger, firms bring about an urban center as the number of its employees expands. Meanwhile firms that do not have increasing returns to scale may very likely remain small. However they still have strong motivations to move together to form an urban center, because they cut their costs by sharing public inputs. More often, even firms with increasing returns to scale, find it beneficial to locate themselves in an existing urban center to further cut their production costs. By doing so it is beneficial to the whole society and to the firms themselves because they can share existing public inputs there.

Once firms, with or without increasing returns to scale, locate themselves in an urban environment, as long as commuting is costly, most people choose to live nearby. It is not surprising that in developed nations, more than 70 per cent or 80 per cent of the population lives in metropolitan areas (Table 9.1).

Table 9.1: The Degree of Urbanization in Selected Developed Countries

	1950	1990	2025
UK	84.2	92.1	93.8
W. Germany	72.3	86.4	88.6
France	56.2	73.8	77.3
Italy	54.3	68.3	75.8
Spain	51.9	78.0	86.3
US	64.2	74.1	77.0
Japan	50.3	76.9	80.6

Source: United Nations (1987), from Lo and Yeung (1998).

According to Bairoch (1988), as early as 1850 the level of urbanization had already reached 37.1 per cent in England. In 1910 urbanization reached 41 per cent in North America, and in 1950, it reached 38 per cent in Japan. In developing nations, such as those in Latin America, the urbanization rate has also been rising rapidly (Table 9.2). In many poor nations that cannot afford to build many cities, usually a few cities expand rapidly due to the fact that new firms and their employees try to benefit from the agglomeration effects by moving into these cities.

Urbanization not only raises the efficiency of an economy by generating agglomeration effects for a given level of conventional inputs and technologies, it also promotes technical progress by facilitating spillover

Table 9.2: Urbanization in Latin America

	1940	1960	1980	1990
Argentina	n.a.	74	83	86
Brazil	31	46	64	75
Chile	52	68	81	86
Cuba	46	55	65	75
Mexico	35	51	66	73

Source: Wilkie et al. (1991); UNDP (1992), see Lo and Yeung (1998).

effects. Lucas (1988), Romer (1986, 1990), and many others emphasize the importance of technical spillovers in generating endogenous growth. However such technical spillovers are most effective in city settings because of intensive and extensive interaction of people (Glaeser et al. 1992). The most recent work by Hassler and Mora (2000) shows that high growth and a social allocation of human resources based on innate ability instead of social background can reinforce each other. Their findings have important implications for the benefit of urbanization. High urbanization allows most people to be liberated from the land to pursue their best opportunities for their talents. A society with high urbanization has high mobility, and therefore, exposes people to changing and challenging situations. They accumulate and update their human capital much faster. Urbanization also enables people to find the best venues for their ability and knowledge. By bringing together people of diverse talents with different educational, ethnical, cultural and linguistic backgrounds, cities provide a most favorable setting for technical progress and spillovers. The latter is exactly the source of endogenous growth. Evidence shows that overwhelmingly most technical advances are achieved in urban areas.

Cities also form for other reasons, but not all towns and cities can grow. Only towns and cities with the potential for endogenous growth can survive or grow into big cities. Cities could be created artificially, such as political or military centers. Towns and cities of this type survive only because of tax revenues collected from rural areas or from other cities. They are following an exogenous growth path. Brasilia and Ankara, among others, are examples. These cities survive mostly on the financial support of tax revenues collected from the rest of the nation. A nation can always have one or two such artificially created cities, but it cannot afford to have too many of them, as the growth of such cities is exogenous, and hard to sustain in the long run. They may collapse once the tax revenues shrink or stop. When China decides to accelerate its urbanization, it must be very careful to avoid taking such a path.

THE UNIQUE PATTERN OF URBANIZATION IN CHINA

Given that historically China has had some large cities, many of which were located in areas more accessible to foreigners, China could give a false first impression that this is a country with many megacities. Actually, according to Kunzmann (1998, Table 3.1), between 1700 and the mid-1980s, no Chinese cities were listed among the world's largest cities. Compared with the general trends observed in most nations, China's pattern of urbanization is quite different from that of other nations at a similar stage in the following aspects.

First, while most developing nations made significant progress in their urbanization, China's urbanization stagnated, if not regressed. During the period 1949–1979, except for the Great Leap period, urbanization proceeded very slowly. For example, the share of town and city population in China's total population was 19.7 per cent in 1960. It fell to 17.3 per cent in 1962, and then stagnated (Table 9.3). It took almost two decades for China to see this figure surpass that of 1960 once again. Since the early 1980s, China has accelerated its urbanization. In 1998 the share of towns and cities in China's total population rose to 30.4 per cent (SSB 1999).

Second, China's town and city population is much bigger than its urban population. Statistics on China's city population must be treated with caution because in China, the town or city population is defined as the total population living within the administrative boundaries of a town or a city (SSB 1990 p. 89). Under China's administrative system a city typically includes a large rural area, which is divided up into a number of counties and townships. Therefore population living in these areas will be included as city population despite the fact that they are farmers. However even if we accept this inflated definition as a measurement of urbanization, according to Chen, China is still lagging behind the world average of 47 per cent (Chen 1999).

In order to avoid the overestimation problem, we need to separate the agricultural population from the total city population. Fortunately the SSB separately reports the non-agricultural population of a city from a city's total population, which covers only those who live in a typical urban setting. Here an urban setting can be described as a built-up area with the provision of public infrastructure such as paved streets, a sewage system, a water and electricity supply system, and is occupied by non-farming residents, industries and commerce (SSB 1999). Clearly in China's context, data on the non-agricultural population within a city are a much closer measurement of urbanization than city population. Therefore, I will only use this definition to measure the size of a city.[2]

Based on this definition, the share of urban population can be as low as 20 per cent of a city's total population. For instance, Chongqing boasts a population of 30 million inhabitants, which would make it the largest city in China. However, 80 per cent are engaged in agriculture. Even Shanghai, the

Table 9.3: China's Population and its Composition

	Urban Population		Rural Population	
	Millions	Share	Millions	Share
1952	71.6	12.5	503.2	87.5
1953	78.3	13.3	51.0	86.7
1954	82.5	13.7	520.2	86.3
1955	82.9	13.5	531.8	86.5
1956	91.9	14.6	536.4	85.4
1957	99.5	15.4	547.0	84.6
1958	107.2	16.2	552.7	83.8
1959	123.7	18.4	548.4	81.6
1960	130.7	19.7	531.3	80.3
1961	127.1	19.3	531.5	80.7
1962	116.6	17.3	556.4	82.7
1965	130.5	18.0	594.9	82.0
1970	144.2	17.4	685.7	82.6
1975	160.3	17.3	763.9	82.7
1978	172.5	17.9	790.1	82.1
1980	191.4	19.4	795.7	80.6
1985	250.9	23.7	807.6	76.3
1986	263.7	24.5	811.4	75.5
1987	276.7	25.3	816.3	74.7
1988	286.6	25.8	823.7	74.2
1989	295.4	26.2	831.6	73.8
1990	301.9	26.4	841.4	73.6
1991	305.4	26.4	852.8	73.6
1992	323.7	27.6	848.0	72.4
1993	333.5	28.1	851.7	71.9
1994	343.0	28.6	855.5	71.4
1995	351.7	29.0	859.5	71.0
1996	359.5	29.4	864.4	70.6
1997	369.9	29.9	866.4	70.1
1998	379.4	30.4	868.7	69.6

Sources: SYOC 1987 and 1999

most urban city in China, has a rural share as high as 27 per cent of its total population. Unexpectedly, the cities with the highest and the second highest shares of non-agricultural population are respectively Urumqi, the capital of Xinjiang Autonomous Region, and Haikou, the capital of Hainan province.

Third, for a long period of time until the late 1970s, China's distribution of city size differed from most countries, where city size distribution usually follows the Pareto distribution.[3] From 1953 to 1978 the number of cities with a population of half a million to one million increased from 16 to 36. The number of cities with a population of one million or more increased from nine to 29. However, the number of cities with a population below 100 thousand decreased from 63 to ten (Zhou 1998 p. 87). This means that while most Chinese are living in rural areas, if one is an urban dweller, then it is most likely that the person is living in a big city. These big cities most likely grew out of the pre-existing medium and small cities.

Since the 1980s, the Chinese government has been encouraging the growth of towns and small cities. As a result, by 1998 out of 668 cities China had in that year, only 13 had a population of more than two million, 24 had a half to one million; 205 had 200 000 to half of a million, 378 had less than 200 000 (Table 9.4).

According to SSB (1999), only 3 per cent of China's total population live in urban areas with a population of one to three millions. During the period 1989–1996, the number of cities increased by 50 per cent and the total urban population increased by 42 per cent. However the number of cities with a population of one to two million only increased by 10 per cent. The total population that lives in these cities increased only by 16 per cent (Wang 1999).

Fourth, China pushed its industrialization at a much faster pace than its urbanization by locating many of its new firms in remote areas or deep mountains. Some of the firms did grow into company towns with heavy government financial support. However under the market conditions prevailing today, many of them may not only not grow into main urban centers, they may actually collapse if financial subsidies are cut off

Since the 1980s when China decided to open up and to reform the economic system, there has been an explosion in the number of TVEs. TVEs produce one third of China's total output, and employ more than one hundred million rural residents (SSB 1999). In addition, every year more than one hundred million of the floating population travel to coastal areas to seek jobs. In other nations, these firms and workers would have been an important source of urbanization. However this is not the case in China.

Most TVEs are located in China's coastal areas, such as the Yangtse Delta and the Pearl River Delta, where we see a high concentration of cities and a high population density. However TVEs are mostly located in the rural areas of these regions. Cities there seem to be wasting their agglomeration effects. The geographical dispersion of these firms clearly shows that even today, China's urbanization is lagging behind its industrialization.

Table 9.4: Some Important Indices of China's Urban Areas (1995)

Millions I	Number of cities	Population (million) II		Area (million km²) III		Pop density (person /km²) IV	Employ in service (%) V	GDP (billion yuan) VI	Service share in GDP (%) VII	Industrial and commercial tax revenue (billion yuan) VIII
		City total	Non- farming	City	Urban	Urban	Urban	Urban	Urban	Urban
All cities	640	500.0	200.2	1.68	0.020	298	28.9	3998.0	36.3	155.9
>2	10	50.6	39.7	0.03	0.003	1664	42.4	737.5	46.4	55.8
1–2	22	40.2	30.3	0.05	0.003	870	39.4	496.6	43.0	21.3
.5–1	42	43.1	29.7	0.07	0.003	609	33.8	504.2	37.8	24.3
.2–.5	192	151.1	57.6	0.39	0.006	385	27.2	1111.2	33.4	32.2
<.2	373	215.1	42.9	1014.00	0.007	189	22.9	1148.4	29.0	22.2

Source: Urban Statistical Yearbook of China, China Statistical Press, Beijing, 1996.

Fifth, China's service sector was discouraged before the late 1970s by a government that believed then that anyone who was not producing industrial goods should grow his own food. Compared with other nations, China's service sector still lags even today. Typically the service sector expands faster than the manufacturing sector in terms of the number of people employed. The experience of the developed nations shows that it is exactly the service sector that has absorbed most of the laborers released either from the agricultural sector or the manufacturing sector (Table 9.5). But in China, after witnessing a rapid increase after the 1980s and the early 1990s, this sector has stagnated in recent years. This untimely stagnation is ominous

Table 9.5: Shares of Service Sector in GDP, 1970–93

	1970	1993	% change
USA	63	75	19.1
UK	52	65	25.0
France	52	69	32.7
Germany	47	61	29.8
Australia	55	67	21.8
Japan	47	57	21.8
Canada	59	71	20.3
Italy	51	65	27.5

Source: Table 1.2 in Lo and Yeung (1998).

when employment pressure has never been higher. The stagnation in the service sector is closely linked with urbanization. The service sector benefits most from a high concentration of population. The low level of urbanization makes the cost of providing services to the majority of the population more expensive than it should be.

THE MAIN CONSTRAINTS TO CHINA'S URBANIZATION

Without international trade urbanization depends on how big a portion of the population can be released from agricultural activities without creating a food shortage. In this sense the agricultural surplus determines the level of urbanization in autarky. Although urbanization may be independent from industrialization, as we see in the case of Ancient Greece or the Roman Empire, industrialization contributes greatly to the acceleration of urbanization for two reasons. First, it greatly increases grain surplus by enhancing the efficiency of agricultural production. Second, it provides urban employment opportunities. However in China, industrialization seems to have contributed little to the acceleration of urbanization. Let's find out what are the main constraints to China's urbanization.

After 1949 China gradually nationalized all properties in urban areas, and collectivized properties, including land, in rural areas. China also installed a central planning system and followed a heavy industry biased development strategy. Meanwhile China also adopted an isolationist policy. All of these factors played a role in slowing down China's urbanization and made China's quest for modernization more difficult than otherwise, as is reflected in the fact that the share of primary sector in total labor force remained high up to 1080 (Table 9.6). But the question is why China stood out as the country that experienced the most difficulties in its modernization before the late 1970s, especially given the fact that almost all the former communist countries adopted similar ownership structures, economic systems, development strategies, and isolationist foreign policies. For example, urbanization and industrialization proceeded smoothly without too many setbacks in the former Soviet Union and many other East European nations.

To explain the big difference between the other former communist nations and China in their urbanization performance, we have to point to the different constraints of natural endowments that they face respectively. All the East European nations have abundant arable land that generated adequate or more than adequate grain surpluses. In these nations it was not the grain surpluses, but the urban job opportunities that determined the level and speed of urbanization. In this sense, the public ownership structures, central planning system, heavy industry-biased strategy, and isolationist foreign policy, were damaging to the speed of industrialization. However it is in China that these institutions and policies had the most damaging effect on both industrialization and urbanization. It is also in China where we find the harshest policies being imposed on residents, especially rural residents.

The change in employment composition from 1952 to 1998 is shown in Table 9.6. Under a free market system, given China's resource endowment, factors would first flow into labor-intensive sectors. The heavy industries would not have received capital, labor and other resources in the amount that the government would like to see (Lin et al. 1997). In order to allocate resources in a way that was infeasible under a free market system, the Chinese government turned to extremely restrictive policies on the flow of production factors. These policies were unnecessary in other former communist countries in East Europe. For example, in order to get as large an agricultural surplus as possible to feed the workers engaged in heavy industries, the government monopolized the procurement and marketing of the main agricultural products. Farmers were only allowed to sell their products to the government at artificially suppressed prices. Since such a policy would lead farmers to desert their land or refuse to deliver agricultural goods, a threat to the success of the development of heavy industries, the

Table 9.6: Employment Composition (per cent)

	Primary	Secondary	Tertiary
1952	83.5	7.4	9.1
1957	81.2	8.9	9.9
1962	82.0	7.8	10.1
1965	81.5	8.3	10.2
1970	80.7	10.1	9.2
1975	77.1	13.3	9.6
1978	70.5	17.3	12.2
1980	68.7	18.2	13.1
1985	62.4	20.8	16.8
1986	60.9	21.9	17.2
1987	60.0	22.2	17.8
1988	59.3	22.4	18.3
1989	60.1	21.6	18.3
1990	60.1	21.4	18.5
1991	59.7	21.4	18.9
1992	58.5	21.7	19.8
1993	56.4	22.4	21.2
1994	54.3	22.7	23.0
1995	52.2	23.0	24.8
1996	50.5	23.5	26.0
1997	49.9	23.7	26.4
1998	49.8	23.5	26.7

Source: Table 5.2, SYOC (1999)

government took two measures. It took away land ownership from individual farmers by collectivizing all the rural arable land, so that it could control the agricultural surplus and guarantee the food supply of the urban workers. In addition, the government installed a de facto segregation between rural and urban residents by introducing a most restrictive household registration system and food coupon system. Without special permission from the government, a farmer had no right to leave his village to work in a city. He even had no right to buy food in urban areas because he was not entitled to receive food coupons required when purchasing food there.

Under such circumstances a farmer had no choice but to remain confined to his native village. Even there he had little say because land was collectively owned and products belonged to the collective. Quotas, taxes, collective accumulation funds and collective welfare funds, etc., had to be deducted first by the government or the collective before a farmer could expect to get his meager share of grain rationing from what was left.

Because of their capital-intensive nature, heavy industries created limited non-farming employment opportunities. Actually China's industrialization not only failed to transfer a large number of rural laborers to urban areas, it even encountered problems fully absorbing the newly added urban population. Millions of urban youth had to be sent to rural areas to avoid aggravating the problem of urban unemployment. Given the fact that most people had to make a living out of the limited arable land, many were forced to move into remote areas. In some areas farmers were so desperate to produce enough grain that they even converted parts of rivers or lakes into farmland. Such reckless efforts caused serious environmental problems.

The Chinese government adopted a much harsher attitude toward urbanization particularly after early 1961 in the wake of the Great Leap Famine (Chang and Wen 1997). This famine is unprecedented in terms of its magnitude. This disaster gave the Chinese government a lesson on why the size of the agricultural surplus was the final determinant of the speed and level of urbanization. Since then the Chinese government has become obsessed with the issue of how to feed one fifth of the world population with 9 per cent of the world arable land. Unfortunately, instead of abandoning the wrong economic system and policies, the Chinese government in its response, chose to further tighten its control over the growth of all cities, and sent millions of urban people to remote areas to reclaim land from mountain slopes, grassland, even shoals in rivers and lakes. This is why China's industrialization proceeded with little, if any, progress in urbanization.

WTO, GEOGRAPHICAL RELOCATION OF POPULATION AND URBANIZATION

China has been using 9 per cent of the world's arable land to feed more than 20 per cent of the world population living within its boundaries. While this is a remarkable achievement, China has also paid an enormous price. First, in doing so, China forced more than half of its labor force to be tied to the land. Many of them are making a meager living out of barren or mountainous terrain. Unless most of them can be moved from the farming sector and can be relocated in non-farming sectors, its plan to lift the whole nation's living standard to the world average by the middle of this century is unlikely if China continues to follow an isolationist line. The prospect looks even dimmer if we take into consideration the fact that in terms of per capita timber resources, per capita petroleum resources, per capita water resources, and many other crucial natural resources, China is significantly below the world average too. Second, China's environment has already been severely abused under the pressure of population over the centuries. Using a well below average per capita amount of resources to achieve world average living standards, while a heroic effort, turns out to be too overwhelming for China to achieve by itself. Any nation that does so is actually making an overdraft from the resources that future generations are entitled to.

The accession of China to the WTO will greatly raise China's chances to transform successfully its society into a modern, industrialized and urbanized one. For the first time in the last 150 years, the prospect for achieving this national goal has never become brighter for the following reasons. First, China will have a more secure way to obtain grain from the world market. The WTO is a multilateral arrangement to protect and facilitate free trade among its members. In the past, Chinese had deep concerns regarding its food security, and rejected the idea of relying on foreign food. However China obtained its food security at the expense of its farmers' income and its environment. The accession to the WTO will remove China's fears. In case it needs to import more food China will not subject itself to unilateral sanctions. Its access to the world food markets is protected by the regulations of the WTO. The security in the world food market will unlock China from the desperate situation where it has to abuse its environment in order to feed its growing population. Therefore China can accelerate its urbanization and make urbanization irreversible, even if its food production experiences a temporary but severe decline.

Second, the existing restrictions on its labor-intensive products imposed on China by many nations, especially the highly developed nations, will be relaxed over time after China enters the WTO. Without exporting its labor China, can expect the whole world to help absorb part of its huge rural labor pool through importing its exports. Increased employment opportunities in exporting industries will facilitate the relocation of rural laborers and their families into China's urban areas.

Third, the accession to the WTO is beneficial even to those who remain in the farming sector, although they may face pressure from competing foreign products. As most rural laborers move out of the farming sector, those who stay will have more land and other resources at their disposal. Farmers can gradually increase their operation scale, lower their production cost and increase their income. They will also benefit from the fact that they will no longer be forced to grow only grain. If grain crops cease to be profitable in areas where they live, local farmers will have the freedom to grow other crops. Chinese farmers still have cost advantages in producing labor-intensive crops, such as paddy rice, many vegetables, certain fruits, flowers and herbs. The Chinese farmers also have cost advantages in meat and seafood production. However the majority of Chinese farmers will still produce grain because for a country as big as China, its grain prices are endogenously determined. A small percentage increase in the amount of its total imports will significantly and upwardly influence the world grain prices, making grain production back in China profitable again. Therefore it is unlikely, based on world relative prices and comparative advantages, that Chinese farmers will suddenly and substantially reduce their grain output.

Fourth, as urbanization accelerates, the service sector, a sector that benefits most from a high concentration of population will find fertile soil for expansion. Simple mathematics shows that if urbanization proceeds smoothly, it can absorb much more surplus labor than now, given that China's service share in the total labor force is significantly lower than the world average. As we pointed out above, by the middle of this century, China's population will peak at 1.6 billion. If its labor participation rate is 55 per cent, China will have a labor force of 880 million by that time (Table 9.7), or increase by 180 million over 1998. We assume that China is willing

Table 9.7 Changes in the Labor Shares of Three Sectors and Projected Changes in Their Absolute Numbers

100 Million	Total	Primary	Secondary	Tertiary
1998	100% (7.0)	50% (3.5)	23% (1.6)	27% (1.9)
2050	100% (8.8)	10% (0.9)	30% (2.6)	60% (5.3)
Change	0% (1.8)	–40% (–2.6)	+7% (+1.0)	+33% (+3.4)

Source: SYOC 1999

to further restructure its economy along its comparative advantage to explore employment opportunities in labor-intensive production in the decades to come. We also assume that by that time 10 per cent of its labor force, or around 90 million, will still be engaged in agriculture, 30 per cent, or 260 million, will work in manufacturing. Then China will need to find non-farming jobs for 530 million laborers. That amounts to 60 per cent of its labor force. Currently China already has 190 million working in the service industry. Therefore China needs to find jobs in the service industry for 340 million laborers. Of these, 180 million are newly added during this period, and 260 million are released from other sectors, mostly from the farming sector. At first glance, it is a formidable task to absorb them. However according to the experience of developed nations, as many as 80 per cent of the labor force can find jobs in the service industry. If China successfully develops its service sector, there will be little trouble absorbing most of its surplus labor. Of course this task depends to a large extent on the speed and level of China's urbanization. Column V of Table 9.4 clearly illustrates that the bigger the cities are, the higher the share of the service sector in total employment will be. Therefore in order to create more urban service jobs, China should not discourage the growth of big cities.

Fifth, China will also have the opportunity to relocate its population to reduce pressure on its water resources. At the present time, the geographical distribution of population in developed nations is increasingly shaped by the location of water resources. Looking at the distribution of the population in Australia, the US and many other nations, we see how important the availability of water resources is in determining population density. Most of China's water resources and precipitation are concentrated in the south, east, central and southwest areas. Currently, the spatial distribution of the

Table 9.8: Geographical Distribution of China's Arable Land

Region (k hectares)	Population	Arable Land
Northeast, North, Northwest	51919 (42%)	577201 (61%)
East, South, Southwest, Central	71363 (58%)	37250 (39%)

a. Including Beijing, Tianjin, Hebei, Shanxi, Inner Mongolia, Liaoning, Jilin, Henan, Heilongjiang, Shandong, Shaanxi, Gansu, Qinghai, Ningxia amd Xinjiang.
b. Including Shanghai, Jiangsu, Zhejiang, Anhui, Fujian, Jiangxi, Hubei, Guandong, Hunan, Guangxi, Hainan, Sichuan, Guizhou, Yunnan and Tibet.

population is partially shaped by the distribution of arable land. In Table 9.8 we can see that despite the fact that there is a severe water shortage in China's north and northwest, 42 per cent of China's total population has to live in these areas because 61 per cent of arable land is located there. Once they are released from the farming sector they do not need to stay there. They can move to the coastal areas or the south where water is abundant, precipitation is greater and more evenly distributed throughout the year. Therefore towns and cities in these areas should be given priority to grow first, and new towns and cities should also be located mostly there to avoid future water shortages.

Sixth, accession will also allow China to import land-intensive products, and enable it to shift to production that matches its factor endowment. The reduced pressure on land, in turn, will help reduce deep-rooted fears over the prospect that some part of its arable land will inevitably be lost to urbanization. China should realize that one square kilometer of land acquires a much higher value, and accommodates a much bigger population, if it is used for urban development than when it is used as farmland. In addition, by concentrating its population in urban areas, China actually may save a lot of arable land. Column III in Table 9.4 shows that currently the total acreage of urban areas of all cities is only 20 000 square kilometers. Their share in China's total territory is trivial for a country as large as China. In the future China will surely lose some of its arable land to the expansion of the existing cities and to the construction of new cities. However the country will also regain a lot of land by consolidating millions of villages throughout the nation after most of the rural population leaves for urban areas and the size of an average farm expands. We can also see in Column IV of Table 9.4 that the population density is much higher in big cities than in small ones. This fact provides more evidence that in order to save arable land, China should not discourage the growth of big cities.

CONCLUSION

Urbanization is an important institutional innovation that allows firms and populations to benefit from the agglomeration effect. A high level of urbanization means that an economy can produce much more efficiently for a given level of technology and resources. Constrained by its factor endowment, particularly the scarcity of arable land, China can generate only limited grain surpluses. This means that in autarky, China cannot go far in urbanization without damaging severely its ecology. In order to control population from moving into urban areas, it has to impose most restrictive policies on its rural residents and rural business such as TVEs. China's water resources and arable land resources are also distributed extremely unevenly. Arable land is mostly located in the north and west, but water resources are concentrated in the south and east. However a large portion of its population has been tied to the land such that they cannot move to areas where water is abundant.

The arrangement of the WTO allows China to have more leeway to move out of this trap. China can trade its labor-intensive products freely for natural resources and food products. Therefore China no longer needs its own capacity to generate grain surpluses that in turn will dictate the speed and level of its urbanization. Under the multilateral arrangement of the WTO, China will feel more secure in importing a large amount of grain in case such need arises. China will also find it easier to optimize the distribution of its population once most people are no longer tied to the land. They can gradually move to where water resources are concentrated. While the expected increase in its labor-intensive products will help vent part of its labor surplus, it will mainly be the service sector that will absorb most of its labor pool. The experiences of rich nations as well as many developing nations show that the service sector is the largest employer of labor, and the acceleration of urbanization will provide ample opportunity for growth in the service sector.

However in order to reap the benefit of an open world and free trade, China must follow the lead of the market mechanism, including its pursuit of urbanization. That is, the growth of cities should be market oriented and based on the result of agglomeration effects and spillover effects. A city should be allowed to emerge or grow as long as firms believe that by being located there or moving there, they can bring down their production costs. It is inappropriate to restrict the growth of such cities if the gains reaped by newly arriving firms can more than compensate for the losses suffered by the existing firms.

The accession of China to the WTO provides China with a golden opportunity to accelerate its urbanization. Urbanization is vital to raising its economic efficiency, dampening the expected rise in unemployment in the immediate future and eventually absorbing its huge surplus labor pool. It is high time for the Chinese government to adopt bold and forward-looking policies on urbanization, migration and land zoning. Through successful urbanization, China will not only thoroughly change its own image, but will also significantly change the world landscape.

NOTES

1. I will discuss this figure in a more detailed way later in the chapter, where I will explain why caution should be exercised.
2. A more detailed discussion on this issue can be found in the article entitled 'The Key to the Establishment of a Statistical Index System for the Development of China's Small Cities and Towns' by Zou (1996). His article is included in 'The Policy Highlights of the Reform Experiments of towns and Small Cities' edited by the Department of Rural Areas, the State System Reform Commission, and published by Gaige Printing House in 1996.
3. According to Auerbach (1913) and Singer (1936), the city size distribution could be represented as a Pareto distribution $y = Ax - a$, where y is the number of cities with populations greater than x. Here x is a particular population size, A and a are constants. Therefore, the number of cities with populations greater than x goes up when A goes up, but goes down when x and A go up. A special, but frequently referred to, distribution is when An equals the size of the largest city in the nation, and A equals 1 (Cheshire and Mills 1999).

REFERENCES

Auerbach, F. (1913), "Das Gesetz der Bevolgerungskoncentration", Petermanns Geographische Mitteilungen 59:74-76 cited in. Cheshire, Paul and Edwin S. Mills (1999), *Handbook of Regional and Urban Economics*, Vol. 3, Amsterdam: North-Holland.

Bairoch, Paul (1988), *Cities and Economic Development*, Chicago: University of Chicago Press.

Chang, Gene and Guanzhong James Wen (1997), 'Communal Dining and the Causation of the Chinese Famine of 1958–1961', *Economic Development and Cultural Change*, October, pp. 1–34.

Chen, Wenling (1999), 'The Tertiary Sector Urgently Waiting for the Support from Urbanization', *Jingjixue Xiaoxibao*, 3 December 1999.

Cheshire, Paul and Edwin S. Mills (1999), *Handbook of Regional and Urban Economics*, Vol. 3, Amsterdam: North-Holland.

Glaeser, Edward L. et al. (1992) 'Growth in Cities', *The Journal of Political Economy*, 100 (6), Dec., pp. 1126–1152.

Hassler, John and Jose V. Rodriguez Mora (2000), 'Intelligence, Social Mobility, and Growth', *American Economic Review*, September, pp. 888–908.

Johnson, D. Gale (2000), 'China's Agriculture and WTO Accession', paper No. 00-02, Office of Agricultural Economic Research, University of Chicago.

Kunzmann, Klaus R. (1998), 'World City Regions in Europe: Structural Change and Future Challenges', included in *Globalization and the World Large Cities*, Fu-Chen Lo and Yue Man Yeung (eds), New York: United Nations University Press.

Lin, Justin Yifu, et al. (1997), *China Miracle*, Hong Kong: The Chinese University of Hong Kong, cited in Lo, Fuchen and Yue-man Yeung, *Globalization and the World of Large Cities*, the United Nations University

Lo, Fuchen and Yue-man Yeung (1998), *Globalization and the World of Large Cities*, the United Nations University.

Lucas, Robert E. Jr. (1988), 'On the Mechanics of Economic Development', *Journal Monetary Economics*, 22 (July), pp. 3–42.

Renmin Ribao, 19 March 2001.

Romer, Paul M. (1986),'Increasing Returns and Long-run Growth', *Journal of Political Economy*, 94 (October), pp. 1002–1037.

— (1990),'Endogenous Technological Change', *Journal of Political Economy*, 98, October, S71 S102.

Singer, H. W. (1936), 'The "courbe des population": a parallet to Pareto's law', *Economic Journal* 46: 254-263, cited in Cheshire, Paul and Edwin S. Mills (1999), *Handbook of Regional and Urban Economics*, Vol. 3, Amsterdam: North-Holland.

State Statistics Bureau (SSB) *Statistical Yearbook of China*, 1990, 1996 and 1999, Beijing: China Statistical Press.

Sun, Jinxin (1994), 'The Population of China towards the 21st century', Beijing: The Statistical Publishing House of China.

Wang, Yixin (1999), 'On the Hollowing of Some Cities in Sunan', *Jingjixue Xiaoxibao*, 26 November 1999.

Wilkie, J. et al. (1991), 'Statistical Abstract for Latin America 28'. University of California, Los Angeles cited in Lo, Fuchen and Yue-man Yeung (1998), *Globalization and the World of Large Cities*, the United Nations University.

Zhang, Haoruo (1996), 'Deepen Reforms, Vigorously Search to promote an all-round development of towns and small cities in China', included in *The Policy Highlights of the Reform Experiments of the Small Cities and Towns*, edited by the Department of Rural Areas, the State System Reform Commission, Beijing: Gaige Printing House.

Zhou, Nongjian (1998), *Chinese Rural Areas and Urbanization Study*, China: Guangxi Renmin Printing House.

Zou Yixing (1996), 'The Key to the Establishment of A Statistical Index System for the Development of China's Small Towns and Cities', included in *The Policy Highlights of the Reform Experiments of the Small Cities and Towns*, edited by the Department of Rural Areas, the State System Reform Commission, Beijing: Gaige Printing House.

PART 3

Linkage with the World

10. The Impact on the US and Other Countries

Zhi Wang

INTRODUCTION

With the conclusion of the agreements on the terms of China's entry into the World Trade Organization (WTO) between China and most of its trade partners, especially the United States and the European Union, most people now expect that both China and Taiwan will join the organization early in the 21st century. The potential impact of China's WTO membership on the global economy has become the subject of newspaper headlines and a hot topic in academic and policy discussions both in China and abroad. While the major Chinese leaders appear to be committed to opening China further and to actively pursuing WTO entry, many in China are still wary of the consequences of WTO entry on the domestic economy. Outside China, especially in the United Sates, most union members perceive China's rising trade power as a threat to American welfare and jobs, despite the explicit support of the Administration for China's accession to the WTO. The debate over China's WTO accession raises the importance of having a relatively comprehensive quantitative assessment of the impact of China's WTO entry on patterns of world production and trade, structural adjustments and income distribution in the world economy, based on the market access commitments that China has made to date. An objective estimate of the benefits and costs of China's commitments on rest of the world will help China's trade partners to understand better the real economic consequences of China's WTO entry on their economies and thus adjust rationally their policies to meet the challenges and seize the opportunities arising from such forthcoming events.

Both China and Taiwan are important players in international trade. By the end of 1998, the volumes of China's exports and imports had reached $183.6 billions and $140.3 billions respectively. Comparable volumes in Taiwan were $121 billions and $114 billions respectively. The combined volumes of total exports and imports in China, Hong Kong and Taiwan are more than half of those in the US and have exceeded those of Japan since 1995. Relative volumes will likely increase as integration among the three Chinese economies intensifies following the recent unification of Hong Kong and Macao with China and as China continues to grow and industrialize.

To satisfy their membership requirements with respect to the world trade body, both China and Taiwan will have to follow through on their commitments to adopt broad and deep trade liberalization measures to make their trade regimes consistent with the rules of the WTO. Implementation of these liberalization measures implies a substantial reduction in tariffs and non-tariff barriers across all economic sectors in one of the world's largest and most rapidly expanding markets. Obviously, it will not only change China's resource allocation among its domestic production and export sectors, but it will also affect the structure of China's trade with its trading partners. World trade patterns and production structures in other economies will have to adjust to accommodate such changes. What opportunities will the growth and liberalization of Chinese markets likely bring to developing and developed countries around the world? What challenges will other countries face as the tremendous and low-cost Chinese labor force is integrated into the world economy? How will the increase in the export competitiveness of Chinese products affect world markets? Who will gain? Who will lose? What are the geographical and sectoral distributions of these gains and losses? And what are the economic consequences of these gains and losses for workers in China's major trade partners? To better understand the future of the global economy into the 21st century, it is an important intellectual task to analyze how and to what extent China's WTO accession would influence patterns of world production and trade. Similarly it is essential to evaluate the benefits and costs of Chinese and Taiwanese access to the WTO for other major players in the world economy.

This chapter evaluates the impact of China's WTO accession on the US and other countries in the world economy. It estimates aggregate and sectoral gains and losses to production and trade for the US and China's other major trading partners using a recursive dynamic, multi-region, multi-sector computable general equilibrium (CGE) model. The model includes China's major trading partners, both developed and developing countries, and covers major production and trade activities in the world economy from 1997 to 2010 in order to capture third country and accumulation effects. The rest of the chapter is organized as follows: the next section outlines the basic structure of the model used in the evaluation. The section that follows lays out major assumptions in the baseline calibration and scenarios. Major simulation results and underlying economic forces shaping those results are presented and discussed in the next section. The last section concludes the paper by presenting major policy implications and limitations.

STRUCTURE OF THE MODEL

The model used in this chapter is an extension of the CGE models used in the China's WTO accession study by Wang (1997a, 1997b, 1999) with import embodied technology transfer and trade policy induced TFP growth. It is part of a family of models used widely to analyze the impact of global trade liberalization and structural adjustment programs. It focuses on the real side of the world economy and incorporates considerable detail on sectoral output and real trade flows, both bilateral and global. However, this structural detail is obtained at the cost of not explicitly modeling financial markets, interest rates, and inflation. While not designed to generate short-term macroeconomic forecasts, the model could be linked to a macroeconomic model including asset flows and generating macro scenarios. Given a macro scenario, however, this model could then be used to determine the resulting real trade flows and sectoral structural adjustments for each region in a recursive dynamic framework. Under assumptions on the likely path of future world economic growth, it generates the pattern of production and trade resulting from world economic adjustment to the shocks specified in the alternative macro scenarios.

In this study 17 fully endogenized regions and 22 production sectors in each region are specified to represent the world economy. The 17 regions are: (1) the United States, (2) Canada, (3) West Europe (4) Japan, (5) Australia and New Zealand, (6) Mexico, (7) Korea, (8) Singapore, (9) Taiwan, (10) Hong Kong, (11) China, (12) South East Asia (ASEAN, includes Malaysia, Thailand, Philippines, Indonesia, and Viet Nam), (13) South Asia (India, Bangladesh, Nepal, Pakistan, and Sri Lanka), (14) Latin American MFA restricted countries (Central America and Caribbean, Brazil, Colombia, Peru, Uruguay), (15) Mid-east and South African MFA restricted countries (Turkey, Botswana, the rest of the South African Customs Union, and the rest of Middle East), (16) Low income southern African countries (Malawi, Mozambique, Tanzania, Zambia, and rest of sub-Saharan Africa) and (17) the rest of the world.

The 22 sectors are: (1) grain and oilseeds, (2) plant based fiber, (3) other non-grain crops, (4) livestock, (5) meats and dairy products, (6) processed food, (7) beverages and tobacco, (8) forestry and fishery, (9) mineral products, (10) energy products (11) textiles, (12) wearing apparel, (13) leather, shoes and sports goods, (14) other light manufactured goods, (15) wood and paper products, (16) manufactured intermediates, (17) motor vehicles and parts, (18) other transport equipment, (19) electronic equipment, (20) other machinery, (21) utilities, housing and construction, (22) transportation and traded services, a portion of which is allocated to international shipping.

There are six primary factors of production: agricultural land, natural resources, capital, agricultural labor, unskilled labor, and skilled labor. Skilled and unskilled labor have basic education in common, but skilled labor usually has more advanced training. Agricultural labor has little or no education and works only in the farm sectors. Natural resources are sector specific, while other primary factors are assumed to be mobile across sectors, but immobile across regions. Land and agricultural labor are only used in the agricultural sectors.

Three types of gains from trade liberalization are captured by the model.

1. Gains from more efficient utilization of resources, which lead to a one-time permanent increase in GDP and social welfare.
2. More rapid physical capital accumulation from a 'medium-run growth bonus' which compounds the efficiency gain from trade liberalization and leads to higher saving and investment.
3. The model incorporates capital and intermediate goods imports embodied technology transfer among regions, which links sector specific TFP growth with each region's imports of capital and technology intensive products. The technology transfer is assumed to flow in one direction specifically, from more developed regions to less developed regions. Empirical evidence suggests that there is strong positive feedback between trade expansion and productivity growth. Trade liberalization increases the prevalence of technology transfer as trade barriers are reduced. Firms in the liberalized regions will import more capital and technology intensive goods as both investment and intermediate inputs from abroad at cheaper prices. Those goods are usually embodied with advanced technology from other countries, thus stimulating productivity growth for all production factors. As pointed out by Lewis, Robinson and Wang (1995), however, while there is fairly widespread agreement that linkages between imports of intermediate inputs and TFP do exist, there is less evidence of the size of the feedback. In our simulation exercises, the elasticities used for developed countries are one third the values used for developing countries.

Accumulation patterns for capital stock in the model depend upon depreciation and gross real investment rates, the latter set exogenously based on forecasts from the Oxford world macroeconomic model (Oxford Economic Forecasting, 1999). However, household savings, the government surplus (deficit), and foreign capital inflows (foreign savings) are assumed to be perfect substitutes and collectively constitute the source of gross investment in each region. Given the assumption that aggregate real investment is determined as a share of real GDP, changes in the trade balance, which directly affect foreign savings, are assumed to have only a partial effect on aggregate real investment in the region. Instead they lead to an equilibrium adjustment in the domestic savings rate, which partially offsets the change in foreign savings.

Household savings decisions are endogenous in the model. They represent future consumption goods for the household with zero subsistence quantity (by assuming inter-temporal separable preferences, ELES demand systems). The government surplus (deficit) is the difference between government tax revenues and its expenditures, the latter fixed as a percentage of each regions real GDP based on forecasts from the Oxford model.

Foreign capital inflows or outflows are determined by the accumulation of the balance of trade, which is also fixed as a percentage of GDP in each region based on the Oxford model's projections except for the United States. The model does not include financial markets or portfolio investment. The trade balance is the only source of foreign savings (either inflow or outflow). There is no explicit specification of foreign direct investment (FDI). However, it is counted in the trade flows, because in order to convert FDI into production capital, technology and equipment have to be purchased via domestic or international trade.

Agricultural labor and urban unskilled labor are not substitutable in the production functions, but are linked by rural–urban migration flows. These flows are endogenous in the model and are driven by the rural–urban wage differential and structural changes in production and trade. The increase in the skilled labor force is based on the growth in the stock of tertiary educated labor in each region, as estimated by the World Bank (Ahuja and Filmer, 1995), which provides an indication of changes in the number of those qualified for employment as professional and technical workers. That is, as tertiary education grows, the share of the skilled labor force grows correspondingly.

There are economy-wide and sector-specific TFP growth variables for each region in the model. The economy-wide TFP variable is solved endogenously in the baseline calibration so as to match a pre-specified path of real GDP growth in each region based on forecasts from the Oxford model. Then the economy-wide TFP variable is fixed when alternative scenarios are simulated. In such a case, the growth rate of real GDP and the sector-specific TFP variables that link productivity growth and imports are solved endogenously.

Similar to Hertel et al. (1995), rents associated with MFA quotas are assumed to be captured by exporting countries through export taxes, and these export tax rates are adjusted endogenously to equate with the quotas. Such treatment assumes that all quotas are binding constraints at equilibrium. Consistent with this modeling practice, we divide developing countries subject to MFA quota restrictions into quota binding and non-binding regions[1] based on historical trade statistics. Quantity constraints only apply to those regions with binding quotas.

BASELINE CALIBRATION AND SIMULATIONS DESIGN

China's market accession commitments for WTO entry include a complex package of trade and investment liberalization measures. In this chapter, however, only five aspects of these measures are considered: (1) tariff reduction in both agricultural and manufacturing products; (2) elimination of non-tariff barriers in industrial sectors; (3) agricultural trade liberalization including the accelerated growth in import quotas for grains and plant based fibers and the elimination of such import quotas at 2005; (4) the opening up of major service sectors and (5) the phase out of MFA quotas on textiles and clothing. Once China becomes a member of WTO, its exports of textiles and apparel to North America and European markets will be subject to accelerated MFA quota growth from 2001–2004 similar to other developing countries that are WTO members. The remaining quota restrictions will be eliminated in the year 2005 according to the Agreement on Textiles and Clothing (ATC).[2]

Because China's market accession commitments for WTO entry will be phased in over a transition period, a baseline from 1998–2010 is established first as Scenario I (the Uruguay Round case) under a set of assumptions. It generates a reference growth path for the world economy with the implementation of the Uruguay Round trade liberalization, but without China and Taiwan's participation. This calibrated 'benchmark' will serve as a basis of comparison for the counter factual simulation conducted in Scenario II. Table 10.1 summarizes the major macroeconomic assumptions and results from the baseline calibration. It uses the economy-wide TFP variable in each region as a residual and adjustment mechanism to match the pre-specified real GDP growth rate under assumptions on the three major macroeconomic variables in the model: gross investment, government spending, and balance of trade. It incorporates the impact of the recent Asia financial crisis by imposing the negative GDP growth and the current account surpluses of the affected regions. All three macro-variables are specified as a percentage of GDP and based on forecasts by the Oxford model. China's imports of grains and plant-based fiber are subject to quota control with a 3 per cent annual growth rate. Because China and Taiwan are excluded from the WTO under this scenario, their exports in textiles and clothing are subject to a constant growth in MFA quotas and the quantity restriction continues after 2005. All other MFA quota restricted regions are subject to accelerated quota growth and the termination of the quota system in 2005. The base quota growth rates are calculated from bilateral data provided by the International Textiles and Clothing Bureau at Geneva. The accelerated annual quota growth rate is 25 per cent for WTO members during 1998 to 2001, then an additional 27 per cent is applied to the last three years of ATC implementation.

In Scenario II (the accession case), all the macroeconomic assumptions and exogenous growth factors are the same as in Scenario I, but with both China and Taiwan joining the global trade liberalization process by applying the same liberalization measures specified in the Uruguay Round agreement. The extent of China's tariff reduction is aggregated from the Harmonized Commodity Description and Coding System (HS) tariff schedules based on

US–China agreement (November, 1999) and weighted by 1998 import data from China's Customs. The import quotas for grains and plant fiber are assumed to grow at a 5 per cent annual rate and will be eliminated at the year 2005, replaced by a 15 per cent uniform tariff. All non-tariff barriers on industrial products in China are assumed to be reduced by 20 per cent each year from 2001and set at zero in 2005. A 50 per cent cut in traded service sector protection is also assumed so as to represent the opening up of the major service sectors as specified in China's WTO offer. The base year service sector protection rate in China was adopted from Hoekman (1995). A 15 per cent tariff cut is assumed for grains in Taiwan, while a 36 per cent reduction is assumed for all other products. China's initial NTB rates for industrial products and tariff rates for all sectors each year in the simulation period are listed in Table 10.2. Because China and Taiwan become WTO members under this scenario, their exports of textiles and apparel are subject to the same treatment as other developing countries. For each of the two scenarios, the CGE model generates the effects on social welfare, terms of trade, the volume of trade, output, consumption, the real wages paid to each factor, and changes in prices and resource allocation. The differences in results generated by the two simulation scenarios provide estimates of the impact of China joining the WTO on the world economy. However, these estimates should be regarded as outcomes from conditional projections rather than as forecasts. In reality, actual trade and output patterns are affected by many more factors than just trade liberalization, including domestic macroeconomic and income policy changes.

SIMULATION RESULTS

Basic Economic Forces Shaping Results

Trade theory suggests that world trade patterns are determined by the relative costs of producing and delivering commodities by trading nations. Although many factors, such as distance, technical efficiency, prices of intermediate inputs, etc., may influence such costs, the relative scarcity of factor endowments is the most basic determinant. A country tends to export commodities that require relatively intensive use of its relatively abundant factors of production and tends to import commodities that use its scarce production factor(s) intensively. In other words, the direction of net tradeflows is a function of the relative factor-intensity of production, and the relative factor scarcities among countries. The scarcer the production factor, the higher its cost in production.

Figure 10.1 illustrates the relative size of the arable land, capital and labor endowment in the major regions across the world. It shows that the five

Table 10.1: Major Assumptions for Baseline Calibration in the Model

	US	W Eur	JPN	Aus & NZ	Can	Mex	Kor	Sing	HK	Tai	PRC	ASE AN	S Asia MFA	LA MFA	ME & Afr. MFA	Oth. Af	Rest of Wrld	Wrld Ave
Average annual growth rate, %, 2000–2010																		
Real GDP	3.0	2.5	2.5	3.3	2.8	4.9	4.9	5.1	5.3	4.6	7.6	5.1	5.8	3.8	6.6	3.8	5.6	3.5
Labor	0.8	-0.1	-0.2	1.0	0.6	2.4	1.1	0.3	0.2	0.8	0.8	1.9	2.2	1.8	3.1	3.0	1.5	1.5
Skilled	3.1	3.7	2.9	6.7	5.6	2.4	1.1	0.1	4.0	4.1	2.9	5.6	2.2	1.8	6.4	6.4	5.7	4.0
TFP	0.7	1.0	1.2	1.0	2.0	0.1	2.0	1.6	1.9	1.1	3.2	1.1	2.4	1.2	3.4	0.5	3.1	1.4
Cap stock	4.7	2.7	2.5	3.8	3.6	6.6	5.3	6.5	4.5	6.6	8.6	5.8	5.2	3.1	2.7	2.6	3.6	3.7
Gross inv	4.4	3.5	2.7	2.9	3.5	10.5	5.1	5.1	6.4	3.6	7.6	5.1	5.8	3.8	6.6	3.8	5.6	4.4
Govt	1.9	1.4	1.9	2.6	2.2	3.0	2.8	5.1	7.1	3.4	8.3	5.1	5.8	3.8	6.6	3.8	5.6	2.6
Exports	3.9	3.5	1.3	3.6	2.9	4.8	3.9	5.0	3.6	4.5	7.8	6.7	8.9	4.3	7.2	3.0	6.1	4.5
Imports	3.5	3.6	3.6	3.2	3.2	6.2	5.3	5.3	5.1	4.3	6.9	5.8	7.5	4.6	6.5	3.8	5.6	4.5
HH Cons	2.7	2.3	2.9	3.3	2.8	3.4	5.9	6.4	5.8	5.2	7.7	4.9	5.8	3.8	6.6	3.9	5.6	3.4
Absorp	3.0	2.5	2.5	3.3	2.8	4.9	4.9	5.1	5.3	4.6	7.6	5.1	5.8	3.8	6.6	3.8	5.6	3.5
Average annual agricultural labor force migration, 1000 persons, 2000–2010																		
Agr labor migration	39	78	61	5	3	152	56	0	0	16	2998	2090	4046	470	1428	1451	1866	14761

162

Table 10.1 Continued

	US	W Eur	Jpn	Aus & NZ	Can	Mex	Kor	Sing	HK	Tai	PRC	ASE AN	S. Asia MFA	LA MFA	ME & Afr MFA	Oth Afr	Rest of Wrld	Wrld Ave
Labor composition, %, 2000																		
Agr labor	2.2	4.5	4.3	5.4	2.7	21.8	11.4	0.3	0.7	8.8	68.1	52.0	60.6	22.7	30.0	65.9	27.7	45.8
Unskilled	64.2	66.0	78.1	60.1	58.3	66.8	77.9	74.4	78.8	76.4	24.0	42.2	35.2	67.8	56.9	29.9	55.7	43.0
Skilled	33.6	29.5	17.6	34.5	39.0	11.4	10.7	25.4	20.5	14.8	7.9	5.8	4.1	9.6	13.1	4.2	16.6	11.3
Labor composition, %, 2010																		
Agr labor	2.0	4.2	3.7	5.0	2.5	19.0	9.5	0.3	0.7	7.5	65.1	44.2	55.0	19.6	20.0	60.9	23.5	42.2
Unskilled	55.7	53.1	72.4	35.2	34.5	69.6	79.8	74.9	69.5	71.9	25.1	47.5	40.9	70.9	62.0	33.3	51.6	43.4
Skilled	42.3	42.7	24.0	59.9	63.0	11.4	10.7	24.8	29.9	20.6	9.8	8.3	4.1	9.6	18.1	5.8	24.9	14.4
Gross investment as % of real GDP																		
2000	20.7	19.9	25.5	22.8	19.8	22.9	29.7	44.7	28.9	24.0	37.2	32.4	22.8	20.2	22.1	15.1	20.9	
2010	23.6	21.9	26.0	22.1	21.2	38.3	30.3	44.7	32.0	21.8	37.2	32.4	22.8	20.2	22.1	15.1	20.9	
Government spending as % of nominal GDP																		
2000	17.0	19.5	9.6	17.9	18.8	9.3	8.7	11.3	7.8	12.4	12.4	9.5	11.0	17.2	21.7	10.6	12.1	
2010	15.2	17.5	9.0	16.8	17.6	7.7	7.1	11.3	9.2	11.1	13.2	9.5	11.0	17.2	21.7	10.6	12.1	
Balance of trade as % of nominal GDP																		
2000	-3.0	1.2	2.9	-1.7	2.7	0.4	4.9	12.3	3.5	1.6	2.0	6.3	-1.3	-1.1	-0.4	-5.2	-2.2	
2010	-2.3	2.2	0.9	0.1	2.8	-4.2	0.5	8.5	-3.5	1.7	0.9	8.0	-1.3	-1.4	-0.4	-5.4	-2.1	

Table 10.2: Tariff and Non-tariff Protection Rates in China for its WTO Accession (per cent)

	2000	2001	2002	2003	2004	2005–2010	Reduction	Initial NTB
Grains & oilseeds	27.7	26.2	24.6	23.0	21.5	21.5	22.5	
Planted fiber	73.5	67.7	61.9	56.1	50.3	50.3	31.6	
Non-grain crops	22.1	19.7	17.5	15.4	14.5	14.5	34.4	
Livestock	21.4	20.5	19.5	19.3	19.2	19.2	10.4	
Dairy and meats	16.7	14.9	13.2	11.5	11.4	11.4	31.8	
Processed food	34.3	31.1	27.8	24.7	22.4	22.4	34.8	2.7
Tobacco & beverages.	50.0	44.8	39.6	34.4	29.2	29.2	41.6	2.7
Forest and fishery	4.4	3.1	2.7	2.6	2.6	2.6	40.8	
Minerals & energy	1.3	0.3	0.3	0.3	0.3	0.3	74.7	9.4
Textiles	25.4	22.0	18.5	15.2	12.4	12.4	51.2	7.0
Clothing	32.1	28.5	24.9	21.4	17.9	17.9	44.3	
Leather & shoes	12.2	10.5	9.1	8.6	8.6	8.6	29.6	
Other light manufacturing	13.7	12.8	11.9	11.2	10.7	10.7	21.9	
Wood & paper	11.4	9.1	7.0	5.1	4.3	4.3	62.2	5.5
Intermediates	11.8	9.8	8.2	7.1	6.9	6.9	41.8	12.0
Motor vehicle	33.3	29.2	25.1	21.1	18.4	18.4	44.7	26.3
Other transportation	4.9	3.8	3.7	3.6	3.5	3.5	29.1	11.2
Electronics	11.6	9.0	6.3	3.7	3.0	3.0	74.5	7.8
Machinery	13.5	11.4	9.6	8.1	7.4	7.4	45.5	5.1
Traded services	29.7	25.8	21.9	18.1	14.2	14.2	52.0	
Average	17.0	14.5	12.2	10.2	8.9	8.9	47.6	

Source: China's tariff cut is aggregated from 6 digit Harmonized Commodity Description and Coding System (HS) tariff schedules based on US–China Agreement (November, 1999) and weighted by 1998 import data from China's Customs. China's non-tariff barrier (NTB) on industrial products is based on Zhang et al. and Li et al. (1998).

high-income regions (US, Western Europe, Japan, Canada, and Australia/New Zealand) account for less than 20 per cent of the global labor force, but possess more than 75 per cent of the world's capital stock. In contrast, more than half of the global labor force, with about 6 per cent of the world's capital, resides in the low-income developing countries in Asia (China, the ASEAN, and South Asia). Japan, Korea, Taiwan, Singapore, Hong Kong, and China are poorly endowed with arable land relative to labor.

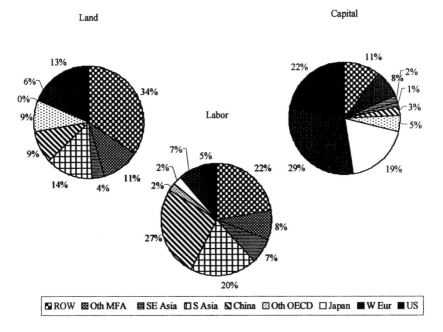

Figure 10.1: Structure of Factor Endowments in Major Regions

Conditions are just opposite in the United States, Canada, Australia/New Zealand, where land is abundant and cheap. West Europe, Mexico, the Caribbean and other MFA restricted countries, the ASEAN and South Asia have intermediate amounts of arable land per worker, placing these countries between the two extremes.

The relative scarcities of factor endowment in trading nations are quite important for understanding the direction of net trade flows. Figure 10.2 presents the correspondence between land intensity and the direction of net trade flows in four broad categories of food and agricultural products. It shows clearly that the United States, Canada and Australia/New Zealand, as land abundant countries, are net exporters of almost all food and agricultural

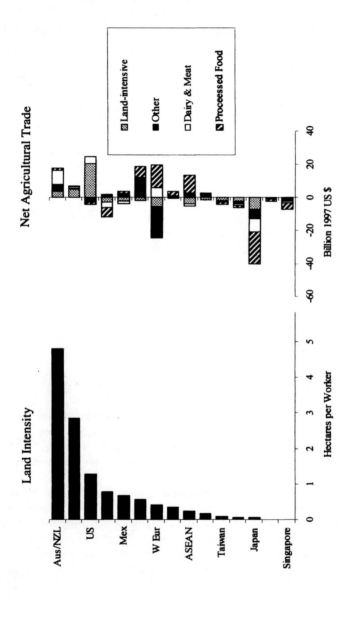

Figure 10.2: Countries with Abundant Land Tend to Export Agricultural Products

products, especially those land-intensive products such as grains, cotton and oilseeds. Japan, Korea, Singapore, Hong Kong, and Taiwan, as land scarce economies, are net importers of all food and agricultural products. Western Europe, Mexico and the other Latin American MFA restricted countries, the ASEAN and South Asia, with intermediate land endowments, are each net exporters and net importers of different agricultural products. The European countries are net exporters of meat and milk products and processed food, but net importers of land-intensive products. The ASEAN, South Asia and other MFA restricted countries are net exporters of non-grain crops, and processed food, which are often labor-intensive, but net importers of land-intensive agricultural products.

China's situation seems consistent with this pattern as market forces play a more and more important role in determining production and trade, driven by its market oriented economic reform. As a land-scarce economy, China is a net importer of land-intensive agricultural products, but a net exporter of labor-intensive agricultural commodities, such as non-grain crops. The on-going domestic economic reforms and trade liberalization as China implements its WTO commitments, will reinforce market forces and further push China's agricultural production and trade away from its current grain self-sufficiency policy in the years to come.

Figure 10.3 shows the correspondence between capital intensity and direction of net trade flows for different kinds of manufactured goods. This shows that labor-intensive manufactured goods (textiles, apparel, shoes, and other light manufactures) are the major net imports for Japan, West Europe, and the United States, while capital and skill-intensive manufactured goods (manufactured intermediates, motor vehicles, machinery and other transport equipment) are their major net exports. The trade patterns of labor abundant MFA restricted developing countries such as China, the ASEAN, and South Asia are quite similar. They are net exporters of labor-intensive manufactured goods and net importers of capital-intensive manufactured goods. At an intermediate level of capital intensity, Korea, Mexico and Taiwan, are net suppliers and net demanders of different skill/capital-intensive manufactured goods, while remaining net exporters of labor-intensive manufactured goods. However, upstream products such as textiles are a major portion of their net exports of such products, with more labor intensive exports such as apparel, playing smaller and smaller roles as they further shift such production to China and other developing countries. Obviously, industrial countries such as the United States and China are generally not competing economically for international trade at their current stages of development because their comparative advantages differ greatly. Their different factor endowment structures make their trade complementary. Other developing countries compete with each other and with China for exporting labor-intensive goods and electronic products to industrial countries, and attracting FDI from these

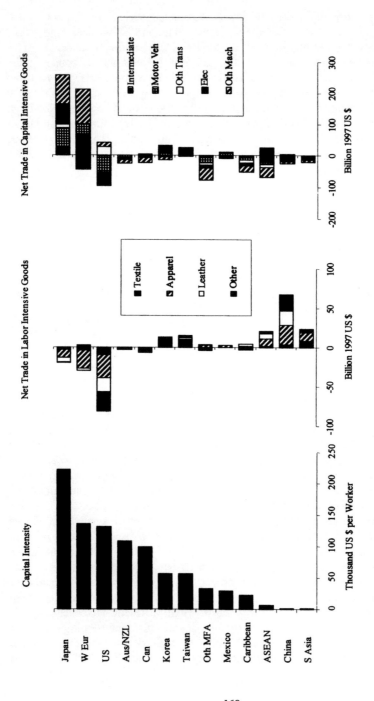

Figure 10.3: Counties with Abundant Labor Tend to Export Labor-intensive but Import Capital-intensive Manufacturers (1997)

countries. Similarly, Japan, Western Europe, and the United States compete to meet the demand for technology / capital intensive goods in China and other developing countries and to benefit from investment opportunities there.

The. structure of factor endowments in China and its major trading partners is also the basic economic force shaping the effects of China's WTO accession on the world production and trade. Joining the WTO, especially when industrial countries eliminate restrictions on imports of labor-intensive manufactured goods such as textiles and apparel from China, would further contribute to China's comparative advantage in producing such goods and increase its net exports. The expansion of labor-intensive manufactured goods in China would cause resources to be bid away from farming and drive up demand for agricultural and capital/technology intensive goods. This would increase China's net agricultural and capital/technology intensive imports and push up world market prices for such products. The opposite effect would occur in most developed economies because of their different endowment structures. Developing countries whose endowment structure is similar to China will encounter keener competition in the world labor-intensive goods market and face lower prices for their exports

The impact of China's WTO accession is also affected by China's current import protection structure and the structure of the tariff cuts in China's WTO offer, which are listed in Table 10.2. The larger the initial distortion and the deeper the tariff cuts in the offer, the greater the induced impact. However, the relative factor scarcity and intensity in production discussed above are the more fundamental forces driving the impact and the resulting adjustment pattern in the world economy. Production resources will be released from those previously highly protected industries in China and drawn into sectors where China has comparative advantages, thus enabling China to become a more efficient supplier in the world manufactured goods market.

Impact on World Net Trade Patterns

Figure 10.4 shows the time path of net trade flows in agricultural, labor-intensive and capital-intensive products for China under the two scenarios during the simulation period. Even in the case in which China is excluded from the WTO, China's net exports of labor intensive products and net import of food and agricultural products will continue to increase because of its rapid industrialization and population growth. WTO accession will accelerate this trend. The annual growth rate of China's net exports of labor-intensive goods will increase from 3.4 per cent to 6 per cent, and the annual growth rates of its net food and agricultural imports will increase from 18 per cent to 22 per cent. This will result in $165 billion additional net exports of

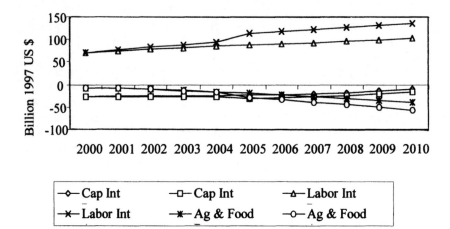

Figure 10.4: Impact of WTO Accession on China's Net Trade Patterns

labor-intensive manufactured goods and $80 billion in additional net imports of food and agricultural products during the 10 year simulation period (Table 10.3). In the same period, China's net imports of capital-intensive products will increase by 47 billion because of its accession to the WTO. There is however a general decline in the trend of China's net capital-intensive imports over time under both simulation scenarios.

Where do these additional net labor-intensive exports from China go and where do the additional net imports in food and agricultural products by China come from? Figure 10.5 shows that part of the increase in labor-intensive exports from China will go to markets in industrial countries, where import demand increases because of the elimination of MFA quotas, while part will be substitutes for net exports originally from other MFA restricted developing countries in Asia and Latin America. Figure 10.6 shows that a large part of the increased net imports of land-intensive agricultural products into China after its joining the WTO will come from land-abundant developed countries such as Australia, Canada and the United States, but a significant portion will come from other developing countries. The major underlying reason is that China's entry into the WTO will divert exports of labor-intensive products from other developing countries to China. The labor-intensive sectors in these regions cannot attract as many production resources as they could when China and Taiwan were not in the WTO, so more factors of production will remain in the agricultural sectors in those countries. At the same time, increased agricultural import demand from China and Taiwan will push up world food prices, while at the same time the increased export supply

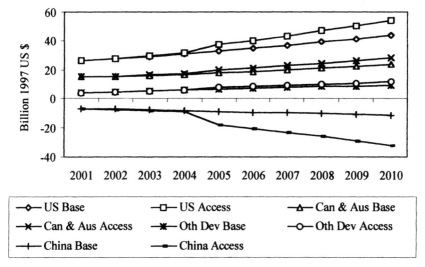

Figure 10.5: Impact of China's WTO Accession on Net trade in Labor-Intensive Manufacturers

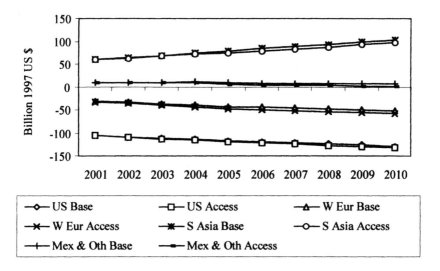

Figure 10.6: Impact of China's WTO Accession on Net Trade in Land-Intensive Products

of production will remain in the agricultural sectors in those countries. At the same time, increased agricultural import demand from China and Taiwan will push up world food prices, while at the same time the increased export supply of labor intensive manufactured goods from China will reduce the prices of these goods in the world market. As a result agricultural exports will become relatively more profitable and agricultural imports will become relatively more expensive, resulting in an expansion of production and exports of agricultural products in these countries. However, the increase in the production of labor-intensive sectors in China will also demand more manufactured goods inputs from the world market, causing the manufacturing sector to expand and agricultural production to decline in Japan, Korea and Taiwan, thus increasing their net imports of food and agricultural products. Another underlying reason for this disparity, other than the relative scarcity of agricultural production factors in these countries, is that they are at a higher stage of economic development and have the technology to produce the goods demanded by China's manufacturing sector. Because they are at a lower stage of economic development, most developing countries do not have such capacity or are not able to produce what China's manufacturing sector needs at a competitive cost.

Why do China's net imports in capital-intensive products show a declining trend over time in both simulation scenarios (Figure 10.4)? This indicates that exports of some capital-intensive products from China are rising and that there is an industrial upgrade process going on as China imports more capital-intensive products from industrial countries. There are three fundamental factors that contribute to this trend. First, there are quantitative constraints such as MFA quotas in developed countries markets that have limited China's growth potential in producing labor-intensive products and forced China to divert its production resources to other manufacturing activities, including capital-intensive sectors. Second, China is undergoing a period of rapid investment growth and capital accumulation. From 1991 to 1995 investment in fixed assets grew at an annual rate of 36.1 per cent, averaging 20.6 per cent a year in real terms. During the same period China was the largest FDI recipient among developing countries, with over $100 billion in foreign capital inflows. Strong growth in capital-intensive manufacturing is a direct consequence. As pointed out in trade theory, an increase in the supply of capital will lead to an increase in the output of the sector which uses capital intensively and a reduction in the output in other sectors that use other factors intensively (Rybczynski theorem). Finally, a notable feature of China's manufacturing exports is their high import content reflecting the rapid growth of processing trade in recent years fueled by inflows of FDI. More than half of China's exports of machinery and electronics are processing exports with low value-added, which may tend to exaggerate the extent of industrial upgrading in China's exports.[3]

Joining the WTO cannot fundamentally change this trend, because China ultimately will upgrade its industrial structure during its modernization, as most newly industrialized countries are doing now. But as shown in both Figure 10.4 and Table 10.3, joining the WTO will increase China's net imports of capital-intensive products by about $47 billion over the 10-year simulation period. This is because the expansion of the labor-intensive sector will bid productive resources away from capital-intensive production on the one hand, and increase domestic demand for such products on the other hand, causing exports to decline and imports to increase.

Aggregate and Growth Effects

Table 10.3 summarizes major aggregate economy-wide effects between a WTO with and without China. Admitting China and Taiwan into the WTO will accelerate world economic growth. Thus according to the model results the average annual growth rate of world real GDP would be 0.03 percentage points higher and the cumulative total world GDP growth would be 0.33 percentage points higher in 2010 than in the baseline scenario. However, the strongest stimulus to economic growth will occur in China and Taiwan. China's real GDP growth rate would increase by 0.36 percentage points (0.03 percentage point for Taiwan) per year from 2001 to 2010, and its GDP would be 7 percentage points higher (0.5 per cent point higher for Taiwan) in 2010 than would be the case if it were excluded from the WTO. Real GDP growth in all developed countries and most developing countries would also increase from China's WTO accession. These increases may seem small in annual terms, however, the cumulative effects are notable when extended over the whole simulation period. In 2010 real GDP would be 0.16 per cent higher in the United States and 0.11 per cent higher in West Europe than the case of a WTO without China. Newly industrialized economies such as Singapore, Hong Kong, and Korea, that have close ties with China and Taiwan, would benefit more and grow faster because of China's WTO accession, while some developing countries that have a similar endowments and export structures as China would be slightly negatively affected, especially those MFA quota restricted countries in the ASEAN and South Asia. They would have to divert resources from manufacturing to food and agricultural products because stronger Chinese competition would reduce their export share in the world market. However, this result may be partially attributed to the highly aggregated sectors in our model. We will further discuss this point in some detail in next section.

The gains to economic growth from China and Taiwan's trade liberalization are mainly generated from three sources that reinforce each other: (1) more efficient allocation of production factors, including the migration of agricultural labor to manufacturing activities, which increases

Table 10.3: Differences Between a WTO With and Without China: Accumulated Sectoral Net Trade by Region During 2001–2010.

Billion US $	US	W Eur	JPN	Aus & NZ	Can	Mex	Kor	Sing	HK	Tai	PRC	ASEAN	S Asia	LA	ME & Af MFA	Oth Af	Rest of Wrld
Grains & oil seeds	33.1	1.4	-0.5	6.2	13.2	0.2	0.3	0.0	0.0	0.2	-67.2	0.4	1.4	8.6	0.4	0.0	2.1
Planted fiber	11.2	0.3	0.0	1.3	0.0	0.3	-0.1	0.0	0.1	-0.1	-21.8	0.4	1.2	0.2	0.6	2.4	4.1
Non-grain crops	-5.3	0.6	-0.4	-0.7	-1.4	0.5	-0.1	0.0	0.0	-1.1	4.5	0.2	1.5	0.8	0.6	-0.4	0.6
Livestock	-2.0	-1.0	-0.2	-2.9	-1.1	0.1	0.0	0.0	-0.1	0.2	7.0	0.1	0.2	-0.2	0.2	0.0	-0.3
Dairy & meat	-0.1	0.2	-0.2	-0.4	-0.4	0.0	0.0	0.0	0.0	-0.4	0.4	0.2	0.1	0.0	0.2	0.0	0.2
Processed food	-0.7	-0.3	-0.8	-0.2	-0.2	0.1	-0.1	0.2	0.2	-0.9	-0.8	1.2	0.9	1.2	0.0	-0.2	0.3
Tobacco & bev	1.0	3.1	0.2	-0.1	0.0	0.1	-0.1	0.2	0.1	-2.4	-2.6	0.1	0.0	0.1	0.1	0.0	0.2
Food & agr	37.4	4.4	-1.8	3.1	10.1	1.3	0.0	0.4	0.4	-4.4	-80.4	2.4	5.3	10.9	2.0	1.8	7.2
Forest & fish	-0.1	-0.2	-0.1	0.1	0.0	0.0	-0.2	0.0	0.0	-0.2	1.1	-0.2	0.4	0.0	0.0	-0.4	-0.3
Energy products	-0.5	-0.1	0.0	-0.6	-0.5	0.3	-0.8	-0.6	-0.1	-2.0	3.6	1.0	1.0	0.5	-0.9	-0.3	-0.1
Mineral products	-1.4	-2.2	-1.1	-0.4	-0.6	0.0	-0.5	-0.2	-0.1	-0.5	6.8	0.5	0.8	-0.1	-0.2	-0.1	-0.7
Textiles	-0.4	-4.0	7.4	0.4	0.8	-0.5	6.3	0.1	4.8	6.9	-26.3	3.4	-0.5	-0.2	0.5	0.0	1.2
Clothing	-12.6	-13.3	-10.6	-0.7	-1.8	-3.0	-2.9	0.0	-5.3	-2.7	107.2	-10.7	-12.9	-10.1	-6.2	-0.2	-14.4
Leather & shoes	-2.8	-11.2	-1.4	-0.3	0.2	-0.5	-1.4	-0.2	-0.4	-0.7	47.7	-15.1	-1.5	-5.2	-0.9	-0.2	-6.0
Other light mfg	-1.4	-13.0	-3.9	-0.3	-0.4	-0.6	-1.5	-0.2	-0.6	-1.8	36.1	-2.2	-2.2	-0.7	-4.2	-1.2	-1.7

174

Table 10.3 Continued

	US	W Eur	JPN	Aus & NZ	Can	Mex	Kor	Sing	HK	Tai	PRC	ASEAN	S. Asia MFA	LA MFA	ME & Afr MFA	Oth Afr	Rest of Wrld
Total labor-intensive	-17.1	-41.6	-8.6	-0.9	-1.2	-4.6	0.5	-0.3	-1.5	1.7	164.7	-24.7	-17.1	-16.2	-10.8	-1.6	-20.8
Wood & paper	-1.7	-1.7	-1.0	-0.4	-2.2	0.3	-0.1	-0.3	0.0	-0.5	5.7	1.3	0.3	0.1	0.2	-0.1	0.0
Intermediate prod.	6.7	2.6	15.4	0.5	-1.2	0.9	8.6	1.0	2.2	8.7	-63.3	7.3	3.2	0.7	1.7	0.0	5.1
Motor vehicles	2.0	6.7	4.9	-0.6	-0.4	2.1	-1.8	-0.3	-0.3	-7.0	-10.1	1.4	0.3	1.2	0.7	0.0	1.2
Oth trans equip	-7.6	-2.8	-3.0	-0.3	-0.6	0.1	-2.9	0.2	-0.1	-0.2	17.0	0.8	0.6	0.0	0.0	0.1	-1.3
Electronics	-0.9	-0.3	0.3	0.4	-0.9	-0.7	-2.1	0.8	2.1	2.1	-0.1	-0.4	0.4	0.1	0.0	0.1	-0.8
Machinery	-4.9	-8.0	-2.7	-0.3	-1.9	-0.4	-1.9	-0.7	0.7	3.1	9.5	3.6	1.1	0.5	1.6	0.5	0.2
Traded services	3.7	19.6	-2.1	-0.5	-0.4	1.5	-2.7	-1.0	-3.7	0.0	-32.1	4.7	3.2	2.2	3.4	-0.4	4.9
Housing & const.	-0.2	-1.1	-1.0	0.0	0.0	0.0	0.0	0.0	-0.1	0.0	2.3	0.1	0.0	0.1	0.0	0.0	0.0
Total	15.3	-24.7	-0.6	0.1	0.8	0.8	-4.0	-1.0	-0.6	0.8	24.6	-2.2	-0.5	-0.1	-2.3	-0.4	-5.4

Table 10.4: Differences Between a WTO With and Without China: Aggregrated Economic Indicators by Region

	US	W Eur	JPN	Aus & NZ	Can	Mex	Kor	Sing	HK	Tai	PRC	ASEAN	S Asia	LA MFA	ME & Af MFA	Oth Afr	Rest of Wrld	Wrld Ave
Cumulative growth 2000–2010, percentage point change from baseline																		
Real GDP	0.2	0.1	0.1	0.4	0.3	-0.2	0.4	1.4	1.2	0.5	7.0	-0.3	-0.6	0.0	-0.1	0.0	-0.1	0.3
Real exp	0.6	-0.3	0.9	-0.3	-0.5	-0.7	0.5	-0.2	1.3	7.4	74.5	-1.3	-2.9	-0.7	-1.0	-0.8	-0.8	3.7
Real imp	2.8	1.8	3.0	1.9	0.9	-0.7	3.2	1.5	3.9	7.9	53.7	-0.2	-2.0	0.4	0.5	1.3	0.7	3.5
TFP	0.0	0.0	0.0	0.0	0.0	-0.1	-0.1	-0.4	0.0	0.1	2.8	-0.2	-0.2	-0.1	-0.2	-0.1	-0.1	0.2
Cap stock	0.1	0.0	0.0	0.1	0.1	-0.1	0.2	0.7	0.4	0.3	3.5	-0.1	-0.2	0.0	0.0	0.0	0.0	0.1
Average annual growth rate 2000–2010, percentage point change from baseline																		
Real GDP	0.0	0.0	0.0	0.0	0.0	0.0	0.0	0.1	0.1	0.0	0.4	0.0	0.0	0.0	0.0	0.0	0.0	0.0
Export	0.1	0.0	0.1	0.0	0.0	0.0	0.0	0.0	0.1	0.5	3.3	-0.1	-0.1	-0.1	-0.1	0.0	0.0	0.3
Import	0.2	0.1	0.2	0.1	0.1	0.0	0.2	0.1	0.3	0.5	2.6	0.0	-0.1	0.0	0.0	0.1	0.0	0.3
TFP	0.0	0.0	0.0	0.0	0.0	0.0	0.0	0.0	0.0	0.0	0.2	0.0	0.0	0.0	0.0	0.0	0.0	0.0
Cap stock	0.0	0.0	0.0	0.0	0.0	0.0	0.0	0.0	0.0	0.0	0.2	0.0	0.0	0.0	0.0	0.0	0.0	0.0

Table 10.4: Continued

	US	W Eur	JPN	Aus & NZ	Can	Mex	Kor	Sing	HK	Tai	PRC	ASEAN MFA	S Asia MFA	LA MFA	ME & Af MFA	Oth Afr	ROW	Wrld Ave
Agricultural labor force migration, 2001–2010, 1000 persons																		
Accum	-60	-37	-12	-8	-13	-47	-3	0	0	11	6299	-401	-322	-244	-86	-542	-421	4113
Real consumption, investment and trade balance, change from baseline, 2001–2010, billion 1997 US$																		
Accum	84	64	36	10	10	-4	13	7	10	12	385	-8	-17	-4	-4	0	-7	586
Real exports, change from baseline, 2001–2010, billion 1997 US$ in fob price																		
Accum	40	-14	34	-1	-6	-4	6	-3	8	70	1127	-23	-13	-6	-15	-2	-17	1182
Real imports, change from baseline, 2001–2010, billion 1997 US$ in fob price																		
Accum	144	99	77	9	8	-5	29	9	19	67	726	-8	-11	1	3	3	12	1182
Nominal trade balance, change from baseline, billion 1997 US$																		
Accum	-2.6	1.9	2.2	-0.1	0.2	0.5	0.6	0.6	-0.3	-0.1	-2.9	-0.9	0.2	0	-0.3	0.1	0.0	
Terms of trade, change from baseline, per cent																		
2004	0.2	0.2	0.5	0.4	0.1	-0.1	0.5	0.3	0.8	-0.6	-2.5	0.2	0.0	0.1	0.2	0.1		
2010	0.4	0.1	0.6	1.0	0.7	-0.3	0.8	0.5	1.1	-0.5	-4.3	0.2	-1.0	0.1	0.0	0.9	0.2	

177

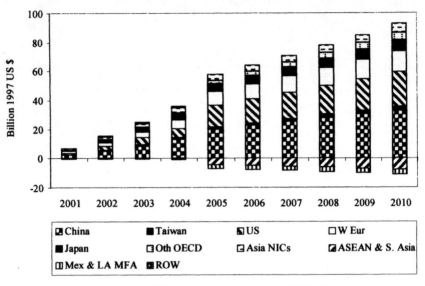

Figure 10.7: Gains in Real Purchasing Power with WTO Accession

labor productivity; (2) more rapid physical capital accumulation from trade liberalization, which induces higher income for economic agents and lowers the price of capital goods and leads to higher savings and investment so that there will be a larger physical capital stock available in the economy; and (3) more rapid growth of total factor productivity (TFP) due to the speeding up of technology transfer via expansion of capital and intermediate goods imports from advanced industrial countries. The additional capital accumulation and TFP growth in each region because of China's WTO accession are reported in the first half of Table 10.3. Since both China and Taiwan are assumed to adopt dramatic liberalization measures to meet WTO entry requirements in the simulation exercises, it is expected that they will be subject to the largest impact from the above three sources and gain the most from their WTO membership. For instance, physical capital accumulation in China will be 3.5 per cent higher in year 2010 and an addition 6.3 million agricultural laborers will become production workers in various manufacturing sectors over the 2001–2010 period if China is admitted to the WTO.

As indicated in classical trade theory, removing trade distortions leads to further realization of each region's comparative advantage, more efficient allocation of production factors and expansion of trade. These types of efficiency gain are driven by each region's comparative advantages, resulting in structural adjustments in each regional economy and reshaping the world net trade pattern. In addition, there will be strong positive feedback between trade expansion and productivity growth. As China expands its labor-intensive exports to the world market after joining the WTO, Chinese firms will import more capital and technology-intensive goods, as both investment and intermediate inputs from abroad, at cheaper prices. These goods usually embody advanced technology from other countries and thus stimulate productivity growth for all production factors. The simulation results show that WTO membership will accelerate China's TFP growth by about 0.2 percentage points a year and contribute significantly to the additional real GDP growth due to its entry into the WTO over the whole simulation period.

Households in China and its major trade partners would benefit from further realization of each region's comparative advantage in a freer trade environment with faster economic growth. As shown in the second half of Figure 10.7 and Table 10.4, real purchasing power, measured by real consumption and real investment, adjusted by the real balance of trade, rises by about $59 billion a year on average for the world as a whole over the period from 2001 to 2010. Almost all regions share in these gains. Similar to other trade liberalization exercises, the liberalizers, in this case, China and Taiwan, gain the most. However the rest of the world also gains substantially, especially the industrial countries. For example, US real purchasing power would increase more than $84 billion across the whole simulation period and about $14 billion annually after 2010. Only MFA quota restricted developing counties in Asia, South America and Mexico would suffer losses due to China's WTO entry because trade will be diverted away from these countries to China as will be discussed in next section. The size of these losses would be small.

Impact on US and World Labor-intensive Markets and Implications for Other Suppliers of Such Products

Figures 10.8 and 10.9 plot world market shares of textiles and apparel for period from 2001 to 2010. Almost all regions share in these gains. Similar to major country groups. The figures illustrate the differences between the two simulation scenarios. China faces a declining world textile market share and a slowly increasing world apparel share during the simulation period if it is excluded from the WTO. Other MFA quota restricted suppliers such as the ASEAN and South Asia would benefit the most under such a scenario, as their market share in apparel would increase from 33 per cent in 2000 to about 37per cent in 2010. However, if China joins the WTO and obtains the benefits from phasing out MFA quotas for its textile and apparel exports, its share of the world market for apparel would increase from 20 per cent to 22 per cent during the MFA phase out period, and jump to 28 per cent when MFA is eliminated in the year of 2005 and to 30 per cent in the year of 2010. This gain would be at the expense of all other suppliers but especially those MFA restricted suppliers, such as countries in Asia and South America. In contrast

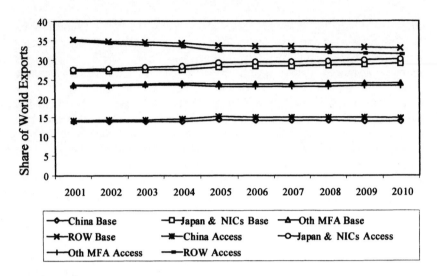

Figure 10.8: Changes in Shares of World Textile Markets with WTO With and Without China

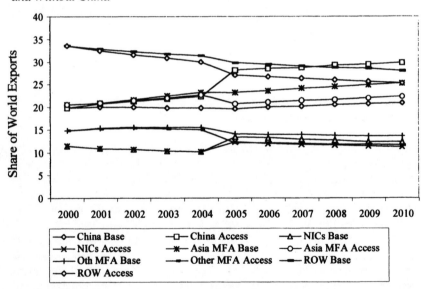

Figure 10.9: Changes in Shares of World Apparel Markets with WTO With and Without China

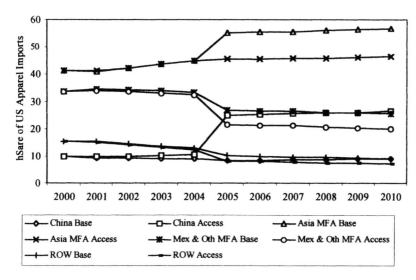

Figure 10.10: Changes in Share of US Apparel Import Market with WTO With and Without China

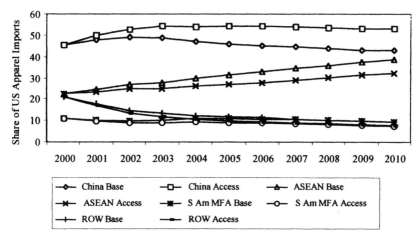

Figure 10.11: Shares of US Leather, Shoes and Travel Goods Import Market with WTO With and Without China

apparel production is relatively labor-intensive and more consistent with China's overall factor endowment structure and comparative advantages. Comparing the performance of China's labor-intensive exports in restricted and unrestricted US markets helps to further highlight the differences between the cases with and without the benefits from phasing out MFA quotas for exports of China and other MFA quota restricted suppliers in developed country markets. Figures 10.10 and 10.11 plot China and other major suppliers' shares of apparel and leather products, footwear and travel goods in the US market over the simulation period. Apparel represents the restricted market in the model since imports are under strict quota constraints in the United States.[4] Leather products, footwear and travel goods represent he unrestricted market, with no quantitative restrictions. Figure 10.11 demonstrates clearly that China's exports out-perform both other Asian and South American suppliers in the unrestricted market by a large margin during the entire simulation period whether China joins the WTO or not. However, access to the WTO will increase the growth of China's share of the US import market by about 10 per cent, sustaining China's market leading position after the year 2010.

In the restricted apparel market, WTO membership will make a significant difference both for China and for other restricted suppliers. If China is excluded from the WTO (Scenario I), the share of its apparel products in the US market would decline gradually (Figure 10.10) during the whole simulation period. Other apparel suppliers, especially those MFA restricted suppliers in Asia, would increase their share more than 10 percentage points and take more than half of the US market in 2010. If China enters the WTO and obtains the benefits from eliminating MFA quotas, its share in the US apparel import market will dramatically increase in the year 2005 by nearly 15 percentage points when quantitative restrictions are removed. The market share of other Asian restricted suppliers only increases about 1 percentage point. Such results highlight the high substitutability of labor-intensive products among developing countries, especially between China and other

Impact on China's Imports and Implications for Major Land and Capital-intensive Product Suppliers

Entering the WTO China will obtain the benefits of WTO membership, such as MFA quota phase out under the ATC, but in exchange it will have to follow through on its commitment to further open its vast market to all of its trade partners. The reduction of import protection and expansion of labor-intensive manufacturing will stimulate China's imports, especially in land and capital intensive products. Figures 10.12 and 10.13 illustrate the difference in China's real food and agricultural imports between the two scenarios by sectors, time and geographic origin. It shows that if China enters the WTO at the beginning of 2001 and fulfills its major market access commitments by 2005, its total imports of food and agricultural products will increase by about $36 billion over the 10-year simulation period. More than 90 per cent of these imports are land-intensive products (grains, oilseeds and

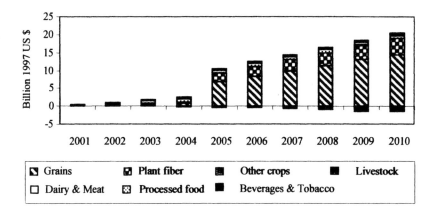

Figure 10.12: Change in China's Imports of Food and Agricultural Products With and Without WTO

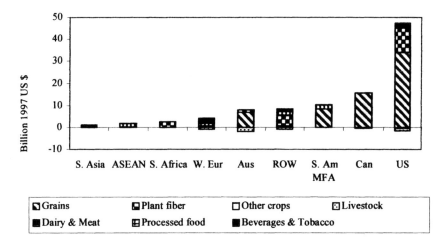

Figure 10.13: China's Imports of Food and Agricultural Products by Region

plant fiber). Only about 5 per cent of the total gains by world agricultural product suppliers will occur during the first four years when the quota system for grain and cotton is still in place. This is despite the fact that China's commitment on tariff reduction is concentrated during the first four years. This implies that quantity constraints and non-tariff barriers will have a more profound impact on agricultural imports than tariffs in China. The geographic

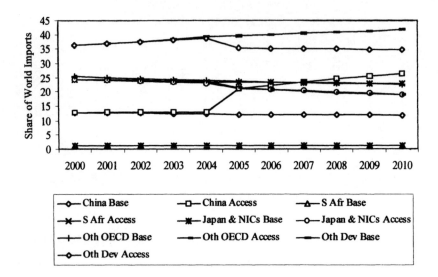

Figure 10.14: Share in World Markets for Land-Intensive Products

distribution of these gains is consistent with the factor endowment structure of the supplier countries. All land-abundant major agricultural commodity suppliers (Australia/New Zealand, Canada, the United States and the rest of the world) gain significantly, with more than 50 per cent of those gains going to the United States alone. Countries with relatively less land endowment such as Western Europe and the ASEAN mainly benefit from exporting

Because China's trade is currently only about 5 per cent of total world trade the change in China' exports and imports due to its entry into the WTO should only have a moderate impact on the world market in general. However, there are at least two exceptions. As discussed earlier, changes in China's trade in textiles and apparel products will have a significant impact on the world market for labor-intensive exports. Another example is the impact on the world market for land-intensive agricultural products. Figure 10.14 plots the shares of world land-intensive agricultural imports for China, low-income southern Africa countries and other major agricultural import regions during the simulation period. It shows that WTO accession will dramatically increase China's share in world land-intensive agricultural imports from less than 13 per cent in 2000 to more than 26 per cent in 2010. The reduction of agricultural protection, especially the elimination of quota restrictions according to WTO rules, is the direct reason for such an import boom. There is another indirect general equilibrium drive: the expansion of labor–intensive manufacturing in China due to its WTO accession and migration of agricultural labor to production jobs during industrialization will increase China's domestic demand for agricultural products while at the same time bidding away other scarce resources such as land and capital from agricultural production, thus lowering the growth rate of domestic supply. Both effects together will lead to increased imports and higher world prices for agricultural products. However, the impact on food imports by the least developed economies such as those in low-income southern Africa is very limited as shown in Figure 10.14.

Figures 10.15 and 10.16 present the difference in China's real imports of

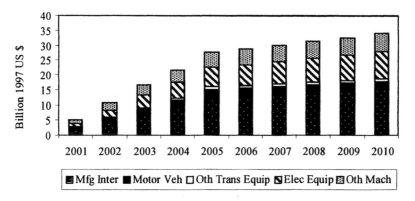

Figure 10.15: China's Imports of Capital-Intensive Goods with WTO With and Without China

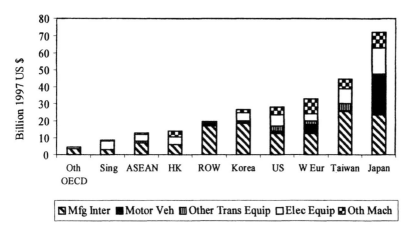

Figure 10.16: Change in China's Imports of Capital-Intensive Goods by Region

capital-intensive products between the two scenarios. Over the 10-year simulation period, China will import about $238 billion more capital-intensive manufactured goods if it joins the WTO. Nearly 45 per cent of these imports will be intermediate goods and 11 per cent will be motor vehicles and parts. Electronics and other machinery will constitute another 25 and 19 per cent respectively. The three major industrial regions (W. Europe, the United States, and Japan) gain the most, seizing 50 per cent of these new sales to China. Asian newly industrialized countries (Taiwan, Hong Kong, Singapore and Korea) and ASEAN also gain significantly, accounting for another 41 per cent, while all other developing countries in the world take less than 7 per cent. The sectoral structure of these new imports is also consistent with the capital endowment and technology development of the economies that supply these products. For example, the three advanced industrial counties would capture about 85 per cent of the gain in motor vehicles and parts, and more than 60 per cent of the gain in machinery and equipment, while about a half of the gain by the Asian NICs and the ASEAN would be intermediates and electronic products. However, the Asian NICs are in the process of upgrading their industrial structures and are becoming more and more important suppliers of capital-intensive goods to China. For instance, the simulation results show that they take about one third of the new machinery sales to China after China joins the WTO.

In order to modernize its economy and raise productivity, China needs to import large amounts of technology and capital-intensive goods, estimated at about $263 billion (US dollars) a year by the year 2010, if it enters the WTO in 2001. As its export-oriented industries create more and more foreign exchange during its modernization, China's import capacity for such commodities will tend to grow continuously. This will convert its massive infrastructure needs into effective demand and thus extend the export market for firms in industrial countries. To capture such rising opportunities for US firms, the United States needs to adopt a more active economic and trade policy to further engage China. Admitting China into the WTO is an important step in this direction. It will end the annual debate on China's MFN trade status, reduce uncertainty in US–China trade relations, and encourage US companies to adopt long term investment strategies in China in order to obtain a larger share in this the world's largest potential market.

CONCLUSIONS AND LIMITATIONS

This chapter provides a relatively comprehensive assessment of the impact of China's WTO accession on other economies in the world based on market access commitments that China has made to date. It estimates aggregate and sectoral gains and losses to production and trade for China's major trade partners by using a recursive dynamic, multi-region, multi-sector computable general equilibrium (CGE) model. The simulation results show that major gains from China's WTO accession would accrue to China itself. However, the rest of the world, especially the developed countries and the Asian newly industrialized economies, also benefit. This is because these countries have different factor endowment structures and are at different stages of technology development compared to China. Integrating China into the global trading system could induce more competition in labor-intensive products and reduce their prices. The expansion of labor-intensive sectors in China could increase its net imports of agricultural and capital-intensive products, drive up their prices and improve the terms of trade of industrial and land abundant countries. Some developing countries with a similar endowment structure to China, such as those in South America and Southeast Asia, would experience keener competition in labor-intensive exports and lower prices for their products. More production factors will remain in their food and agricultural sectors and increase their net agricultural exports.

The simulation results also show that China's WTO entry will have a profound impact on world labor-intensive exports and the primary agricultural import market. China's share of the world market for apparel will increase by about 10 percentage points and thereby reduce the shares of other countries across the world. China will also increase its land-intensive agricultural imports dramatically as its share in total world imports will double. However, its impact on food imports into the least developed countries is very limited because of the expansion of agricultural production worldwide.

The results of this chapter provide useful insights for understanding the impact of China's accession to the WTO and demonstrate that a CGE model can be a valuable tool for trade policy evaluation. However, there are several obvious limitations that need to be mentioned. First, this analysis does not take into account other major aspects of WTO membership, such as reduction of barriers in foreign investment, protection of intellectual property rights, securing market access, enforcement of commitments and cooperation in dispute settlement. It at best captures only one aspect of the issue at hand. Second, China had not finalized all of the terms for its WTO entry when this analysis was finished. There were still uncertainties regarding the size of its trade concessions, the time schedule of implementation for each of the liberalization measures, and the length of the phase-in period, especially with regard to quantitative restrictions on imports and barriers to services. A relatively stylized representation of trade liberalization measures in these areas was adopted in the simulation design. Third, the CGE model used in this chapter is a highly stylized simplification of the world economy and is far from perfect (Wang, 1997a). Finally, there are uncertainties about the size of key parameters, such as elasticities of substitution of products from different sources and the elasticities between capital goods imports and TFP growth. The actual size of the effects is very sensitive to these key parameters. Therefore, the results reported in this paper need to be interpreted with caution: they can be viewed as indicative but not as precise real outcomes.

NOTES

1. There are 11 developing regions in the model, nine of which are subject to binding MFA quotas. They are Korea, Singapore, Taiwan, Hong Kong, China, ASEAN, South Asia, Latin American MFA restricted countries, and Mid-east and African MFA restricted countries. Low income African countries and rest of the world are modeled as MFA quota non-binding countries.
2. On 1 January 1995, the ATC entered into being and replaced the old Multi Fiber arrangements (MFA). The ATC provides for the elimination of the quotas and the complete integration of textiles and apparel into the WTO regime over a 10-year transition period ending on 1 January 2005. All WTO countries are subject to ATC disciplines, and only WTO members are eligible for ATC benefits.
3. For example, the largest items of electronics exports in 1995 were radio cassette players and telephone sets. They are produced from imported semi-processed materials and assembled by spare parts from abroad for re-export. The portion of the production process conducted in China was basically labor-intensive in nature.
4. Estimates of price effects of US quotas on China's exports of apparels and historical data on quota fill rates during the 1990s suggest that the quotas are very restrictive. Based on weekly license prices and 1996 US import level, the tax equivalents for China's exports of apparel were estimated at 37 per cent. In contrast, tax equivalents for other restricted countries only range from 0.5 to 26.

REFERENCES

Ahuja, V. and D. Filmer (1995), 'Educational Attainment in Developing Countries: New Estimates and Projections Disaggregated by Gender', World Bank Policy Research Working Paper 1489, Washington, DC.

Hertel, Thomas, Will Martin, Koji Yanagishima, and Betina Dimaranan (1995) 'Liberalizing Manufactures Trade in a Changing World Economy', in Martin, Will and Alan Winters (eds), *The Uruguay Round and the Developing Economies*, World Bank Discussion Papers 307.

Hoekman Bernard (1995), 'Assessing the General Agreement on Trade in Services', in Martin, Will, and Alan Winters (eds), *The Uruguay Round and the Developing Economies*, World Bank Discussion Paper 307.

Lewis, Jeffrey D., Sherman Robinson, and Zhi Wang (1995), 'Beyond the Uruguay Round: The Implication of an Asian Free Trade Area', *China Economic Review – An International Journal*, 7(1), pp. 35–90.

Li, Shantong, Zhi Wang, Fan Zhai and Lin Xu (1998),'The Global and Domestic Impact of China joining the World Trade Organization', Washington Center for China Studies and Development Research Center, the State Council, People's Republic of China, December.

Linkins, Linda (1999), ' Estimating the Tax Equivalents of U.S. Textile and Apparel Quotas', Research Note No. 99-08-A, Office of Economics, U.S. International Trade Commission.

Oxford Economic Forecasting (1999), *The Oxford World Macroeconomic Model, An Overview*, Oxford: Abbey House.

U.S. International Trade Commission (1999), 'Assessment of the Economic Effects on the United States of China's Accession to the WTO', Investigation No. 332-403, Publication 3229.

Wang, Zhi (1997a), 'The Impact of China and Taiwan Joining the World Trade Organization on US and World Agricultural Trade: A Computable General Equilibrium Analysis', Technical Bulletin, No. 1858, USDA, Economic Research Service.

Wang, Zhi (1997b), 'China and Taiwan Access to the World Trade Organization: Implications for U.S. Agriculture and Trade', *Agricultural Economics*, 17, pp. 239–264.

Wang, Zhi (1999), 'Impact of China's WTO Entry on Labor Intensive Export Market – A Recursive Dynamic CGE Analysis', *The World Economy*, 22(3), pp. 379–405.

Zhang, Shuguang, Yansheng Zhang and Zhongxin Wan (1998), *Measuring the Costs of Protection in China*, Washington DC: Institute for International Economics.

11. The Impact on Taiwan

Chen-yuan Tung

INTRODUCTION

Economic relations between Taiwan and China have developed rapidly. According to China's statistics, as of December 1999 Taiwan's cumulative realized FDI in China was $23.9 billion. According to Taiwan's statistics, as of December 1999 China was the largest recipient of Taiwan approved outward investment receiving $14.5 billion and accounting for 40 per cent of Taiwan's total outward investment. According to an estimate by Taiwan's Mainland Affairs Council (MAC), two-way trade between Taiwan and China reached $25.8 billion in 1999. That same year Taiwan enjoyed a huge trade surplus of $16.8 billion with China, the third largest buyer of Taiwan's exports.

Economic exchange across the Taiwan Strait has accelerated the ongoing economic restructuring process in Taiwan. There are many economic concerns raised by the cross-Strait exchange, which this chapter will address. This chapter will also review how cross-Strait economic relations, driven by Taiwan's foreign direct investment (FDI) in China, contribute to Taiwan's economic transformation and contribute to a new international division of labor among Taiwan, China, and the rest of the world.

THE EVOLUTION OF TAIWAN'S OUTWARD INVESTMENT

In 1987 Taiwan's government deregulated control over foreign exchange and this led to a rapid increase in outward investment by Taiwan's enterprises. As Taiwan's labor-intensive industries began to lose their comparative advantage, Taiwan firms began investing in the Southeast Asian countries (SEACs).[1] According to Taiwan's Investment Commission, Taiwan's FDI in the SEACs was 15 per cent of Taiwan's total FDI in 1987 and 39 per cent of its total FDI at its highest point in 1991. By the end of 1997, Taiwan's cumulative FDI in the SEACs was $3.7 billion, 14 per cent of Taiwan's total FDI.

Although Taiwan's entrepreneurs began investing in China in the late 1980s, Taiwan did not compile formal statistics until 1991. According to Taiwan's official figures, in 1991 Taiwan's FDI into China was $174 million.

In 1993 it jumped to nearly $3.2 billion, which was 66 per cent of Taiwan's total FDI for that year. By the end of 1999, Taiwan's cumulative FDI in China was $14.5 billion, 40 per cent of Taiwan's total FDI. China became the place with the highest accumulated Taiwanese FDI. Overall Taiwan's FDI in the late 1980s and early 1990s involved mainly small and medium, labor-intensive enterprises looking for overseas manufacturing bases, mostly in the SEACs and China. (Kuo 1997, pp. 57–59)

BALANCE OF PAYMENTS

According to a United Nations (UN) report, the direct effect of Taiwan's FDI on its balance of payments can be estimated using the following formula (UN 1993, p. 59):

Change in balance of payments = – (outflow of FDI) + (FDI-driven exports) + (FDI income)

Beijing's figures for Taiwan's FDI in China are more accurate than those kept by Taipei because Taiwan firms must report their investments to Chinese authorities, but often do not notify the Taiwan government. From 1991 to 1997, Taiwan's realized FDI in China averaged $2.6 billion per year. Beijing's figures might be exaggerated, therefore, an inflated figure for the Taiwan's FDI in China would give us a more negative estimate of its impact on Taiwan's balance of payments. This is because the first item (outflow of FDI) in the formula is negative.

Taiwan does not keep official statistics on FDI income from China (payments of royalties, fees and salaries to the patent and repatriation of dividends, equity interest and loan principal). Therefore the income from Taiwan's FDI in China must be estimated using figures for Taiwan's total FDI income. For Taiwan's total FDI, the income–investment ratio is 0.71 dollar per each dollar of investment (Table 11.1). The amount of Taiwan's FDI in China multiplied by this ratio would indicate that Taiwan's income from its FDI in China averaged $1.9 billion every year from 1991 to 1997 (Table 11.2).

As for FDI-driven exports, there are many different estimates. According to the Chung-Hua Institution for Economic Research (CIER), FDI-driven exports in 1990 accounted for 34 per cent of Taiwan's total transit exports to China. (CIER 1993, p. 176) According to several other studies, the figure was between 32 per cent and 46 per cent in the early 1990s (K. Kao 1994, p. 26; C. Kao 1994, pp. 164–166; Chung 1997, p. 143). In fact most of Taiwan's exports to China consist of raw materials, parts, machinery and equipment. According to various investigations, 68 per cent to 86 per cent of the machinery and equipment used by Taiwan-invested enterprises in China are

Table 11.2: The Impact of Taiwan's FDI in China on Its Balance of Payments ($ US millions)

	1985	1986	1987	1988	1989	1990	1991	1992	1993	1994	1995	1996	1997	Ave.
FDI	263	261	10	-3160	-5347	-3913	-734	-1088	-1694	-1265	-1424	-1979	-2974	-1773
Inflow	-79	-65	-705	-4121	-6951	-5243	-2005	-1967	-2611	-2640	-2983	-3843	-5222	-2957
Outflow	342	326	715	961	1604	1330	1271	879	917	1375	1559	1864	2248	1184
Portfolio investment	-46	71	-372	-1712	-902	-1006	45	444	1067	905	493	-1112	-8283	-801
Assets	0	-4	-363	-1171	-967	-937	-741	-705	-1332	-1997	-2236	-4368	-6729	-1658
Liabilities	-46	75	-9	-541	65	-69	786	1149	2399	2902	2729	3256	-1554	857
Net Investment income	1115	1983	2281	3400	3823	4388	5018	4778	4336	4138	4302	4237	3461	3635
Credit	2115	2875	3759	5260	6598	6878	7300	7327	6674	7007	7977	7586	7857	6093
Debit	-1000	-892	-1478	-1860	-2775	-2490	-2282	-2549	-2338	-2869	-3675	-3349	-4396	-2458

Notes: Steps in estimation
A. 1987 is base year. Assume income on pre 1987 investment is $2875 million per year after 1987.
B. Cumulative FDI from 1987 to 1997 was $38291 million; cumulative portfolio investment, $21546 million. Cumulative outward investment was $ 59837 million.
C. Total investment income (credit) was $74223 million from 1987–1997
D. Net investment income (subtracting investment income for the investment before 1987) was $42598 million (74223 – 2857 x 11) from 1987–1997.
E. Every dollar of outward investment from 1987–1997 was $0.71 (= 42598/59837).
F. The annual average income of direct investment was $2478.1 million (=[0.71*38291]/11) from 1987–1997.

Source: Central Bank of China (Taiwan), Balance of Payments Quarterly, February, 1999.

purchased from Taiwan, and 36 per cent to 71 per cent of the raw materials, parts and semi-finished products are purchased from Taiwan (Chung 1997, p. 143; Kao and Huang 1995, p. 105; MoEA 1997, pp. 89–98; MoEA 1998, pp. 135–138). If we use the 34 per cent figure calculated by the CIER as a multiplier, we can derive a fair estimate of Taiwan's FDI-driven exports to China as averaging $5.4 billion every year. Thus from 1991 to 1997 Taiwan's FDI in China contributed an average of $4.6 billion per year in net foreign exchange to Taiwan's balance of payments (Table 11.2).

DOMESTIC INVESTMENT

The above section explains that Taiwan's FDI in China does not create a so-called 'capital crowding-out effect'. On the contrary, it has increased foreign exchange earnings by an average of $4.6 billion per year, which was 60 per cent of Taiwan's trade surplus in 1997. Therefore if Taiwan's domestic investment did not increase, Taiwan's FDI in China is not to blame.

Taiwan's gross domestic investment was already declining rapidly before 1986 – from 34 per cent of GDP in 1980 to 18 per cent at its lowest point in 1986. Thereafter, it increased slightly – to 25 per cent at its new high point in 1993 and 22 per cent in 1998 – still higher than in 1986. The annual rate of change annual rate of change in private gross fixed capital formation was –3.5 per cent in 1982 and –6.2 per cent in 1985. It was an average of 4.8 per cent for the period between 1980 and 1986. By comparison, although the annual growth rate for private gross fixed capital formation was –7.7 per cent in 1990, it was 10.7 per cent on average from 1987 to 1998. Hence, while Taiwan's entrepreneurs were investing heavily overseas, they did not halt their domestic investment. Rather, they simultaneously expanded both FDI and domestic investment.

Taiwan's Ministry of Economic Affairs (MoEA) has conducted two major surveys of enterprise managers to determine their motivation to invest in foreign countries. In 1996 managers from 2800 companies were polled and the same survey was repeated with 3280 enterprises in 1998. According to these two surveys, after enterprises began investing abroad only a minority of small enterprises lessened their domestic investment. In addition, the MoEA has created an 'index of the FDI impact on domestic investment'[2] to measure the impact of Taiwan's FDI on domestic investment (MoEA 1998, p. 21). If the index is positive, then Taiwan's FDI did not have a negative impact on domestic investment. In other words, after investing abroad, the portion of enterprises that continued to invest domestically and expanded domestic production exceeded the portion that reduced or terminated their domestic operations.

The index of small enterprises was –5.8 per cent in 1996 and –6.6 per cent in 1998, and around 55 per cent of them still maintained the original scale of

Table 11.2: Impact of Taiwan FDI in China on its Balance of Payments ($ millions)

	1985	1986	1987	1988	1989	1990	1991	1992	1993	1994	1995	1996	1997	Total	Ave[e]
Taiwan's FDI in China[a]	n.a.	n.a.	n.a.	n.a.	n.a.	n.a.	-869	-1050	-3139	-3391	-3162	-3475	-3289	-18375	-2625
Investment income[b]	n.a.	n.a.	n.a.	n.a.	n.a.	n.a.	617	746	2229	2408	2245	2467	2335	13046	1864
Taiwan's trade surplus with China[c]	870	667	937	1764	2745	3629	6368	9429	12890	14164	16342	17668	18540	106013	13629
Taiwan's exports to China[c]	987	811	1227	2242	3332	4395	7494	10548	13993	16023	19434	20727	22455	123668	15811
E. FDI-driven exports @ ratio of 34%[d]	336	276	417	762	1133	1494	2548	3586	4758	5448	6608	7047	7635	42047	5376
F. Impact on Taiwan's BoP[f]	336	276	417	762	1133	1494	2296	3282	3847	4464	5691	6039	6681	36718	4614

Notes:

a. Use China's statistics on Taiwan's realized investment; the 1991 figure includes investment before 1991.
b. Income per dollar of investment is $0.71.
c. According to the estimate of Taiwan's Mainland Affairs Council.
d. According to the 1993 estimate of the Chung-hua Institution for Economic Research
e. From 1991 to 1997
f. Balance of Payments: A+B+C

Sources: Taiwan Economic Research Institute, Cross-Strait Economic Statistics Monthly, 73, September 1998.; Central Bank of China (Taiwan), Balance of Payments Quarterly, February, 1999.; Chung-hua Institution for Economic Research (1993), Cross-Strait Economic Yearbook.

their domestic operations (Kao 1998, p. 242). For the larger enterprises, the index of the FDI impact was more positive: 11.7 per cent and 18.2 per cent for medium and large enterprises in 1996, and 24.4 per cent and 25 per cent in 1998, respectively. After investing abroad, some small enterprises were forced to reduce or terminate domestic operations because of a lack of capital and managers. However for medium-large enterprises, outward investment was done for the purpose of increasing competitiveness by taking advantage of the international division of labor. These companies did not sacrifice domestic investment but rather expanded both domestic and foreign operations.

The index of the FDI impact on domestic investment was 2.5 per cent for those who began to invest abroad before 1986, −2.8 per cent for those from 1987 to 1991, 0.9 per cent for those from 1992 to 1994, and 8.7 per cent for those from 1995 to 1996 (MoEA 1997, p. 188). These results are consistent with the trend of Taiwan's overall outward investment. From the mid-1980s to the early 1990s, most enterprises with FDI were labor-intensive small firms. Some of these smaller companies closed their Taiwan production bases and shifted to overseas operation. After the mid-1990s, the scale of the enterprises investing abroad grew larger. This investment was conducted to facilitate international division of labor, not to close domestic factories. This kind of FDI expanded such that the index became 8.7 per cent in 1995 and 1996. This kind of FDI did not crowd out domestic investment as both outward and domestic investment increased.

For all enterprises, the index was 1 per cent in 1996 and reached 5.9 per cent in 1998. That is, Taiwan's FDI expanded along with domestic investment. Looking at FDI recipient countries, the index for Taiwan's FDI in China was −3.5 per cent in 1996, but turned out to be 1.8 per cent in 1998. By contrast, the indices for Taiwan's FDI in Vietnam and Indonesia were still negative in 1998. These negative indexes are a cause for true concern (MoEA 1997, p. 188; MoEA 1998, p. 21).

Basically when Taiwan's entrepreneurs conducted outward investment, except for a few small and medium enterprises that reduced or closed domestic production and thus reduced domestic investment, the majority of enterprises did not reduce domestic investment when investing outside of Taiwan. Some small and medium enterprises that did cut domestic investment were mostly labor-intensive industries that began to invest abroad from 1987 to the early 1990s. They were forced to reduce or close their original factories because of a lack of capital and a weak managerial base. The impact of these closures and reductions was very limited. The annual growth rate in private investment of this period remained higher than pre-1987 rates.

INDUSTRIAL UPGRADING

The question of whether or not Taiwan's FDI in China facilitated Taiwan's industrial upgrading should be addressed in two parts. First, did Taiwan experience industrial upgrading? Second, if Taiwan experienced industrial upgrading, how was this related to Taiwan's FDI in China?

According to the Taiwan MoEA's 'Index of Manufacturing Industrial Upgrading', there are three concrete indices to measure whether or not Taiwan's industries are upgrading: (1) the ratio of output of heavy chemical and technology-intensive industries to total output of manufacturing industries (output ratio); (2) the ratio of exports of heavy chemical and technology-intensive industries to total exports of manufacturing industries (export ratio); and (3) labor productivity in manufacturing industries (productivity).

The output ratio was 57 per cent in 1982 and 77 per cent in 1997. The export ratio was 50 per cent in 1982 and 74 per cent in 1997. Thus, both the output and export ratios increased dramatically between 1982 and 1997 rising 30 per cent and 24 per cent, respectively. The productivity (in 1991 dollars) was $9600 in 1982 and $31 000 in 1997, increasing by $25 000. These basic figures clearly demonstrate how fast Taiwan's industries have upgraded.

A closer examination of the output and export ratios and productivity reveals a link between Taiwan's industrial upgrading and FDI. The output ratio increased 3.7 per cent from 1982 to 1986, 5.8 per cent from 1986 to 1990, 5.5 per cent from 1990 to 1994, and 7 per cent from 1994 to 1998. The export ratio increased 5.1 per cent from 1982 to 1986, 9.1 per cent from 1986 to 1990, 5.7 per cent from 1990 to 1994 and 4.3 per cent from 1994 to 1998. Productivity (in 1991 prices) increased $2800 from 1982 to 1986, $8600 from 1986 to 1990, $6300 from 1990 to 1994 and $3700 from 1994 to 1997.[3]

Taiwan's entrepreneurs began to invest heavily in China (and the SEACs) after the mid-1980s. Labor-intensive industries migrated to China (and the SEACs) in mass between the mid-1980s and early 1990s. The period from 1986 to 1994 coincided with the period when Taiwan's industries were upgrading most rapidly. Explicitly, there is a positive relationship between Taiwan's FDI in China and industrial upgrading.

Before the mid-1980s, Taiwan always had a 'dual economic structure'. Taiwan's small and medium enterprises produced labor-intensive goods for export, and its large enterprises were in charge of supplying intermediate and capital goods in a monopolized domestic market. After 1987 when Taiwan began to invest abroad heavily, the domestic economic structure changed significantly: labor-intensive, small and medium enterprises migrated, and capital and technology-intensive large enterprises replaced small and medium enterprises as Taiwan's prime exporters. The share of exports of the small and medium enterprises to Taiwan's total exports was 67 per cent in 1987 and declined to 49 per cent in 1997. By comparison, from 1982 to 1987 the share of the small and medium enterprises declined by only 3 per cent. In the next decade the share of the small and medium enterprises declined by 18 per cent.

In terms of Taiwan's export structure – if divided into labor intensity, capital intensity, technology intensity, heavy industrial products, and high-technology products – Taiwan's export structure has shifted in the past decade to less labor-intensive, higher capital-intensive, and higher technology- intensive products. In particular, the share of heavy industrial and high technology exports increased tremendously. From 1982 to 1988, the share of the heavy industrial products to total exports increased by 7 per cent and the share of the exports of high technology products increased by 8 per cent. From 1988 to 1998 the share of the exports of heavy industrial products increased by 22 per cent and the share of the exports of high technology products increased by 16 per cent.

In addition, there was another explicit change in Taiwan's export structure. From 1987 to 1998 the share of intermediate goods in Taiwan's total exports increased by 26 per cent (to 60 per cent in 1998), and the share of machinery exports increased by 8 per cent. In the same period the share of Taiwan's consumer goods in Taiwan's total exports declined by 31 per cent. In particular the share of consumer non-durable goods decreased significantly, that is by 23 per cent. By comparison, from 1981 to 1987, the export share of intermediate goods decreased by 3 per cent, that of consumer goods decreased by 2 per cent and the share of machinery increased by 7 per cent.

Thus the momentum of Taiwan's industrial upgrading came from the enormous export expansion of heavy chemical, capital and technology-intensive products, or intermediate goods and machinery, which were mainly supplied by large enterprises. Therefore the output ratio of heavy chemical and technology-intensive industries, which are primarily composed of large enterprises, increased rapidly, that is by 16 per cent, and the export ratio of these industries increased by 19 per cent from 1986 to 1997. The expanded demand for intermediate and capital goods by the small and medium enterprises which invested overseas (including in China) led to the expanded output of these goods produced by Taiwan's large enterprises.

The division of labor existing inside Taiwan before the mid-1980s has basically been transformed into a global division of labor driven mainly by the FDI of Taiwan's small and medium enterprises. Labor-intensive, small and medium enterprises established production bases overseas (including in China), with the provision of intermediate and capital goods, in effect, handled by large enterprises in Taiwan. This new international (inter-firm) division of labor had considerable benefits for Taiwan's industrial upgrading (Kao and Wu 1995, pp. 402–416; Kao 1998, pp. 237–253; Tu 1998, p. 98).

In addition to the inter-firm (inter-industry and intra-industry) global division of labor discussed above, there was intra-firm international division of labor[4] (Chen, Chen and Ku 1995, pp. 103–104). According to the 1998 investigation report, 32 per cent of Taiwan's enterprises with FDI explicitly stated that their products produced in Taiwan were superior or higher value added than those made by their overseas bases, and only 4 per cent gave the opposite response. Divided by major investment area, among Taiwanese entrepreneurs investing in China and the SEACs, 26 per cent to 44 per cent said that their products in Taiwan were superior or higher value added, while at most 7 per cent said the opposite.

The third possibility of industrial upgrading is that after Taiwan's labor-intensive industries invest heavily abroad, they will release domestic resources (including labor, land, and capital) that used to be employed in those industries. Adding investment income repatriated by overseas production and FDI-driven export income, this will facilitate the more efficient use of Taiwan's factors of production and lead to expanded production capacity.

As argued in general international trade theory, when a country opens up to free trade, that country will specialize in industries where it has a comparative advantage. In turn, the industries where it has less comparative advantage will decline and their resources will then be absorbed by the more competitive industries. The opening country thus acquires benefits from both commodity exchange and specialization of production.

Similarly, when its wage–rental ratio increases, Taiwan's labor-intensive industries can no longer compete with those of the SEACs and China, and hence tend to lose their comparative advantage. On the one hand, entrepreneurs and managers can achieve higher returns by investing part of their capital and utilizing their limited technology in China's export processing industries. In turn, the entrepreneurs repatriate investment income, which facilitates domestic capital accumulation in Taiwan. In addition, FDI-driven exports expand foreign markets for Taiwan's products (particularly intermediate and capital goods), which promote economies of scale in Taiwan's industrial development.

On the other hand, a large amount of labor, land, and capital employed by the original labor-intensive industries can be transferred into capital and technology-intensive industries. Because Taiwan's wage–rental ratio is higher than China's (and the SEACs') its capital rental cost is relatively cheaper, and there is a higher ratio of highly trained technicians. Therefore Taiwan's enterprises would tend to employ capital and technology-intensive production factors (Lin 1998, pp. 139–151).

Furthermore the migration of the labor-intensive industries would facilitate forming a domestic environment in favor of technology and capital-intensive industries, and this in turn would attract foreign multinational companies in such industries to invest in Taiwan. All of this would facilitate

Taiwan's industrial upgrading.

As for the FDI of capital and technology-intensive industries, Taiwan's investment style is similar to the FDI experiences of developed countries. The international literature has analyzed these experiences and basically concluded that outward FDI makes a positive contribution to the home countries. Japan is a good example of this phenomenon. For Taiwan, capital and technology-intensive enterprises engaged in FDI are essentially large and medium enterprises. Their FDI is intended to expand production capacity, expand the market base, increase competitiveness and establish a global production network and division of labor. These FDIs would essentially contribute to Taiwan's economic development, especially industrial upgrading (Chen and Chen 1995, pp. 433–462; Li and Fu 1997, pp. 5–6; Kao 1994, pp. 219–227).

NO INDUSTRIAL HOLLOWING-OUT

Taiwan's industrial structure has experienced a great transformation. One of the major characteristics of this change is that the share of the manufacturing industry's output to GDP has declined significantly and the share of the service industry has increased tremendously. From 1982 to 1986 the manufacturing industry's contribution to total GDP increased from 35 per cent to 39 per cent. Nevertheless the ratio declined to 27 per cent in 1998, a reduction of 12 per cent. Relatively, the service sector's share of GDP increased from 47 per cent in 1986 to 63 per cent in 1998, an increase of 16 per cent.

However it is natural that the service sector should grow as an economy becomes more developed. For example, the share of service sector output in the United Kingdom and the United States was over 70 per cent of GDP in 1993, nearly 70 per cent in France, 83 per cent in Hong Kong in 1994 and 63 per cent in Singapore in 1995.

Taiwan is no exception. Of special note, Taiwan began to promote the 'Asia-Pacific Regional Operation Center' (APROC) plan in 1995 in the hopes of establishing six major operation centers. Five of these centers belong to the service sector.[5] Therefore we cannot assert that Taiwan has an 'industrial hollowing-out' syndrome just because the share of the service sector in GDP has increased rapidly, while the share of the manufacturing sector has gone down (Kao and Wu 1995).

Nevertheless the dramatic change in economic structure leads to suspicions that capital outflows are creating either an unwillingness to upgrade or non-competitiveness, without upgrading, which is reducing the share of the manufacturing sector in GDP. As explained in the previous section, Taiwan's industries have been upgrading over the past decade and Taiwan's FDI explicitly contributes to the upgrading process. Compared with other countries, Taiwan's performance is quite satisfactory: from 1993 to 1998, the annual growth rate of Taiwan's industrial output was 4.5 per cent, slightly below that of the United States, but far exceeding the –0.1 per cent to 2 per cent average of other industrial countries. Therefore Taiwan's industries are still strongly competitive and there is not evidence of the so-called 'hollowing-out' syndrome.

NO HIGHER UNEMPLOYMENT

In the past, there was always a concern that Taiwan's FDI would increase its domestic unemployment rate, since most labor-intensive industries would move abroad. As a matter of fact Taiwan's unemployment rate did not increase along with the increase of its overseas FDI (including in China). Taiwan's unemployment rate averaged 2.6 per cent from 1982 to 1986, 1.6 per cent from 1987 to 1994, and 2.5 per cent from 1995 to 1998. The labor reallocation problem would have been most serious from 1987 to 1994, when the migration of labor-intensive industries was at its peak. Yet in this period Taiwan's unemployment rate was 1 per cent lower than the average rates from the periods between 1982 to 1986 and 1995 to 1998. Hence, FDI did not have a significant negative impact on Taiwan's unemployment rate.

The real problem for Taiwan was labor reallocation. Furthermore it is the declining international competitiveness of some domestic industries that creates the need for labor reallocation and FDI. It is not the case that FDI leads to higher unemployment. We should not confuse the cause with the result (UN 1993, pp. 57–88).

NO WORSENING WAGE INEQUALITY

From 1987 to 1997 Taiwan did increase its imports from developing countries, including the Southeast Asian countries and China, while reducing its imports from developed countries. In 1987 the share of the OECD-7 [6] of Taiwan's total imports was 67 per cent and that of both the ASEAN-4[7] and China was 6 per cent. In 1997 the share of the OECD-7 shrank to 59 per cent and that of both the ASEAN-4 and China increased to 12 per cent. In terms of value Taiwan imported $2.1 billion from both the ASEAN-4 and China in 1988, while importing $13.6 billion in 1997. The absolute value of Taiwan's imports from both the ASEAN-4 and China increased by 6.4 times over 10 years.

Although some trade theories predict that increased trade between Taiwan and the developing countries would lead to worsening wage inequality, from 1987 to 1996 Taiwan's wage inequality did not worsen. In 1987 the average monthly earnings of employees with less than a college level education was

NT\$12 755 and that for college graduates was NT\$23 503 (Richardson 1995, p. 44).[8] That is, the ratio of wage inequality was 0.84 [(23 503 − 12 755)/12 755]. Thereafter the wage inequality lessened significantly through 1995. In 1995 average monthly earnings of non-college graduates was NT\$28 730 and that for college graduates was NT\$44 770. The ratio of wage inequality was 0.56. In 1996 the wage inequality ratio worsened slightly to 0.62.

COMPETITION IN INTERNATIONAL MARKETS

Taiwan's export structure has changed dramatically since Taiwan began investing heavily abroad in 1987. In the past labor-intensive consumer goods were manufactured by small and medium enterprises in Taiwan and were then exported to developed countries such as the United States, Japan and Europe. Now it is very common for small and medium enterprises to establish overseas bases to produce labor-intensive consumer goods, with the inputs of intermediate and capital goods coming from Taiwan's large enterprises.

The final products are still exported to the United States, Japan and Europe. For example, according to the author's estimate, in 1996 Taiwan-invested entrepreneurs in China exported \$27.8 billion worth of goods, about \$7.2 billion to \$11.2 billion of which was exported to the US market alone. This would mean that Taiwan enterprises accounted for 14 to 22 per cent of China's exports to the United States (Tung 1999, pp. 220–235).

Therefore Taiwan's shrinking market share in the developed countries is due to the change in its role in the international division of labor in which Taiwan no longer produces most of its competing labor-intensive goods. This shrinkage is not because Taiwan's exports are less competitive.

CONCLUSION

According to China's statistics, as of December 1999 Taiwan's cumulative realized FDI in China was \$23.9 billion. According to Taiwan's estimates, trade between Taiwan and China reached \$25.8 billion in 1999. Many concerns arise from the complex process of Taiwan's globalized economic development and are exacerbated by the political confrontation between Taiwan and China. This chapter argues that Taiwan's investment in China is a part of the global division of labor and concludes that Taiwan's investment in China makes a net positive contribution to Taiwan's economic development.

Using empirical evidence, this article analyzes seven major concerns voiced in Taiwan about cross-Strait economic exchange. Cross-Strait economic exchange driven by Taiwan's FDI did contribute positively to Taiwan's balance of payments and did not crowd out domestic investment.

From 1991 to 1997 Taiwan's FDI in China contributed $4.6 billion net additions to foreign exchange on average every year for Taiwan's balance of payments. When Taiwan's entrepreneurs conducted outward investment, except for a few small and medium enterprises that reduced or closed domestic production and thus reduced domestic investment, the majority of enterprises expanded both FDI and domestic investment simultaneously.

In addition Taiwan's FDI in China helped domestic industrial upgrading and did not lead to industrial 'hollowing-out'. The expanded demand for intermediate and capital goods by the small and medium enterprises, which invested overseas (including in China), in fact, led to the expanded output of these goods produced by Taiwan's large enterprises. This new international (inter-firm) division of labor generated considerable benefits for Taiwan's industrial upgrading. Furthermore intra-firm division of labor exists: Taiwan's enterprises produce superior or higher value-added goods while their subsidiaries in China manufacture labor-intensive products. The more efficient reallocation of resources in Taiwan, trigged by outward investment, also contributed to Taiwan's industrial upgrading. Finally, there is no so-called 'hollowing-out' in Taiwan; as Taiwan's industries are still strongly competitive and growing rapidly in the 1990s.

Taiwan's FDI in China did not increase unemployment and worsen wage inequality from the mid-1980s to the mid-1990s. From 1987 to 1994, when the migration of labor-intensive industries was at its peak, Taiwan's average unemployment rate was 1 per cent lower than it was from 1982 to 1986 or from 1995 to 1998. Further the ratio of wage inequality in Taiwan fell from 0.84 in 1987 to 0.56 in 1995, and to 0.62 in 1996.

Finally, China and Taiwan did not compete head-to-head in the international market because they produced different types of products. Taiwan's shifting position in the global division of labor explains why Taiwan's market share in the developed countries is shrinking.

NOTES

1. The SEACs include the Philippines, Indonesia, Thailand, Malaysia, and Vietnam.
2. According to studies by Taiwan's Economic Ministry, the index ratio of expanding domestic investment – the ratio of suspending or planning to suspend domestic all operation – the ratio of reducing the current scale of domestic enterprise) + 2.
3. Labor productivity in 1998 was $27 792 (in 1991 dollars), which deviated significantly from the trend. This article adopts the 1997 figure.
4. FDI may result in three kinds of industrial restructuring: intra-firm, intra-industry, and inter-industry.
5. Including financial center, telecommunication center, media center, navigation transit center, and aviation transit center.
6. The OECD-7 includes Japan, the USA, Germany, United Kingdom, France, Canada, and Netherlands.
7. The ASEAN-4 includes Malaysia, Indonesia, Thailand, and the Philippines.
8. Richardson and some other economists suggest the measurement by differentiating workers

with and without 12 years of education. Below college education includes illiterate, self-educated, primary school, junior and senior high school, and senior vocational school. College education includes junior college, college, and graduate school.

BIBLIOGRAPHY

Chen, Tain-Jy, Yi-Ping Chen, and Ying-hua Ku (1995), 'Taiwan's Outward Direct Investment: Has the Domestic Industry Been Hollowed Out?' in Nomura Research Institute and Institute of Southeast Asian Studies (compiled), *The New Wave of Foreign Direct Investment in Asia*, Singapore: Institute of Southeast Asian Studies, pp. 87–110.

Chen, Tain-Jy, and Yi-Ping Chen (1995), 'The Impact of Taiwan's Outward Investment on Its Industrial Development' (in Chinese), in Ya-Huei Yang (ed), *Taiwan's Industrial Development and Policy*, Taipei: Chung-Hua Institution for Economic Research, pp. 433– 62.

Chung, Chin (1997), 'Double-edged Trade Effects of Foreign Direct Investment and Firm-Specific Assets: Evidence from the Chinese Trio', in Y.Y. Kuen (ed.), *The Political Economy of Sino-American Relations*, Hong Kong: Hong Kong University Press, pp. 135–162.

Chung-Hua Institution for Economic Research (CIER) (1993), *Cross-Strait Economic Yearbook* (in Chinese), Taipei: Chung-Hua Institution for Economic Research.

Council of Labor Affairs (Taiwan) (1987-1996), *Yearbook of Labor Statistics*.

Investment Commission, Ministry of Economic Affairs (Taiwan) (1999), *Statistics on Outward Investment and Indirect Mainland Investment*, September 1999.

Kao, Charng (1994), *Mainland Economic Reform and Cross-Strait Economic Relations* (in Chinese), Taipei: Wu-Nan.

Kao, Charng and Chi-Tsung Huang (1995), 'The Analysis on the Relationship between Taiwan's Investment in Mainland and Cross-Strait Trade', in Kuang-Shen Liao (ed.), *The Potential Danger and Opportunity in the Cross-Strait Economic Interaction*, Hong Kong: Hong Kong University Press, pp. 95–120.

Kao, Charng and Shi-Ying Wu (1995), 'The Impact of Cross-Strait Economic Relations on Taiwan's Industrial Development' (in Chinese), in Ya-Huei Yang (ed.), *Taiwan's Industrial Development and Policy*, Taipei: Chung-Hua Institution for Economic Research, pp. 391–432.

Kao, Charng (1998), 'Taiwan Entrepreneur Investment of Manufacturing Industry in Mainland and Cross-Strait Industrial Labor Division' (in Chinese), in Mee-kau Nyaw, Si-ming Li, and Kao Charng (eds), *Economic China*, Hong Kong: Chinese University Press, pp. 237–254.

Kao, Kong-lien (1994), *The Current Situation and Prospect of Cross-Strait Economic Relations* (in Chinese), Taipei: Mainland Affairs Council.

Kuo, Wen-Chen (1997), 'The Review and Future Prospect of Taiwan's Outward Investment' (in Chinese), *Economic Outlook (Taipei)*, 54, pp. 57–59.

Li, Zhong-Ce, and Fong-Cheng Fu (1997), *The Theory and Practice of Cross-Strait Industrial Labor Division* (in Chinese), Taipei: Chung-hua Institution for Economic Research.

Li, Zhong-Ce, Fong-Cheng Fu, and Zhi-qiang Li (1996), 'The Theory and Practice of Cross-Strait Industrial Labor Division' (in Chinese), in Chin Chung (ed.), *Division of Labor Across the Taiwan Strait: Theoretical Considerations and Implementing*

Schemes, Taipei: Chung-Hua Institution for Economic Research, pp. 1–38.

Lin, Chu-Chia (1998), 'The Comparison of Production Functions for the Cross-Strait Taiwan's Entrepreneurs' (in Chinese), in Mee-kau Nyaw et al. (eds), *Economic China*, Hong Kong: Chinese University Press, pp. 139–151.

Ministry of Economic Affairs (MoEA) (Taiwan) (1997), *The Investigation Report on the Outward Investment by Manufacturing Industry* (in Chinese).

— (1998), *The Investigation Report on the Outward Investment by Manufacturing Industry* (in Chinese).

— (1999), 'Table A-12 The Growth Rate of the Industrial Output in Major Countries' (in Chinese), http://www.moea.gov.tw/~meco/stat/four/a-12.htm.

— (2000), 'The Role of Service Industry in the Economic Development' (in Chinese), http://www.moea.gov.tw/~meco/paper/issue/15.htm.

Ministry of Finance (MoF) (Taiwan) (1993), *Report on the Characteristic Classifications of Tradable Commodities*.

— (1998), *Monthly Statistics of Exports and Imports*, December 1998.

Richardson, J. David (1995), 'Income Inequality and Trade: How to Think, What to Conclude', *Journal of Economic Perspectives*, 9 (3), 33–55.

Taiwan Economic Research Institute (ed.) (2000), *Cross-Strait Economic Statistics Monthly*, no. 92, April 2000, Taipei: Mainland Affairs Council.

Tung, Chen-yuan (1999), 'Trilateral Economic Relations among Taiwan, China, and the United States', *Asian Affairs: An American Review*, 25 (4), 220–235.

Tu, Ying-yi (1998), 'The Retrospect and Prospect of Industrial Internationalization Policy', *Economic Outlook (Taipei)*, 55, pp. 98–101.

United Nations (UN) (1993), *Transnational Corporations from Developing Countries: Impact on Their Home Countries*, New York: United Nations.

12. Foreign Investment in China: Macro Determinants

Kevin Honglin Zhang

INTRODUCTION

In recent years few developments in the globalization of the world economy have been more important than the emergence of China as the most attractive site for foreign direct investment (FDI). In the two decades since economic reform was initiated in 1978 China has become the largest recipient of FDI in the developing world and globally, the second only to the US since 1993. FDI flows were over $27 billion in 1993 alone, which constituted 35 per cent of total FDI in all developing countries in that year (SSB, 2000). By the end of 2000 the cumulative number of registered FDI projects stood at 361 500, the contracted value of FDI was US$663 billion, and the total realized amount of FDI in China reached as much as US$344 billion (SSB, 2001)

The important role of FDI in the Chinese economy might be suggested by the following: FDI inflows in 1995 constituted 26 per cent of gross fixed capital formation. Foreign invested firms employed 18 million Chinese by the end of 1996, constituting 18 per cent of the total non-agricultural labor force (UNCTAD, 1999). In 1997 19 per cent of total gross industrial output was produced by foreign affiliates. In 2000 foreign invested firms created exports of US$236.7 billion, which constituted near 50 per cent of China's total exports (SSB, 2001)

Although a considerable literature on determinants of FDI in China has appeared in recent years (for example, Lardy, 1992, 1994, 1995; Naughton, 1996; Wei, 1995; Zhang, 2000a, 2001a, 2001b), systematic treatments of the issue are still limited. China's adoption of a liberalized policy to allow FDI inflows and the promotion of export oriented FDI, in many respects, are similar to policies pursued by other developing countries as they move away from restricting foreign capital toward more open, externally oriented development strategies. China's real distinctions are threefold: its huge size, its access to massive numbers of supportive overseas Chinese, and its strong government. With the combination of these three factors, the FDI boom raises a host of interesting questions. What attracts multinational corporations to China? How has China taken its advantages in attracting FDI? What FDI strategy should China take after it joins the World Trade Organization? This chapter addresses these questions based on the premise that understanding

China's success in attracting FDI requires attention to China's comparative advantages and disadvantages from an international perspective.

The basic message of this chapter is that China's achievement in attracting and utilizing FDI is real but that it faces severe challenges with its accession to the World Trade Organization in the near future. What most attracts foreign investors are China's huge market, liberal FDI regime, cheap resources (labor, land, and raw materials), and rapid economic growth. Moreover, investments from Hong Kong and Taiwan (HKT), and from overseas Chinese have made an important contribution to the FDI boom.

The rest of the chapter begins with stylized facts regarding FDI in China, which highlight some important characteristics of the operations of multinational firms in China. Then we provide an analytical framework about determinants of FDI location in which various types of FDI are distinguished. The next section explores factors that determine the Chinese FDI boom, focusing on China's locational advantages and important institutional factors. The last section discusses challenges faced by China in the new setup of the WTO and summarizes key conclusions.

STYLIZED FACTS CONCERNING FDI IN CHINA

FDI Boom in the 1990s

Figure 12.1 depicts annual flows and the cumulative amount of FDI over the period 1982–98. The most impressive feature that emerges from the time trend is the sharp rise in FDI in the 1990s in contrast with the moderate growth in the 1980s. Although a surge of interest among foreign investors in China emerged after 1979, large FDI inflows did not occur in the initial period because of China's poor infrastructure and lack of experience in dealing with foreign investors. The period 1984–91 saw steady growth and a relatively large amount of FDI, due in part to the extension of the special economic zones from four to another 14 cities in 1984 and FDI incentives introduced in 1986. In 1992 China seemed to reach its critical threshold of attracting FDI on a large scale. The single year FDI flow in 1993 ($26 billion) exceeded the cumulative flows ($23 billion) of the prior 13 years (1979–91). In 1998 China received $45 billion in FDI and the cumulative FDI flows exceeded $265 billion.[1]

China's FDI boom seems to be more than simply a part of the global expansion of multinationals. Figure 12.2 shows China's position in the world as well as all developing countries during the period 1982–98. China's FDI shares in both developing countries and the world rise significantly over time, particularly in the 1990s. This fact suggests that locational factors play a critical role in China's FDI boom and that China indeed has unique advantages over other potential host countries in attracting foreign investors (Zhang, 2001a).

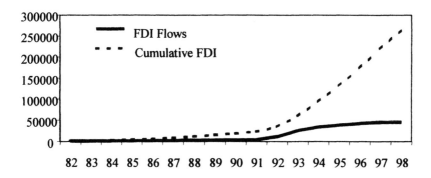

Figure 12.1: FDI Flows and Cumulative FDI in China: 1982–98 (Millions of US Dollars)

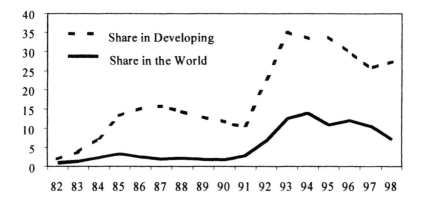

Figure 12.2: Shares of China's Inward FDI in All Developing Countries and the World: 1982–98 (per cent)

Export-oriented FDI Strategy

The evolution of China's FDI policy is summarized in Table 12.1. China's opening to FDI was symbolized by the promulgation of the 'Chinese–Foreign Joint Venture Law' on 1 July 1979. While permitting entry of foreign firms, the law did not create a legal framework that would allow currency convertibility and reduce red tape. In 1986 new provisions, including preferential tax policies, were established to encourage foreign investment.

However FDI was invited exclusively for exports except for offshore oil exploration and the real estate sector (Zhang and Song, 2000). Under such an export promotion FDI regime many export processing and export assembling plants (mainly from Hong Kong and Taiwan) were established in the special economic zones, the open coastal cities, and the economic and technological development zones.[2] At the same time foreign investors that aimed at domestic markets encountered many difficulties and their investments were relatively small (Zhang, 2000a).[3]

Table 12.1: The Evolution of China's FDI Policy

Date	Event
December 1978	Deng Xiao-Ping became China's paramount leader. Justified in terms of the critical importance of foreign capital and technology to Chinese economy, the 'open door' policy was formally adopted at the Third Plenum of Chinese Communist Party's Eleventh Central Committee.
July 1979	The 'Law of the People's Republic of China on Joint Ventures Using Chinese and Foreign investment' ('Law of Sino-Foreign Joint Ventures') was adopted, granting foreign investment a legal status in China.
August–October 1980	Four special economic zones (Shenzhen, Zhuhai, Shantou, and Xiamen) were established in the southeast coast to attract foreign capital and advanced technology. These special economic zones were intended to serve as the testing grounds for bold, experimental economic and social
April 1984	The concept of special economic zones was extended to another 14 coastal cities and Hainan Island.
February 1985	Three coastal 'development triangles' – the Yangtze River delta, the Pearl River delta in Guangdong, and the Min Nan region in Fujian – were also opened to foreign investors.
April 1986	'Law of China on Enterprises operated Exclusively with Foreign Capital' was announced, thus permitting wholly foreign-owned enterprises, in addition to joint venture.
October 1986	New provisions (called 'Twenty-two Provisions on the Encouragement of Foreign Investment') were established. The new incentives included: reducing fees for labor and land use; establishing a limited foreign currency market for joint ventures; and extending the maximum duration of a joint-venture agreement beyond 50 years.
April 1988	(1) Hainan Island became a province, and at the same time it became China's fifth and the largest single special economic zone. (2) 'Cooperative Joint Ventures Law' was adopted.

Table 12.1: Continued

Date	Event
March 1990	Amendments to the 1979 'Joint Venture Law' were passed, greatly improving the investment climate in China. The stipulation that the chairman of the board of a joint venture should be appointed by Chinese investors, for example, was abolished. Also significant was the provision of protection from nationalization.
April 1990	The concept of special economic zones was extended to the Shanghai Pudong New Development Area, which is about the size of Singapore.
June 1992	'Open cities' with FDI incentives were extended to 18 inland provincial capital cities, 6 port cities along the Yangtze River, and 13 border-cities.
June 1995	More sectors including service industries were open to foreign investors.
December 1995	Ending exemptions and reductions of tariffs and value-added taxes for foreign-invested enterprises.
April 1996	National treatment of all foreign investors, removal of duty-free status on capital goods imports by foreign-invested enterprises.
January 1997	Shenzhen allowed foreign-invested enterprises with advanced technology to sell 100% of their products on the domestic market.

Source: Based on what has been compiled by the author.

China began to open gradually its domestic market to multinational firms in certain sectors, including telecommunication, transportation, banking, and insurance. The gradual shift from an 'export promotion' to a 'technology promotion' FDI regime was largely due to pressures from the US and West European countries that had increasing trade deficits with China due to China's export boom through FDI. Moreover China realized that technology transfers from industrial countries might be possible only as market oriented FDI was allowed.

Hong Kong and Overseas Chinese as a Dominant Source of FDI

Considering that over 90 per cent of global FDI originates from industrial countries (UNCTAD, 1996), it is striking that the majority of FDI in China did not come from industrial countries, but came instead from Hong Kong and the overseas Chinese in the region, which control large portions of economic activity in Indonesia, Malaysia, and Thailand.[4] Table 12.2 shows

Table 12.2: Sources of FDI in China 1977–98 (US$ million and percent)

FDI sources	1992–1998			1979–1991		
	Rank	FDI	%	Rank	FDI	%
Developing Asia		173809	74.3		15594	67.5
HK[a]	1	125300	53.6	1	13208	57.2
Taiwan	2	19458	8.3	8	199	0.9
Singapore	5	11626	5.0	6	628	2.7
S. Korea	6	8005	3.4	13	51	0.2
Thailand	10	1876	1.0	11	118	0.5
Others[b]		8085	3.2		1390	6.0
Developed		60097	25.7		7509	32.5
Japan	3	18890	8.1	3	1740	7.5
US	4	17963	7.7	2	2382	10.3
UK	7	5830	2.5	4	862	3.7
Germany	8	3332	1.4	5	655	2.9
Canada	9	2046	0.9	10	146	0.6
France	11	1620	0.7	7	305	1.3
Australia	12	1535	0.7	9	171	0.7
Netherlands	13	1194	0.5	14	32	0.1
Italy	14	1010	0.4	12	83	0.4
Switzerland	15	709	0.3	15	16	0.1
Others		5968	2.6		1117	4.8
		233906	100.0		23103	100.0

*Notes:*All numbers of FDI flows and stock are realized investment in current values.
a. FDI from Macao is included under the name of Hong Kong. Although Hong Kong was transferred to China on 1 July 1997 from the UK, its capital flows into China are still viewed as 'foreign' investment under the policy of 'One country and two systems'.
b. Others include Malaysia, Indonesia, Philippines, and other developing countries.

Sources: Numbers for 1992–98 are computed from *International Trade* (various issues) by MOFTEC of China. The data for Taiwan and South Korea for 1985–91 are estimated in official publications. Others are from *Almanac of China's Foreign Economic Relations and Trade* (various issues) *and China Statistical Yearbook* (1999).

the origins of FDI into China in the period 1979–98. During the boom period (1992–98) the Asian FDI sources included Hong Kong (ranked first), Taiwan (second), Singapore (fifth), South Korea (sixth), and Thailand (tenth), which together accounted for 74 per cent of the FDI flows into China. With the exception of Japan (ranked third) and the United States (fourth), other industrialized countries played a minor role.[5] The unique pattern of FDI sources is a result of China's export oriented strategy and the special links of Hong Kong, Taiwan, and overseas Chinese in Asia with China in culture and history.

Distinctive Features of FDI Projects in Technology, Sectors, and Size

The predominant share of FDI from Asian developing economies raises the question of their competitive edge in the world markets for investment. This is because Hong Kong and Asian developing country firms appear to lack ownership advantages such as advanced proprietary technology and established brand names. It seems that the competitive edge of Hong Kong, Taiwan, and Singapore rests primarily on managerial and marketing advantages in making and selling light consumer goods such as textiles, garments, toys and light electronics, which are their main export products (USCBC, 1990). Overall their investments tend to be small by international standards and also specialized in labor intensive, low technology activities (Zhang, 2000a). Their products tend to be undifferentiated and sold mainly on the basis of price rather than distinct design or performance characteristics (Wells, 1993).

Uneven Regional Distribution within China

While FDI is located in every corner of China, it tends to be highly concentrated in the southern coastal provinces and major metropolitan cities, which account for about 90 per cent of total FDI in China (Table 12.3). The uneven regional distribution of FDI in China is a result of a variety of factors, including the FDI policies and differences in the regional investment environments, particularly the 'hometown connections' of Asian investors. The destinations of the investments from Asian developing economies reflect ethnic factors and the 'Chinese connection' factor is pervasive. Most overseas Chinese originally came from coastal areas (Guangdong and Fujian Provinces in particular) which have received a huge share (67 per cent) of total Asian FDI in China (Zhang, 2001a). Western investors tend to concern themselves primarily with market access and in this context, metropolitan areas (such as Beijing, Tianjin, and Shanghai) and coastal areas have been heavily favored relative to inland regions.

AN ANALYTICAL FRAMEWORK

Based on multinational firms' motives, technology and production structure, it is useful to distinguish between vertical (export oriented) and horizontal (market-oriented) FDI (Caves, 1996; Markusen, 1995). Vertical FDI, motivated by cheap foreign labor, fragments the production process across countries by production stages based on labor intensities; while horizontal

Table 12.3: Regional distribution of FDI in China 1986-97 (US $ million and percent share)

Provinces	1986–1991		1992–1997	
	Flows	Share	Flows	Share
Coastal Areas	14618	92.0	174079	87.5
Beijing	1438	9.1	7010	3.5
Tianjin	380	2.4	7972	4.0
Shanghai	1448	9.1	18254	9.2
Hebei	173	1.1	3774	1.9
Liaoning	859	5.4	8599	4.3
Shandong	544	3.4	13369	6.7
Jiangsu	640	4.0	24007	12.1
Zhejiang	264	1.7	6753	3.4
Fujian	1506	9.5	20316	10.2
Guangdong	6596	41.5	55016	27.6
Hainan	538	3.4	4923	2.5
Guangxi	232	1.5	4086	2.1
Inland Areas	1269	8.0	24935	12.5
Jinlin	45	0.3	1875	0.9
Heilongjiang	136	0.9	2422	1.2
Inner Mongolia	0.0013	0.0	273	0.1
Shanxi	23	0.2	627	0.3
Anhui	41	0.3	2101	1.1
Jianxi	46	0.3	1637	0.8
Henan	166	1.1	2567	1.3
Hubei	133	0.8	3491	1.8
Hunan	60	0.4	3037	1.5
Sichuan	111	0.7	3340	1.7
Guizhou	26	0.2	265	0.1
Yunnan	24	0.2	779	0.4
Tibet	0	0.0	0	0.0
Shaanxi	392	2.5	1797	0.9
Gansu	16	0.1	326	0.2
Qinghai	0	0.0	22	0.0
Ningxi	3	0.0	109	0.1
Xinjiang	47	0.3	267	0.1
Total	15887	100.0	199014	100.0

Sources: Data for 1986–1995 are taken from *China Regional Economy* (1996) by SSB and data for 1996 and 1997 from the *China Statistical Yearbook* (1997 and 1998) by SSB.

FDI, that is induced by foreign market access, builds plants in multiple countries to serve local markets (Zhang, 2000b). In general vertical multinationals use standardized technologies and locate abroad at least one stage of production in which unskilled labor is used intensively. Vertical FDI thus is more likely to be attracted to host countries with low wages relative to source countries. Trade costs (tariffs and transportation costs) would reduce investment to the extent that a subsidiary of the vertical multinationals in the host country would import equipment or intermediate products from its parent country (Zhang and Markusen, 1999). Due to its 'footloose' nature, this type of FDI is also attracted to countries that offer favorable incentives such as tax holidays.

Horizontal multinationals build up similar production facilities abroad for scale economies to gain access to foreign markets. To compete with local producers, horizontal multinationals must possess a certain superior technology that is not available in the host country. Host market size is expected to play a key role in attracting this type of FDI because larger market size offers greater opportunities to realize effectively economies of scale (Zhang, 2000b). As a country's market grows to a critical threshold level, foreign firms start investing and increase sharply their investment. Since this type of FDI involves advanced technology, it generally has higher requirements for human capital and infrastructure in the host country. The substitute relationship between horizontal FDI and exports for a multinational to serve the foreign market implies that import restrictions in the market might induce more horizontal FDI (the 'tariff jumping' hypothesis).

Theoretical studies focusing on locational factors also address how the economic performance of a host country determines the amount of FDI flows into that country. The growth driven FDI hypothesis emphasizes the necessity of growing market size and improving conditions of human capital and infrastructure in attracting FDI (Zhang, 2000b). A country's market size (measured by GDP) rises with economic growth, other things being equal, encouraging foreign firms to increase their investment. Rapid economic growth leads to high levels of aggregate demand that stimulate greater demand for investments including FDI. Moreover better economic performance in host countries tends to provide better infrastructure and greater opportunities for making profits and so greater incentives for FDI.

WHY IS CHINA SUCCESSFUL IN ATTRACTING FDI?

Many observers view China's success in attracting FDI as a puzzle by noting its obvious disadvantages relative to other host countries (Kamath, 1990; Lardy, 1994 and Perkins, 1994): (a) China had little legal system 'infrastructure' so that property rights were not well defined; (b) China's currency was not convertible so that foreign investors had no certain sources of hard currency earnings; (c) corruption in China has been severe and growing so that foreign investors incur additional costs. These negative influences, however, have been offset by China's huge market, large FDI flows from HKT and other overseas Chinese, and its liberalized FDI regime.

Huge Markets

The prospect that China would open what foreign investors had long believed to be its huge potential domestic market made China a highly desirable location for new investment and hence was an extremely strong positive lure for multinationals.[6] The 'market of one billion' was the primary reason why most foreign investors were interested in China, although investors from Hong Kong and other Asian developing economies were also attracted by low cost Chinese labor. Ultimately it is the lure of one billion customers that can offset many worries.

The advantage of market size has been enhanced by China's rapid economic growth in the last 20 years. Table 12.4 shows how outstandingly

Table 12.4: China's GDP and GDP growth rate: 1978–98

	1978	1984	1988	1990	1992	1996	1998
GDP (billion 1990 yuan)	669	1097	1626	1770	2163	3357	3927
Per capita (1990 yuan)	695	1051	1464	1548	1846	2786	3202
Per capita (index)	100	157	226	237	288	427	490
	1978	1984	1988	1978	1992	1994	1992
	–84	–88	–92	–92	–94	–98	–98
GDP growth (% per year)	9.4	11.1	7.9	9.5	12.6	8.7	10.1

Sources: Calculated by applying the indexes in comparable prices from *China Statistics Yearbook* (SSB, various years).

well the Chinese economy has performed since 1978. China's GDP grew annually by nearly 10 per cent for 20 years. The size of the market measured by GDP rose by a factor of almost six and per capita GDP by a factor of nearly five.

Large FDI from HKT and Overseas Chinese

China has a special asset in the large number of supportive overseas Chinese, particularly in Hong Kong and Taiwan (HKT). The unique fact that most FDI in China did not come from developed counties but from developing countries is obviously related to the large overseas Chinese diaspora, particularly HKT and Singapore. This can perhaps be explained by 'Chinese connections' which refer to the special link of overseas Chinese with their homeland such that they would like to identify themselves as part of China in spirit and devote their efforts to making contributions to China's modernization. The Chinese connections are based on the facts that overseas Chinese share the same language, culture and family tradition and that they also have relatives, friends and former business ties in China. Therefore the connections make it much easier for overseas Chinese to negotiate and operate joint ventures relative to other investors in China.[7]

By the end of 1998 there were more than 227 000 registered foreign enterprises established in China. Among them were 165 000 projects invested by overseas Chinese, comprising over 73 per cent of the total number (MOFTEC, 1999). Hong Kong in particular is a key investor in China. By the end of November 2000 the share of Hong Kong in total registered FDI projects totaled 54 per cent and its share by value in both total contracted FDI and total realized FDI was 50 per cent *(The World Journal*, on 20 December 2000). In a world of business that is familiar to overseas Chinese, Western investors often feel lost. The diaspora speaks the right languages and they are relatively untroubled by the absence of a legal and accounting framework or reliable market research.[8]

Liberal FDI Regime and Incentive Policies

China has been systematically liberalizing its FDI regime as indicated in Table 12.1. The attitude of the Chinese government toward multinationals is far more liberal than most other developing counties, especially those in East Asia, such as Japan, South Korea and Taiwan.[9] In the early 1990s China developed one of the most liberal FDI environments among the developing countries (Lardy, 1994). Many sectors such as power generation, transportation, port development, oil exploration and development and services were opened to foreign investors. Liberalization of foreign participation in property development led to particularly significant FDI inflows directed toward the development of residential housing, retail complexes and other projects.

China also offered an impressive package of incentive policies as shown in Table 12.1. Especially in the 1990s some of the special provisions to attract FDI that were only available in the special economic zones were made much more widely available. For example, special tax concessions, liberalized land leasing and other inducements were made available in a growing number of open coastal cities, economic development areas and high technology development zones.[10]

Outstanding Performance of Chinese Economy

China's economic reform and its opening to the outside world since 1978 have been accompanied by rapid economic growth. Real gross domestic product (GDP) grew annually at 9.8 per cent during the period 1978–98, with a rate of over 10 per cent in the 1990s (Table 12.4). Relative to the 1980s the FDI boom in the 1990s is a result of the outstanding performance of the Chinese economy which enabled China's market to grow substantially and improved its investment environment through better infrastructure. In 1992 China seemed to reach a critical threshold in terms of attracting FDI on a large scale. China's market size measured by GDP in 1992 was ten times as large as in 1977, and its annual GDP growth rate during the period 1992–98 was over 10 per cent, the highest in the world. Along with its further liberalized FDI policy, the rapid growth of the Chinese economy made China more attractive to foreign investors with larger opportunities for earning profits.

While market size, overseas Chinese, the FDI regime and rapid economic growth each play critical roles in the FDI boom, the contributions of other factors may not be ignored. These factors include China's cheap resources (labor, land, and raw materials) and the overall expansion of multinationals in the developing world in the 1990s.

CONCLUDING REMARKS: CHALLENGES TO CHINA IN THE FUTURE

Studying the macro determinants of FDI is obviously of interest because more and more developing countries view FDI as an engine of economic growth. China has achieved significant success in attracting FDI since the late 1970s. What most attract foreign investors are China's huge market, liberal FDI regime, rapid economic growth and cheap resources (labor, land and raw materials). More importantly, investors from HKT and from among the other overseas Chinese contribute in a large part to the FDI boom. While the success is impressive, the challenges China faces are severe, particularly with China's accession to the World Trade Organization (WTO) in the near future. China's FDI regime and relevant policies have to adjust to be consistent with the rules of the WTO, resulting in a growing share of FDI made by multinational corporations (MNCs) from the West (the US, Western Europe, and Japan). Two central characteristics of Western MNCs are their large size and the fact that their worldwide operations and activities tend to be centrally controlled by their parent companies. Many MNCs have annual sales volumes in excess of the GDP of the developing nations in which they operate.[11] Enormous size confers great bargaining power on MNCs relative to developing host countries. This power is greatly strengthened by their predominantly oligopolistic positions in worldwide product markets. This situation gives MNCs the ability to manipulate prices and profits, to collude with other firms in determining areas of control, and generally to restrict the entry of potential competition by dominating new technologies, special skills, product differentiation and advertising.

Advanced technology and management skills that China very much wants are frequently found in industries in which oligopolistic MNCs dominate. In many of these industries China has few alternatives and hence its ability to bargain with any one MNC is limited. Moreover MNCs have considerably more experience bargaining with host governments than China has bargaining with the Western MNCs even after China's opening up over the past 20 years.

In many areas of interest, conflicts exist between China and the MNCs. For example, China may desire large investments with export orientation, but the MNCs may prefer small investments aiming at the domestic market; China wants high technology and high value added projects, which may be the opposite of what MNCs are willing to offer. The MNCs desire wholly owned affiliates, rather than Chinese majority joint ventures, which are preferred by China. While China's commitments on entry to the WTO (such as liberalized ownership structures and opening up more sectors including services) may help attract more FDI flows from Western MNCs, the benefits China can draw from these investments depend on changes in China's bargaining power relative to the MNCs. China may develop a regulatory system to manage and control MNC behavior under the WTO framework. Several aspects of MNC behavior may be questioned to make sure that the national welfare is maximized.

Some policy implications emerge from this study: first, since FDI policy is shown to be important for FDI inflows in the coastal areas, a more favorable FDI policy should be helpful for the vast inland areas that have received small amounts of FDI flows relative to the coastal areas. The relatively lower attraction of the inland areas to foreign investors is in large part a result of their lack of incentive policies relative to the coastal areas.

Second, further opening of the domestic market to multinational corporations is needed to attract more FDI flows because it is clear that foreign investors respond positively to both liberalized FDI regimes and to market size. In particular companies in the US, Europe, and Japan (such as Boeing, General Motors, Motorola, Volkswagen, and Toyota) view their investment in China as part of a global strategy, which is designed to secure their sales in China over the long term, but not necessarily to achieve short term profits or reductions in production costs. China has so far not taken full advantage of its market size in encouraging foreign investors because of its many restrictions on market oriented FDI. With China's entry into the WTO, another FDI boom should be expected with more foreign subsidiaries established in China to sell their products locally.

Third, continuing FDI inflows depend largely on the performance of the Chinese economy. Rapid economic growth not only creates large demand for FDI but also improves the investment environment. Since both infrastructure and education turn out to be critical to foreign investors, improvements in these areas seem to be important for continuing FDI flows. Multinational corporations are likely to be attracted to a country that has better infrastructure conditions and more skilled labor.

Finally, it may be noted that in addition to labor cost considerations, 'hometown connections' have played a critical role in the substantial flows of investment into China from overseas Chinese investors. The hometown connections are based on the fact that overseas Chinese not only share the same language and culture with the people in China, but also have relatives, friends and former business ties in China. These connections made it much easier for overseas Chinese investors to negotiate and to operate joint ventures in China than for other investors. Without overseas Chinese, China would not have been successful in attracting so much FDI in the past 20 years. This fact suggests that the Chinese government should maintain its favorable policy for overseas Chinese investors and create a better environment to encourage their investments.

NOTES

1. FDI rose in the early 1990s in part because of the 'round-tripping' of capital of Chinese origin, which was carried out by subsidiaries based in Hong Kong but owned by Chinese central or local governments to take advantage of preferential treatments under the name of foreign capital. While no accurate figures for this type of FDI are available, it is estimated that they are not large relative to total FDI from Hong Kong (UNCTAD, 1996).
2. This strategy was motivated by the success of the export led growth strategy adopted in Japan and the four tigers (Hong Kong, Korea, Singapore, and Taiwan). FDI has been regarded as a powerful engine to expand exports, although FDI was also expected to make a contribution to capital formation and technology transfer.
3. A major difficulty facing foreign investors, for example, was how to reconvert their investments and repatriate their earnings. Firms with export oriented FDI are able directly to earn foreign exchange and have been most successful in avoiding serious foreign exchange deficits. However firms with market oriented FDI are unable to earn sufficient foreign exchange to cover their foreign exchange obligations, including distribution of profits to investors.
4. Although Hong Kong was returned to China on 1 July 1997 from the UK, its capital flows into China are still viewed as 'foreign' investment under the policy of 'one country and two systems'. It should be noted that a part of the reported Hong Kong FDI is actually either Western industrial countries investment through their subsidiaries based in Hong Kong, or Taiwanese investment that is made under the name of Hong Kong for political reasons. The latter was especially true before 1992 when the Taiwanese government officially permitted FDI into China. Moreover in the early 1990s a small part of the reported Hong Kong FDI was carried out by subsidiaries located in Hong Kong but owned by Chinese central or local governments to take advantage of preferential treatment under the name of FDI (UNCTAD, 1996).

5. The US, Japan, and West Europe are the dominant sources of FDI for many developing countries. In comparison with other host countries, Wei (1995) found that China attracted less FDI from major investing countries in terms of both flows and stock measurements. He pointed out, for example, that Chinese hosting of US investment falls short of its 'potential' by almost 89 per cent.
6. There are many empirical studies in which the impact of market size on FDI flows into China are significantly positive (for example, Wei, 1995; Zhang, 2000a, 2001a, 2001b).
7. The Chinese have a long history of overseas immigration, and in almost every country in the world there are Chinese. According to the *Overseas Chinese Economic Yearbook* by the Committee of Overseas Chinese (Taiwan) (1991), the number of overseas Chinese totaled roughly 36 million; most of them (80 per cent) living in Hong Kong and six Southeast Asian countries (Indonesia, Thailand, Malaysia, Singapore, and Burma). Over three million overseas Chinese reside in North America, including two million in the US. Overseas Chinese, except those living in mainland China but including Taiwan and Hong Kong, are estimated to possess assets totaling some US$1500 to 2000 billion (*The Economist*, 30 May 1994).
8. In their study on the location of US FDI, Kravis and Lipsey (1982) found that proximity to the US (e.g. Canada and Mexico) and the use of English as the major language (e.g. Australia, Canada and the UK) appeared to explain the rankings of countries where FDI by US firms is likely to take place.
9. FDI regimes in Japan, South Korea, and Taiwan have been more restrictive than that in China in both comparative development stages and even to this day. For example, foreign ownership in Japan was limited to a maximum of 49 per cent of any joint venture, and FDI explicitly was not allowed to be a presence in a large number of industries. Wholly foreign owned firms were not permitted to operate until 1973.
10. The positive effects of liberal FDI regime and incentive policies on FDI flows into China have been demonstrated empirically (for example, Zhang, 2000a, 2001b, 2001c).
11. For example, the largest MNC in 1994, General Motors had sales revenues in excess of the GDP of Turkey and Denmark. In fact, its gross sales exceeded the GDP of all but seven developing countries (China, India, Brazil, Indonesia, Mexico, Argentina, and South Korea). The five largest MNCs had combined revenues ($871.4) in excess of the GDP of all 48 least developed countries combined by a factor of 11 (UNCTAD, 1995).

REFERENCES

Caves, Richard (1996), *Multinational Enterprises and Economic Analysis*, 2nd edition, Cambridge, MA: Cambridge University Press.

Kamath, S. J. (1990), 'Foreign Direct Investment in a Centrally Planned Developing Economy: The Chinese Case', *Economic Development and Cultural Changes*, 39 (1), pp. 107–130.

Kravis, I. B. and R. E. Lipsey (1982), 'The Location of Overseas Production and Production for Exports by U.S. Multinational Firms', *Journal of International Economics*, 12 (2), pp. 201–223.

Lardy, Nicholas R. (1992), *Foreign Trade and Economic Reform in China: 1978–1990*, Cambridge: Cambridge University Press.

Lardy, Nicholas R. (1994), *China in the World Economy*, Washington, DC: Institute for International Economics.

Lardy, Nicholas R. (1995), 'The Role of Foreign Trade and Investment in China's Economic Transformation', *The China Quarterly*, 144, pp. 1065–1082.

Markusen, James, R. (1995), 'The Boundaries of Multinational Enterprises and the Theory of International Trade', *The Journal of Economic Perspectives*, 9 (2), pp. 169–189.

220 The Globalization of the Chinese Economy

Ministry of Foreign Trade and Economic Cooperation (MOFTEC) of China, *Almanac of China's Foreign Economic Relations and Trade* (various years), Beijing: MOFERT Press.

MOFTEC, *International Trade* (various issues). Beijing: MOFERT Press.

Naughton, Barry (1996), 'China's Emergence and Prospects as A Trading Nation', *Brookings Papers on Economic Activity,* Washington, DC: Brookings Institution, 1996 (2), pp. 273–344.

Perkins, Dwight (1994), 'Completing China's Move to the Market', *Journal of Economic Perspectives,* 8 (2), pp. 23–46.

State Statistical Bureau (SSB) (1996), *China Regional Economy: A Profile of 17 Years of Reform and Opening-Up,* Beijing, China: China Statistics Press.

State Statistical Bureau (SSB) (1992 through 2001), *China Statistical Yearbook* (1992 through 2001), Beijing, China: China Statistics Press.

United Nations Conference on Trade and Development (UNCTAD) (1995, 1996, 1998 and 1999), *World Investment Report 1995, 1996, 1998, and 1999,* New York: United Nations.

U.S.–China Business Council (USCBC) (1990), *Special Report on US Investment in China,* The China Business Forum, Washington, DC.

Wei, Shang-Jin (1995), 'Attracting Foreign Direct Investment: Has China Reached its Potential?', *China Economic Review,* 6 (2), pp. 187–200.

Wells, Louis T. Jr. (1993), 'Mobile Exporters: New Foreign Investors in East Asia', in K. A. Froot (ed.), *Foreign Direct Investment,* Chicago: The University of Chicago Press.

Zhang, Kevin H. (2000a), 'Why is US Direct Investment in China so Small?' *Contemporary Economic Policy,* 18 (1), pp. 82–94.

Zhang, Kevin H. (2000b), 'Human Capital, Country Size, and North–South Manufacturing Multinational Enterprises', *Economia Internazionale/International Economics,* 53 (2), pp. 237–260

Zhang, Kevin H. (2001a), 'What Explains the Boom of Foreign Direct Investment in China', *Economia Internazionale / International Economics,* 54 (2), pp. 251–274.

Zhang, Kevin H. (2001b), 'What Attract Multinational Corporations to China?', *Contemporary Economic Policy,* 19 (3), pp. 336–346.

Zhang, Kevin H. (2001c), 'Roads to Prosperity: Assessing the Impact of FDI on Economic Growth in China', *Economia Internazionale/International Economics,* 54 (1), pp. 113–125.

Zhang, Kevin H. and James Markusen (1999), 'Vertical Multinationals and Host-Country Characteristics', *Journal of Development Economics,* 59, pp. 233–252.

Zhang, Kevin H. and Shunfeng Song (2000), 'Promoting Exports: The Role of Inward FDI in China', *China Economic Review,* 11 (4), pp. 385–396.

13. Foreign Investment in China: Firm Strategies

Minquan Liu, Luodan Xu and Liu Liu

INTRODUCTION

Foreign Direct Investment (FDI) has been one of the key factors contributing to the globalization of the international economy. Flows of FDI help forge strong economic links between home and host countries. According to UNCTAD (1998), from 1983 to 1995 foreign affiliates of multinationals (MNEs) accounted for around one third of worldwide exports. China's accession to the WTO will not only involve the widespread elimination of trade barriers and the opening up of a broad range of sectors, it is also likely to have profound impacts on FDI inflows from various sources, whose linkages to the host economy will depend on their various investment strategies.

This chapter is based on firm level data from a survey of FDI firms conducted in the summer of 1998 in Guangdong Province, China.[1] Forward linkage refers to the sale of an FDI firm's products and services to the host economy; backward linkage means the purchasing of goods and services (Battat et al., 1996).[2] This chapter is mainly concerned with the manufacturing sectors, though the service sectors were also covered by the survey. Investments from four different foreign sources (Overseas Chinese (CN), the European countries (EU), the US, and Japan (JP)) were surveyed. Through a study of the linkage characteristics we identify different investment strategies associated with investment from these sources. Other things being equal, depending on their investment strategies, the effect of China's WTO accession may be to increase or decrease future FDI inflows from these sources. Linkage characteristics themselves, of course, have important implications for the way in which particular investments impact the Chinese economy.

Though the distribution of FDI in China is regionally and sectorally skewed, we can nevertheless use Guangdong as the prism through which to view the whole landscape of FDI in China and China's integration into the global production and trading network. This makes sense since Guangdong Province has been a key FDI host province in China, accounting for close to one third of the total accumulated foreign investments in China since the opening.[3]

The focus of this chapter is the impact of China's WTO accession on the source composition of inward foreign direct investment and its implications for the Chinese economy. The section that follows presents a conceptual framework relating FDI strategies to linkages. The section following that considers the likely effect of WTO accession on inward FDI to China and relates such effects to investment strategies. The next section presents our findings from the Guangdong survey where we use linkage ratios to identify the investment strategies of CN, JP, EU and US investments. The section following that discusses the results and tentatively assesses the likely impacts of China's WTO accession on future inward investment from these sources. The final section provides the conclusions.

FDI, TRADE AND LINKAGES

Investment Strategies

FDI is usually defined as investments in which a home firm acquires a substantial controlling interest in a foreign firm or sets up a subsidiary in a foreign country (Markusen, 1995). There are many motives for a multinational firm to invest abroad. However, two strategies motivate most FDI: in most cases a firm decides to set up affiliates abroad either to serve the local market (market seeking) or to make use of particular production factors (cost reduction) where the host country has comparative advantages (Michalet, 1997). The production in the latter case may be primarily for export.

To achieve these two objectives (market access and cost reduction) two types of investment often occur: horizontal and vertical. This conceptual distinction is provided by Markusen (1995) and Brainard (1993). Horizontal investment replicates in a host country the production of goods and services that formerly took place in the home country (mostly the final stage production) with a view to gaining access to large consumer markets in the host country. The decision to go multinational is described as a trade off between incurring additional costs in setting up a new plant and the saving of variable costs (transport costs and tariffs) (Shartz and Venables, 2000). Brainard (1997) predicts that 'The firms should expand horizontally across borders whenever the advantages of access to the destination outweigh the advantages from production of scale economies at home'. Usually horizontal investment involves countries at a similar income level and a vast market in the host country. Markusen and Venables (1998) show that horizontal investment will be prevalent among more similar economies (in size and in other economic indicators). To compete with local firms, horizontal FDI firms must possess superior technologies that are not possessed by a host country firm. The host market size is expected to play a key role in attracting this type of FDI.

Vertical investment means fragmenting an MNE's production process geographically by stages of production with an aim to minimize costs at each stage. Differences in factor prices encourage such fragmentation. The crucial assumptions for vertical investment are low transportation costs and low tariff barriers, since most of the upstream products are imported into the host country. Major vertical investors carry out much of their investment close to their borders to save on transport costs. Due to its 'footloose' nature, vertical FDI is also attracted to countries that offer favorable incentives and tax exemptions (Zhang and Markusen, 1999).

Horizontal investment is usually considered trade substituting since the products involved could be produced at home to pursue scale economies rather than in the host country (Brainard, 1997). The substitution relationship between horizontal FDI and trade implies that import restrictions of the host country may induce an increase of this type of FDI, that is trying to get around the trade barriers.

Vertical investment is considered trade creating, since stages of a production process are dispersed across countries. Vertical investment usually has high ratios of overseas sourcing and high ratios of sales back to the home country or to a third country, which are reported as imports and exports respectively in a country's balance of payment accounts. In addition, vertical FDI creates country specific external economies, which may result in agglomeration of industrial activities, thereby promoting the exports of domestic firms (Rhee and Belot, 1990).

The above investments are archetypical types. In reality an MNE is likely to have a mix of market seeking and cost reduction objectives. Likewise a firm's investment may display both horizontal and vertical investment characteristics. If the production process of an MNE involves more than one stage, it may replicate one (or several) stages abroad. In this case the objective is to take advantage of low cost inputs and factors and pursue a cost reduction strategy and this type of investment has evident characteristics of vertical investment. On the other hand if an MNE uses few production stages, it may move all the production process to the host country to save costs. This type of cost reduction investment possesses some features of horizontal investment. Moreover market seeking need not necessarily be associated with horizontal investment. An MNE may move only its last production stage (or part of it) abroad in order to avoid trade barriers and increase its market share in the host country, but the investment is typical of horizontal investment. However if the FDI firm replicates the whole set of production stages in the host country but splits them up in different regions of the host country, these production stages are vertically integrated. This type of investment helps both market seeking and cost reduction. Thus the dichotomies given above are best seen as a list of important features of investments that one should consider.

In what follows an investment strategy will refer to both the objective and the vertical–horizontal features of an investment. The following matrix (Figure 13.1) is provided as a guide. It makes clear that market seeking need not necessarily be associated with horizontal investment, and cost reduction need not necessarily be associated with vertical investment. It is also important to stress that the four investment types, given by the four cells, ought to be seen as representing four pure strategy types. In practice the actual investment strategy of a firm is likely to be a mixture of these pure types, although some firms may have pursued strategies closer to one pure type than another.

	Cost reduction	Market seeking
Horizontal	I	II
Vertical	III	IV

Figure 13.1: Matrix of Types of Investment

FDI Strategies and Linkages

It will be helpful to use certain quantifiable indicators to determine investment strategy. Forward and backward linkage indicators serve this function. The ratio of an FDI firm's products and services sold to the host economy (the domestic sales ratio) may be used as an indicator of forward linkage and can be used to determine investment strategy. Market seeking investments are likely to be associated with high forward linkages or high domestic sales ratios or low export ratios. It may also be expected that if a group of FDI firms, on average, display higher forward linkages (a higher average domestic sales ratio or lower average export ratio) than other groups, this group is likely to have pursued a market seeking strategy relative to the other groups. By the same token, firms with lower average forward linkages (a higher average export ratio) are likely to have pursued a less market seeking and a more cost reducing investment strategy.

Combining forward with backward linkage characteristics yields still richer possibilities. Indicators of backward linkages may include the ratio of goods and services purchased from local suppliers in the host country (domestic sourcing ratio) and the ratio of recruitment of local (host country) personnel by a firm. Here we shall only use the former indicator. A firm with a low domestic sourcing ratio (or high overseas sourcing ratio) and at the same time, a high export ratio for its products and services is likely to have pursued a cost reduction strategy.[4] Likewise if a group of FDI firms have both a high average export ratio and a high average overseas sourcing ratio, these firms are likely to have pursued, on average, a cost reduction investment strategy. Moreover the investment is likely to be of a vertical nature.

The combination of a high export ratio and a low overseas sourcing ratio is likely to indicate an 'integrated' strategy. On the one hand a low overseas sourcing ratio indicates that, perhaps because of high tariffs and transport costs but also because of low factor prices, a high proportion of inputs are sourced domestically in the host country. If the MNE in question does not cover many production stages (for example, in the production of unskilled labor-intensive goods), it may move the whole production process to the host country with the 'headquarters' at home only for providing services, such as international sales expertise and information. On the other hand a high export ratio means that the target market is not in the host country. In effect the MNE has used the host country as an 'export platform' to utilize cheap local factor endowments. The investment in question is again cost reducing, but from the perspective of the distribution of production stages, it is not evidence of vertical investment.

A high domestic sales ratio or low export ratio may be matched with two possibilities: a low or high overseas sourcing ratio. As mentioned previously a low export ratio is likely to imply a market seeking strategy. When this is matched with a high overseas sourcing ratio, it suggests a typical horizontal investment strategy. This is likely to occur if the host country's import tariff on the final product is higher than that on the inputs used to produce the final product. The aim of the investment is then to get around the heavy tariff on the final product and to acquire market access in the host country. When a low export ratio is matched with a low overseas sourcing ratio, another 'integrated' investment strategy emerges. In the case of an MNE using many production stages, it may suggest that most (if not all) stages have been duplicated in the host country. The low export ratio may suggest a market penetration motivation, but the low overseas sourcing ratio may also indicate the aim of cost reduction. Therefore it does not have evident characteristics of horizontal investment.

China's WTO Accession and the Likely Effect on Inward Foreign Investment

Given the important contributions FDI makes to a host economy and given the close relationship between FDI and trade, it is natural to raise questions about the effect of China's WTO accession on future FDI inflows. WTO membership will bring about increased trade opportunities. At the same time it will mean a significant reduction of China's tariff and non tariff barriers and an opening up of a broad range of sectors currently closed or semi-closed to international investments. Further, under the new Agreement on Trade-Related Investment Measures (TRIMs), other forms of investment barriers are also likely to be significantly reduced. The combined effect of these factors on future FDI inflows into China will, to an important extent, depend on the nature and objective of foreign investments in question (i.e. investment strategies) and on the respective strengths of these factors.

It is likely that market-seeking investments with high domestic sales and extensive imports of inputs will decline, especially if such investment is subject to significant scale economies. Such investments are often a response to significant trade barriers and a skewed tariff and NTB structure discriminating against imports of final products. Other things being equal a significant reduction in trade barriers relating to the final product (and a less significant reduction relating to the imported inputs) will decrease the inflow of this type of investment. At the same time, of course, WTO membership will open up more sectors to foreign investments and such investment barriers as local content requirements may be eliminated or at least reduced. This will have a positive influence on market seeking investment. However this positive effect may not entirely outweigh the former negative effect.

Cost reduction investments intended mainly to serve overseas markets and with a high content of imported inputs will almost certainly increase. A reduction of trade barriers and protection will mean a further reduction of the cost of production in China making this type of investment more profitable. The opening up of additional sectors to foreign investment and a reduction in various investment barriers are likely to further encourage this type of investment.

It is not easy to predict the impact of WTO membership on inward investments with mixed objectives. The combined effect will depend on the relative degrees to which cost reduction and market seeking objectives play their role. An MNE may pursue both market seeking and cost reducing objectives by replicating all or most of its production stages in the host country, utilizing a high proportion of local resources at each stage and few imported inputs and then selling a high proportion of its final product within the host country. In this case, other things being equal, a reduction in trade barriers should make the trade alternative more appealing. On the other hand the opening up of further sectors and a reduction in investment barriers can also exert a positive impact on this type of investment.

Alternatively an MNE may replicate most or all of its production stages, use a high proportion of local resources, but sell most of its products overseas. In this case a reduction in trade barriers is unlikely to significantly change the incentives for such investment. On the other hand a fall in investment barriers and a further opening up of sectors to foreign investment will have a positive effect on such investments.

China's accession to the WTO is also likely to bring about an improvement in trade and investment policy transparency and standardize and streamline bureaucratic procedures. Besides reducing trade and investment related transaction costs, these will also make international trade and investment a more level playing field, reducing the room for corruption and discretion. All these will help encourage both trade and investment (Wei, 2000). The exact effect on inward foreign investment vis-à-vis trade, however, is difficult to determine.

FINDINGS FROM THE GUANGDONG SURVEY

The Survey and Basic Data

Our survey took place in the summer of 1998 and initially aimed to cover some 600 firms of which half were to be overseas Chinese investment (CN) from Hong Kong, Macao and Taiwan and the remainder equally divided between three other major investment sources: Europe (EU), Japan (JP) and the US (US). At completion, 405 firms were interviewed of which 276 were of CN origin (including seven firms with investment from mainland China registered abroad), and 41 from the EU, 35 from JP and 50 from US sources. There are three firms whose exact source of investment is difficult to determine. The survey took the form of interviews with the help of a detailed questionnaire.

Target firms were selected both according to investment source and according to industrial sector. One of our aims was to carry out a sectoral analysis of FDI characteristics and impacts on the host economy. Here we shall mainly look at the combined non-service (predominantly manufacturing) sector, leaving aside the service sector firms. Of the total sample, 83 are service sector firms, 320 are manufacturing firms and two are agriculture and mining firms.[5] The industrial classification system used is adopted from our collaborator, the Data Management Institute of CFETRGP, which also provided the population data set.[6]

Table 13.1 presents the sample composition by source, form of investment and firm size. Forms of investment include wholly foreign owned enterprises (WFOE), joint ventures (JV), cooperative ventures (CV) and other. Following widespread practice, firms employing 300 workers and above are classified as large enterprises (LEs) and less than 300 workers are classified as small and medium enterprises (SMEs). We note that CN firms have the lowest ratio of WFOEs, while EU firms have the highest ratio, followed closely by the US firms. Table 13.2 reports on the firms' average annual sales, average registered capital, average total investment, average number of employees and average capital intensity (total investment per employee) by source of investment in 1997.

Table 13.1: Form of Investment and Firm Size (by Source), all Sectors, 1997

Number (Percentage)	CN	EU	JP	US
Wholly foreign owned (WFOE)	69 (25.8)	16 (39.0)	11 (32.4)	19 (38.8)
Joint venture (JV)	142 (53.2)	22 (53.7)	20 (58.8)	23 (46.9)
Cooperative venture (CV)	47 (17.6)	3 (7.3)	3 (8.8)	6 (12.2)
Others	9 (3.4)	0 (0.0)	0 (0.0)	1 (2.0)
Number of respondents (NR)	267 (100)	41 (100)	35 (100)	49 (100)
Small and medium (SME)	175 (65.5)	28 (71.8)	20 (60.6)	24 (52.2)
Large (LE)	92 (34.5)	11 (28.2)	13 (39.4)	22 (47.8)
Number of respondents (NR)	267 (100)	39 (100)	33 (100)	46 (100)

Note: The samples for CN, EU, JP and US are 276, 41, 35 and 50 respectively.

Table 13.2: Average Sales, Registered Capital, Total Investment, Employees, Capital Intensity (by Source), all Sectors, 1997

	CN	EU	JP	US
Annual sales	13.07	37.90	24.89	54.56
Registered capital	6.31	14.02	11.38	16.08
Total investment	11.89	21.45	23.75	33.16
Employees	570	415	593	934
Capital intensity	50.03	228.03	86.67	66.05
Sample	276	41	35	50

Note: The unit for annual sales, registered capital and total investment is 10 million RMB, the unit for capital intensity is 10 000 yuan/capita (total investment/employees). Technology intensity is the ratio of technology staff to employees.

Forward Linkage and Investment Strategy

As noted, 'forward linkage' means the ratio of a firm's products and services sold to the host economy. In our study the host market includes Guangdong and 'other places in China'. Table 13.3 reports the average ratios of the products and services of the firms marketed to 'overseas', 'other provinces in China', and 'Guangdong' by source of investment. Note that the firms in question are non-service sector firms only. The average ratios have been calculated without weighting each individual firm's ratios by its share of the total sales of the group, and therefore they do not represent the share of the sum of the total sales of firms of each group to each destination.

Table 13.3: Sales by Source of Investment, Manufacturing Sectors, 1997 (%)

	CN	EU	JP	US
Guangdong	24.7	32.6	30.6	38.4
Other provinces	18.6	44.4	23.4	33.8
Overseas	56.7	23.0	46.0	27.8
Total	100	100	100	100
Respondents	194	21	22	25
Sample	230	30	27	32

Note: The percentages are simple mean averages.

It can be seen that CN firms as a group register the highest average export ratio of 56.7 per cent and the lowest average host–market sales ratio of 43.3 per cent. This contrasts with EU firms that among them report an average export ratio of only 23.0 per cent, which is in fact the lowest among all four groups. US firms show an average export ratio of 27.8 per cent, slightly higher than that for EU firms, but still much lower than the 56.7 per cent reported by CN firms. JP firms have an average export ratio of 46.0 per cent, closer to that for CN firms, but still over nine percentage points lower.

It is of interest to consider the breakdown of sales within the host country market. Of the massive 77.0 per cent of the combined host market sales ratio reported by EU firms, 44.4 per cent are to other parts of China and 32.6 per cent are to Guangdong. The former percentage is in fact the highest among all four groups of firms for sales to 'other parts of China'. The latter ratio, that is sales within Guangdong, is only surpassed by the 38.4 per cent reported by US firms, which have an average ratio of sales of 33.8 per cent to other parts of China, the second highest ratio for that market among the four groups. CN and JP firms, given their fairly low total sales to the combined host market, both have quite low ratios of sales to Guangdong and other parts of China.

We conclude therefore that there exists the least forward linkage from CN firms, and the greatest from EU firms, with US firms being very close to EU firms. JP firms are closer to CN firms than to EU firms. Moreover it appears that EU firms by comparison favored markets across China, rather than within Guangdong, while US firms comparatively favored the Guangdong market.

Compared with JP firms, but especially CN firms, EU and US firms have focused much more on developing the host market. Both EU and US firms appear to have had a strategy of host market penetration or market seeking. Both have very low export ratios. However their investment strategies are not entirely the same. EU firms targeted more the wider China market, while the US firms focused more on the local Guangdong market. Both CN and JP firms appear to have very much followed a cost reduction strategy, with around half of their products sold abroad.

It is worth noting that while US firms appear to have focused more on the local Guangdong market, this may be the result of a 'division of the market' strategy pursued by their parent firm. A US firm in Guangdong and its sister subsidiaries in other parts of China may have 'carved up' the wider China market with separate local target markets. Table 13.4 gives data on the average number of subsidiaries in China. US firms have the highest average

Table 13.4: Number of Affiliates in China: Percentage Distribution and Average by FDI Source

	CN	EU	JP	US
1	101 (48.6)	12 (36.4)	13 (50.0)	9 (22.0)
2–5	69 (33.2)	17 (51.5)	8 (30.8)	22 (53.7)
6–10	25 (12.0)	3 (9.1)	3 (11.5)	5 (12.2)
Above 10	13 (6.3)	1 (3.0)	1 (3.9)	5 (12.2)
Respondents	208 (100)	33 (100)	25 (100)	41 (100)
Sample	276	41	35	50
Average	3.56	2.93	2.84	4.93

Note: The JP average is calculated by excluding an outlier reporting 139 affiliates. EU average is also calculated by excluding one that reported 79 affiliates.

number, which appears to lend support to our conjecture. If so, like their EU counterparts, US parent MNEs may also have extensively pursued a strategy of penetrating the wider China market.

Sourcing and Investment Strategy

One important dimension to assessing backward linkages is sourcing. An FDI firm can purchase inputs from within Guangdong, from other places in China, and from overseas. Purchases from the first two signify backward linkage. Table 13.5 presents our survey findings on sourcing of the firms by source of investment. EU firms record the highest average overseas sourcing ratio at 65.8 per cent, followed by JP firms at 60.2 per cent, CN firms at 49.6 per cent, and lastly, US firms at 44.7 per cent. US firms on average sourced least from overseas.

Of sourcing from within China, among the four groups, US firms on average sourced most from 'other parts of China' (36.4 per cent), followed by CN firms (25.0 per cent). Not far behind the CN firms are the EU firms which on average sourced at 23.5 per cent from other parts of China. JP firms sourced least from 'other parts of China', at 14.8 per cent.

Table 13.5: Sourcing by Source of Investment, Manufacturing Sectors, 1997 (%)

	CN	EU	JP	US
Guangdong	25.4	10.8	25.0	18.9
Other provinces	25.0	23.5	14.8	36.4
Overseas	49.6	65.8	60.2	44.7
Total	100	100	100	100
Respondents	185	20	21	25
Sample	230	30	27	32

Note: The percentages are simple mean averages.

While JP firms on average sourced least from 'other parts of China', they rank only next to CN firms in sourcing from Guangdong, at 25.0 per cent, compared with 25.4 per cent for CN firms. US firms on average sourced from Guangdong at 18.9 per cent and EU firms least at 10.8 per cent.

It appears that with respect to sourcing from China, US and EU firms have favored sourcing from 'other parts of China', while JP firms have done the opposite. CN firms have sourced more or less evenly from the two local sources.

Of the four groups of firms, EU firms are of particular interest. Recall that EU firms as a group also, in fact, had the lowest export ratio and the highest ratio of sales to the host economy. These findings together appear to say that EU firms as a group have engaged in extensive imports of intermediate goods from abroad and then used them to produce goods and services which mainly targeted the host market (in particular the wider China market). The extensive imports may have been necessary for EU firms because they may have required intermediate goods and inputs of a quality and design which were difficult to source locally. On the other hand the practice may well have been part of an overall strategy by the parent firm to penetrate the China market.

The high overseas sourcing ratio and the low export ratio could also suggest that EU parent firms pursued a certain horizontal investment strategy in order to get around the heavy tariffs on their final products (while those on their imported inputs were relatively low), thus making direct investment more cost saving than trade (exporting the final product to China).

JP and US firms may be compared with EU firms. JP firms sourced almost as extensively from overseas as EU firms. However JP firms exported a much larger proportion of their products overseas. It is of interest to examine the major destinations of their exports. Table 13.6 gives percentage distributions of firms from each source group by the first principal export market they reported (Southeast Asia, Japan, Europe, North America, and other). Over 50 per cent of EU, US and CN firms identified Southeast Asia as their first and

Table 13.6: First Export Market: Percentage Distribution of Firms by FDI Source, all Sectors, 1997

	CN	EU	JP	US
Southeast Asia	85 (52.2)	10 (55.6)	6 (28.6)	7 (53.9)
Japan	11 (6.8)	1 (5.6)	12 (57.1)	1 (7.7)
Europe	17 (10.4)	6 (33.3)	1 (4.8)	0 (0.0)
North America	36 (22.1)	0 (0.0)	1 (4.8)	5 (38.1)
Other	14 (8.6)	1 (5.6)	1 (4.8)	0 (0.0)
Respondents	163 (100)	18 (100)	21 (100)	13 (100)
Sample	234	33	27	39

largest export market. However over 57 per cent of JP firms identified Japan as their first principal export market. This implies that a very high proportion of JP firms exports were likely to be destined for their home country, though the exact proportion is not possible to determine. Coupled with the fact that JP firms also reported a very high overseas sourcing ratio (60 per cent) and the second highest export ratio (46 per cent), it appears that JP firms to an important extent used Guangdong as a processing base to produce goods and services in part to serve the host country market but also equally importantly, to serve their overseas and in particular, their home markets. Like EU firms their subsidiaries in Guangdong are likely to use few production stages beyond the last, utilizing China's cheap resources and perhaps especially labor. These firms are likely to be extensively vertically integrated with their parent firms. The export ratio of US firms is close to that of EU firms, while they had the lowest overseas sourcing ratio (EU firms had the highest). Like EU firms US firms appear to have placed emphasis on capturing the host market. However unlike EU firms, they sourced much more from local suppliers. This may suggest that US firms, on average, moved more production stages to Guangdong than the other groups of firms. US firms in Guangdong may be extensive replicates of their parent firms or sister subsidiaries elsewhere. Their investment motives may have included both market seeking and cost reduction.

Finally CN firms had the highest export ratio (57 per cent) and they sourced second least from overseas at just below 50 per cent (higher than that of US firms). CN firms are the most export-oriented group. The principal destination of their exports is Southeast Asia, followed by North America. CN firms, the most numerous group in our sample, had the smallest average size of investment (both in terms of registered capital and total investment; see Table 13.2), and the highest labor intensity ratio (the number of employees of a firm divided by its total investment; see Table 13.2). CN firms appear to have pursued a cost reduction strategy, mainly producing low technological content and labor-intensive products for the host market but especially for exports.

Figures 13.2 and 13.3 provide a summary of the linkage characteristics and investment strategies of the four groups of firms, which we have identified. In Figure 13.3 we have identified JP firms as having pursued archetypical cost reduction and vertical investment strategies, while EU firms pursued an archetypical market seeking and horizontal investment strategy. US firms as a group are close to EU firms in pursuing a market seeking investment strategy. However they do not display as strong a horizontal feature in their investment as EU firms and might even have qualified as vertical investment. In contrast CN firms are close to JP firms in pursuing a cost reduction objective, however, they do not display as strong a vertical feature in their investment as JP firms and might even have qualified as horizontal investment.

	CN	JP	US	EU
Overseas sourcing ratio	Second lowest	Second highest	Lowest	Highest
Export ratio	Highest	Second highest	Second lowest	Lowest
Investment strategy	Cost reduction	Cost reduction	Market seeking	Market seeking

Figure 13.2: Comparison and Contrast of Linkages and Strategies

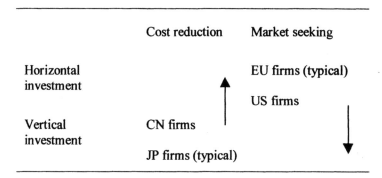

Note: The arrows indicate the directions in which CN and US firms are respectively inclined in their vertical–horizontal investment features.

Figure 13.3 Comparison and Contrast of the Four Groups in Investment Strategy

Sectoral Characteristics and Linkages

We have identified important differences in linkage characteristics between the source groups and on that basis, characterized the different investment strategies adopted by these source groups. One question arises: might such differences in linkage characteristics not be a consequence of source differences, but a consequence of some other underlying factors, for example, form of investment, firm size and industrial sectoral characteristics? The fact that there exist important linkage differences between different source groups might be explained by the differences in the composition of firms of different sources by these factors. In a preliminary study (Liu and Xu, 1999) the possible influences of form of investment and firm size were examined and it was found that both factors could not consistently explain the differences in linkage characteristics between the source groups. Below we briefly consider the possible influence of industrial sector.

The formula below provides a way of extracting away possible sectoral influences.

$$A^j = \sum_i (w_i^j \, a_i^{cn}) / \sum_i w_i^j . \qquad (13.1)$$

a_i^{cn} is the sectoral average of a ratio (for example, export and overseas sourcing) for the i'th sector of the CN group. w_i^j refers to the number of firms in sector i of the j'th source group (JP, EU, US). The summation is over the sectors. A^j is therefore a weighted cross sector average value of the ratio in question, weighted by the ratio of the number of firms in each sector to the total number of firms of j'th source group. The interpretation is that if the firms involved were CN firms and if it is further assumed that such a firm of a given sector would report the ratio to be exactly equal to the CN firms' sectoral average ratio for that sector, then A^j can be interpreted as the cross sector average ratio for the j'th group if its firms were in fact CN firms. Note the important assumption that if a firm were a CN firm of a given sector, the ratio in question it would report would be equal to the CN firms' sectoral average ratio for that sector. Needless to say this is a drastic assumption (since even CN firms, of course, reported different values for the ratio). Therefore at best A^j ought to be seen as an approximate way of predicting the cross sector average value of a ratio for a source group if the firms were in fact CN firms.

Given the above interpretation A^j, the difference between A^j (or the predicted value) and the actual average value of a ratio reported by the group then indicates (approximately) the source influence for the j'th group, relative to the CN group. The choice of the CN group as the reference group is based on the fact that this group is by far the most numerous group in our sample and spans all sectors.

The linkage ratios used for the calculation include the overseas sourcing ratio and export ratio. Table 13.7 presents the results. In regard to overseas sourcing we find that the predicted values for all three non-CN groups are lower than the actual values. The difference for the EU group is the largest. This can be interpreted to mean that source did exert an influence and specifically, it raised the overseas sourcing ratio in all three cases and particularly significantly, in the case of the EU group. Regarding the export ratio, we find that the actual values for all three non-CN groups are lower than their predicted values. This means that the source factor in all three

Table 13.7: Overseas Sourcing and Export Ratios: Actual and Predicted, Manufacturing Sectors, 1997

		EU	JP	US
Overseas sourcing:	Actual	65.75	60.24	44.68
	Predicted	39.49	52.53	36.19
Export ratio:	Actual	22.95	46	27.78
	Predicted	46.96	54.93	39.28

cases did have an effect of reducing the export ratio and in the case of EU and US groups, particularly sharply. The JP group is of interest as the differences between the actual and predicted values for both the export ratio and overseas sourcing ratio are the smallest, indicating that the JP group is comparatively close to the CN firms in export and overseas sourcing characteristics.

DISCUSSION

Using our survey findings on backward and forward linkages, we have been able to identify different investment strategies of the four source groups. We will further examine why these four groups adopt particular strategies in China by relating their strategies to the characteristics of their home economies. This contributes to an assessment of the possible impact of China's WTO accession on inward FDI from these four sources. However the profound change in the social and economic regime that may be expected to be brought about by WTO membership may change the very investment strategies of the MNEs in China. In what follows however we shall ignore such possible changes in strategy and on this basis will offer tentative and broad predictions. Even so it is by no means a straightforward task, given the multi-objective nature of investments and the complex characteristics of the home and host countries. WTO membership can unleash both negative and positive effects. The combined impact will depend on how they balance out.

Investment of CN Firms

CN firms are firms invested by overseas Chinese. Among them investment from Hong Kong dominates.[7] Hong Kong has the geographic, cultural and language proximity to mainland China and particularly, to Guangdong Province. The investment from Hong Kong may not be on the frontiers of the world's technology and organizational complexity. Its particular advantages appear to lie in marketing skills and practices that ensure timely delivery and uniform quality (Wells, 1993) and the adaptation of mature technologies to more labor-intensive contexts, as suggested in Vernon's (1979) product cycle theory. A closer regional integration with mainland China in the run up to 1997 and thereafter also allowed Hong Kong investors to coordinate their production across the border more easily and effectively.

In the late 1970s the structural transformation from labor-intensive to technology-intensive industries in Hong Kong coincided with China's open door policy. The rapid growth of labor costs in Hong Kong caused its labor-intensive manufacturing sectors to lose their traditional competitiveness. This spurred a radical transfer of labor-intensive export industries from Hong Kong to southern China (Sun, 1998), while the 'parent' firms back in Hong Kong became 'headquarters' that collected and processed information and conducted trade using their existing networks in the international market.

Historically Hong Kong was China's main gateway to the outside world. Before FDI was permitted in China, Hong Kong's role for China had been principally as an entrepot. After China actively sought FDI, local Chinese firms joined with Hong Kong firms as joint ventures and this development also coincided with the industrial upgrading in Hong Kong as mentioned above. In this new set-up Hong Kong 'parent' firms have principally served only as trading agents. Today, even though Hong Kong has reverted to China's sovereignty, it still remains a separate customs territory and a separate member of the WTO.

One interesting aspect of China's trade in recent years is that a large part of it is fueled by FDI, particularly investment by Hong Kong firms in Guangdong, which has become an important 'export platform' (Fung, 1996). China's export-oriented trade strategy adopted as a part of the open door policy has had an effect of encouraging the inflow of CN investment vis-à-vis investment from other less export-oriented sources. In 1986 the 'twenty-two' provisions concerning FDI included preferential tax policies and incentives aimed at encouraging foreign investment. Export-oriented FDI firms were allowed duty free imports of raw materials, components and capital equipment intended for export production, as well as other concessionary income tax rates and tax holidays.

According to our survey findings, CN firms appear principally to have made Guangdong an 'export platform' taking advantage of the much lower factor costs. In theory the reduction of trade barriers induced by the WTO accession may accelerate cost reduction investment. However it is unlikely to have a significant influence on CN firms' investment in China, in part due to their low overseas sourcing ratio, but also because many export processing firms have already enjoyed duty exemptions or reductions on their imported inputs designed for export production. At the same time WTO accession will mean a significant loss of the long time entrepot status for Hong Kong and its investors will lose much of their former advantage in international marketing, especially in regard to highly export-oriented investors. The net effect, to a large extent, will be determined by the interaction of these factors. Our basic conjecture is that the latter negative effect is likely to outweigh the former positive effect.

Investment of JP Firms

In contrast to CN firms, JP firms have their own home country characteristics. One feature of Japanese FDI is its 'Wider East Asian Economy' strategy and the extent to which it has involved relocation of Japanese production to lower wage economies as a production base from which to supply the Japanese market and third country markets (Shartz and Venables, 2000). Japan and the Asian host countries, including China, have established a complementary relationship through increased FDI and international trade. Japanese firms manage to preserve and strengthen their international competitiveness through 'slicing value chains' and exploiting comparative advantage at each production stage in Asia. Japanese affiliates in Asia work as export bases to Japan or to third countries to minimize trade frictions with Western countries. Tejima (2000), in an extensive survey, finds that Japanese FDI in China principally aimed at 'strengthening export bases back to Japan'. This may be explained by the fact that JP firms in China have been mainly involved in the production of certain upstream products, perhaps because they would face certain tariff and non tariff disadvantages if they produced downstream products and directly exported these to Western countries.

The appreciation of the yen in the late 1980s and early 1990s after the Plaza Accord in 1985 may have contributed to the boom in Japanese FDI in Asia. Many Japanese firms considered overseas production as a necessary competitiveness enhancing corporate strategy when faced with the more than 25 per cent appreciation of the yen between 1993 and 1995 (UNCTAD, 1996). Japanese FDI firms in developing countries, especially in Asia, aimed at cost reduction, while in the developed countries, they targeted market access by establishing local assembling and distribution networks to avoid trade frictions (Kreinin et al., 1999). The usual pattern of Japanese FDI abroad involves extensive vertical integration on an international scale:

downstream investments in wholesaling and distributing networks in developed countries such as the US, coupled with upstream investment in the production of primary and intermediate goods in developing countries, particularly in Asia. Such a 'globalization' strategy is in part a reflection of the organizational structure of their own industry. A system of production called 'keiretsu', emphasizes vertically structured networks among individual units that concentrate on different tasks in closely connected production processes. Japanese MNEs seem to have established a regional core network in Asia characterized by sophisticated intra firm division of labor and spatial fragmentation of production processes.

The Asian financial crisis had very slight effects on Japanese FDI in China, while it appears to have had a negative effect on Japanese investment in the ASEAN countries because of the perceived greater risk premium, certainly in the short run (Kreinin et al., 1999). China is in a competitive position to attract FDI from Japanese firms vis-à-vis the ASEAN countries. Tejima (2000) finds that Chinese local markets have become more important for Japanese affiliates in China than before. These may suggest a trend that Japanese firms will be motivated to move more stages of production to China after the WTO accession.

Regarding our survey findings, the general reduction in tariffs will enhance JP investment given its high overseas sourcing ratio. However like CN firms, JP firms have also been offered favorable tariff concessions on imported inputs intended for export production. This will negate the otherwise positive effect to some extent. On the other hand WTO accession will involve China opening up more sectors (particularly in automobiles) to foreign investment. With the investment barriers in these additional sectors reduced, JP firms may increase direct investment in China instead.[8]

Investment of US Firms

The United States, like Japan, is closely linked with the Chinese economy through both trade and investment. Access to China's huge consumer market is the principal motive of US firms. The rapidly rising personal incomes brought about by economic reforms have formed a huge domestic market in China. Many US MNEs that face shrinking or saturated markets in mature industrialized economies have been seeking a local presence in the fast growing Chinese market through FDI. Lipsey (1999) finds that 'the most consistent characteristics attracting U.S. direct investment and FDI activity to developing countries was large market size'. This is also consistent with our survey findings.

Compared with CN firms, which are closely related to labor-intensive products (light industry & apparel) aimed at international markets, US firms pay more attention to energy, medical, agricultural, electronics, and heavy industry and service sectors intended to serve China's domestic market. Comparing US and JP investment, Kojima (1978) asserts that while Japanese investment plays the role of a 'tutor' to developing countries, US investment plays the role of a 'competitor' pursuing oligopolistic profit maximization. During the last two decades FDI from the US has been motivated more by a desire for access to emerging markets than for low cost sources of supply (Wheeler and Mody, 1992).

The lower share of small and medium sized enterprises (SMEs) in US investment (Table 13.1) is partly due to its large home economy. Since these enterprises relatively lack distribution and marketing channels abroad compared with LEs, one would expect them to tend to stay with and sell to the home market to save on transaction costs. In analyzing US large modern enterprises Chandler (1997) points out two features: multi operation units and management by a hierarchical administrative staff. These were totally different from those traditional single plant firms. They controlled many operation units at different locations, which engaged in different stages of production. Many of the inter unit transactions were internalized and coordinated by paid employees within a firm. These modern LEs are the origins of present US multinational corporations. The above may shed light on why US FDI firms in China appear to have maintained a certain 'division of market' arrangement between subsidiaries, while collectively they sought market access to the host country. US investment can be viewed as principally being motivated to pursue market share in China.

After China joins the WTO, other things being equal, the reduction of trade barriers will increase the appeal of trade and reduce the appeal of market seeking FDI. However this negative effect may be outweighed by the following positive effect. According to our survey findings, though US firms have the lowest overseas sourcing ratio, it still stands at 44.7 per cent. The discrimination against US firms due to China's export-oriented FDI policies (such as duty exemptions and reductions on inputs intended for export production, from which CN and JP firms have benefited) will be reduced. What is more, the domestic market in China will be further liberalized after accession. With the opening up of more sectors, especially service sectors (principally financial and communications), to foreign investment and reductions in other investment barriers, the inflow of FDI from the US is likely to increase since it is commonly believed that US investors have comparative advantages in these sectors, which are knowledge-intensive with a high rate of intangible assets. (High rates of intangible assets are positively correlated with foreign direct investment since the transaction costs of trade or licensing related to intangible assets tend to be very high.) Given US firms' ambitions with respect to the China market, we believe that there will be an increase of FDI from US firms to China.

Investment of EU Firms

Among the triad members (US, JP and EU), which play a dominant role in the world's FDI, EU firms generally have less experience in China. EU firms have not been as successful in capturing investment opportunities that were opened up in Asian emerging markets such as China since 1980s (UNCTAD, 1996). During the 1980s EU firms focused mainly on the opportunities offered by the European single market process. In the early 1990s more attention was turned to Central and Eastern Europe. In comparison with JP and US firms, EU firms have attached less importance to developing countries. In addition FDI from EU countries to developing countries has been greatly influenced by the cultural ties and colonial heritage related to their imperial history (Shartz and Venables, 2000).

Since the mid-1990s the emerging market of China with almost double-digit economic growth has begun to attract market seeking investment from EU firms. Compared with JP and US investors, European MNEs relied more on direct exports than on opening up subsidiaries and establishing extensive marketing networks (UNCTAD, 1996). Our survey findings indicate that EU firms in China are, to an important extent, designed to facilitate trade, substituting for exports of final products to China, and 'jumping' the heavy import tariffs imposed by China on such products (heavy relative to import duties on intermediate goods). The principal motive of EU firms in China is to sell their products to local consumers. If the tariffs on their final products are greatly reduced, EU firms will be less likely to take the trouble of importing large volumes of inputs to China, conducting the last stage of production and then selling the finished products locally. Rather they are more likely to produce the finished products at home and then export them to China, especially if the production of these products is subject to extensive scale economies.

After China's WTO accession and when trade barriers on final products are significantly reduced (much more than on imported inputs), the inflow of this type of investment is likely to fall.[9] At the same time the opening up of more sectors is likely to encourage EU firms to invest in China. Considering their relative preference for trade, the negative effect on their FDI inflow to China is unlikely to be outweighed by this positive effect. In addition as a later mover compared with JP and US firms, EU firms have yet to familiarize themselves with the Chinese economic and cultural background, which is in fact essential to gaining market accesses to China (for example, setting up effective distribution and marketing networks).

CONCLUDING REMARKS

As a developing country and a transitional economy, China has been gradually integrated into the international network of trade and production, with investments from all three major sources of the world's FDI (US, JP, EU) and overseas Chinese (CN). By examining firm level data from a survey of FDI firms in Guangdong, we begin to get a picture of the characteristics of the investment from these sources.

This chapter aimed to assess the impact of WTO accession on the inflow of FDI in China. Through analyzing linkage characteristics we were able to identify four investment strategies, which respectively characterize investments from the four sources. On the basis of their investment strategies, we then made assessments regarding the impact of China's WTO accession on future FDI inflows from these sources. Needless to say China's WTO accession is expected to bring about profound changes certainly to China's own economic and social environment but also to the world's trading and investment environment. That being so, MNEs may well change their investment strategies in the future. In this chapter we made a limited attempt to assess the impact assuming that the investment strategies of the four source groups of firms we identified will not change.

China is in need of further FDI to upgrade its industrial structure through transfers of advanced technology embodied in FDI to improve enterprise management through transfers of advanced management methods and culture, as well as to create more employment to absorb its abundant labor force. FDI has played a significant role in boosting the growth of the Chinese economy in the last two decades. The policy and institutional support from the government has made an important contribution in attracting FDI. However China is still far from having achieved its potential in receiving FDI from advanced countries (Wei, 1995). Increased globalization, driven by rapid technological developments and a liberalization of investment and trade regimes, will further change the global structure of industry and intensify competition. China is now not only a growing market but also an increasingly competitive producer, in part, thanks to FDI. China's accession to the WTO will no doubt further integrate China into the international system of trade and production and at the same time, subject China to increased competition and more stringent standards.

NOTES

1. The survey was carried out in collaboration with the Data Management Institute of the Guangdong Research Institute, the Commission of Foreign Economic and Trade Relations of Guangdong Province. We would like to thank the following people for their advice and help: Xu Dezhi, Huang Zhiwei, Fu Ge, Long Yaozhang, Chen Zhenquan, Zhu Tingqing, Shi Xiaoyong, Laio Feiyan, Li Xiaoke, Dieter Laumert, Anne IO, Liu Qingseng, Sun Guan, Tony

Perarson, Hao Yajuan, Wu Jianjun, Xu Lefei, Laing Zhicheng, Zeng Jianyu, the students of Linnan College who participated in the survey and Angela Wang for her research.

In this paper an FDI firm in China is defined as an enterprise either wholly or partially funded by a foreign parent firm. An MNE, on the other hand, refers to the parent firm with all its subsidiaries.

2. In our other report on linkages, backward linkage also means the employment of local manpower. Owing to the limitation on chapter length, we have omitted the discussion in this respect. Please refer to Liu and Xu (1999).

3. Guangdong is, of course, the province where China's first experiments with the opening up took place. It was the first province to permit and actively seek inward FDI in the post-Mao era. By 1998, it had attracted a realized value of US$75.3bn of inward investment, accounting for 28.15 per cent of total realized investment in China since the opening up (MOFTEC, 1999).

4. It needs to be said that cost-reducing investments need not necessarily be associated with high overseas sourcing ratios. If the stage or production involved is close to the raw material stage (such as mineral extraction), overseas sourcing ratios need not be high and yet the investment can be cost reducing. However, generally speaking, we would expect cost reducing investments also to be associated with high overseas sourcing ratios (for example, for investments involving productions stages distant from the raw material stage in the whole commodity chain (Gereffi and Korzeniewicz, 1994)).

5. Although one EU firm did not report its sector code, we identified it by its main products.

6. We have examined the representativeness of the sample in another linkage report (Liu and Xu, 1999), which shows that the sample distribution trails closely after the population distribution.

7. Here we shall only consider investment from Hong Kong, since it accounts for most of the investment from the CN source in Guangdong.

8. Strictly, the same factor of investment barrier reduction also applies to CN investment. However we believe that the sectors where CN firms have a 'comparative advantage' (low technology, labor-intensive ones) are already more or less fully opened up, while certain important high tech manufacturing (such as automobiles) and service sectors where JP firms have an advantage are yet to be opened up or to experience significant investment barrier reduction.

9. This is so since in the cascade of tariffs China has applied, those on intermediate goods are generally lower than those on finished final products. The margin of reduction under the WTO membership is correspondingly generally higher for final products than for intermediate goods.

REFERENCES

Battat, J., Frank, I. and Shen, X (1996), 'Suppliers to Multinationals', World Bank, *FIAS Occasional Paper 6*, US: World Bank.

Brainard, S. Lael (1993), 'A Simple Theory of Multinational Corporations and Trade with a Trade-off between Proximity and Concentration', *NBER Working Paper No. 4269*, US: NBER.

Brainard, S. Lael (1997), 'An Empirical Assessment of the Proximity–Concentration Trade-off between Multinational Sales and Trade', *The American Economic Review*, 87 (4).

Chandler, D. Alfred Jr. (1997), *The Visible Hand: The Managerial Revolution in American Business*, Cambridge, MA: Belknap Press.

Fung, K. C. (1996), 'Accounting for Chinese Trade: Some National and Regional Considerations', *NBER Working Paper 5595*, US: NBER.

Gereffi, Gary and Miguel Korzeniewicz (1994), *Commodity Chains and Global Capitalism*, Westport, CT and London: Praeger Publishers.

Kojima, K. (1978), *Direct Foreign Investment: A Japanese Model of Multinational Business Operations*, London: Croom Helm.

Kreinin, E. Mordechai, Shigeyyuki Abe and Michael G. Plunner (1999), 'Motives for Japanese DFI: Survey, Analysis and Implications in Light of the Asian Crisis', *Journal of Asian Economics*, 10.

Lipsey, Robert (1999), 'The Location and Characteristics of U.S. Affiliates in Asia', *NBER Working Paper 6876*, US: NBER.

Liu, Minquan and Xu, Luodan (1999), 'Foreign Direct Investment and Linkages: Some Survey Findings from Guangdong, China', mimeo.

Markusen, James (1995), 'The Boundaries of Multinational Enterprises and the Theory of International Trade', *Journal of Economic Perspectives*, 9 (2).

Markusen, James and Anthony Venables (1998), 'Multinational Firms and the New Trade Theory', *Journal of International Economics*, 46.

Michalet, C. A. (1997), 'Strategies of Multinationals and Competition for Foreign Direct Investment', *World Bank, FIAS Occasional Paper 10*, US: World Bank.

MOFTEC (1999), *Statistics on FDI in China*, Beijing, China.

Rhee, Y. W. and T. Belot (1990), 'Export Catalysts in Low-income Countries', *World Bank Discussion Paper No. 72*, US: World Bank.

Shartz, Howard J, and Anthony J. Venables (2000), 'The Geography of International Investment', mimeo, *The Oxford Handbook of Economic Geography*, Oxford.

Sun, Haishun (1998), 'Macroeconomic Impact of Direct Foreign Investment in China: 1979–96', *The World Economy*, July.

Tejima, Shigeki (2000), 'Japanese FDI, the Implications of Hollowing Out on the Technological Development of Host Countries,' *International Business Review*, 9.

UNCTAD (1996), *Investing in Asia's Dynamism*, European Commission, New York and Geneva: United Nations.

UNCTAD (1998), *World Investment Report 1998: Trends and Determinants*, New York and Geneva: United Nations.

Vernon, Reymond (1979), 'The Product Cycle Hypothesis in a New International Environment', *Oxford Bulletin of Economics and Statistics*, 41 (4).

Wei, Shang-jin (1995), 'Attracting Foreign Direct Investment: Has China Reached Its Potential?', *China Economic Review*, 6 (2).

Wei Shang-jin (2000), 'Corruption and the Composition of Foreign Direct Investment', *World Bank, Working Paper 2360*, US: The World Bank.

Wells, Louise (1993), 'Mobile Exporters: New Foreign Investors in East Asia', in K. A. Froot (ed.), *Foreign Direct Investment*, Chicago: University of Chicago Press.

Wheeler, David and Ashoka Mody (1992), 'International Investment Location Decisions: The Case of US Firms', *Journal of International Economics*, 33 (1–2).

Zhang, Kevin H. and James R. Markusen (1999), 'Vertical Multinationals and Host-country Characteristics', *Journal of Development Economics*, 59.

14. Explosion of Trade Disputes?

Jason Z. Yin and Doowan Lee

INTRODUCTION

For the last half century, international trade has been an important contributor to the growth of the world economy. Similarly, over the past 20 years, after China's decision to pursue a market opening policy, the growth of the Chinese economy has been led by the rapid growth of its exports and imports. However this growth in international trade has been accompanied by an increase in the number of trade conflicts both bilaterally and multilaterally. Trade disputes between China and its major trade partners have been escalating too.

Since the establishment of the World Trade Organization (WTO) in 1995, trade disputes between its country members have escalated sharply. An increasing number of developing countries have become involved in trade disputes, while more conflicts have arisen between the developed countries. In addition more of these disputes have been related to non-tariff barriers and as such, have been more difficult to settle under the WTO than under its predecessor, the GATT. These developments have caused public concern about the consequences of the WTO and this has led to calls for more serious research attention.

At this critical time China is on the verge of WTO membership after completing its successful accession negotiations with its major trade partners. China is expected to become a member of the trade club in 2001. The swelling conflicts within WTO member countries raise a new dimension of concern for China and for the multinationals that have business interests in China on whether it will be overwhelmed by trade disputes after its accession. This chapter is intended to address this issue. It first examines the dispute settlement procedure and the pattern and causes of trade disputes between WTO member countries for the period 1995–2000. It then analyzes the complementary nature of China's trade structures and China's trade disputes with the US, its major trade partner over the past few years, to illuminate the major issues confronting China in its international trade relations and the likelihood that it will be involved in trade disputes after its WTO accession. Based on the results of this analysis, suggestions are made as to strategic actions that China and the multinationals should take to prevent possible trade conflicts and to settle any trade disputes that arise.

WTO TRADE DISPUTES AND SETTLEMENT

International trade has grown dramatically and economic activities have become increasingly integrated globally over the past half century. Economic globalization has resulted in transnational capital and commodity flows of increasing size and speed cascading against relatively discrete national economic jurisdictions. The intertwining of national economic interests and the forces of globalization are creating more conflicts than ever before. This calls for more cooperation among the nations of the world to eliminate protectionist domestic legislation and to promote the free exchange of goods and services (August, 1999). The WTO, as a 'multilateral' trade system, is becoming more and more important in making international trade secure and stable.

In many ways the central pillar of the WTO is its dispute settlement system. The system underscores the rule of law (not the rule of power) and is based on clearly defined rules and timetables for settling disputes. WTO members agree that they will use the multilateral system for settling disputes instead of taking unilateral action if they believe fellow members are violating trade rules. Reducing the scope for unilateral actions is an important guarantee of fair trade for less powerful counties (Ruggierro, 1997). The establishment of the WTO dispute settlement system, allowing independent panels to decide cases put before them on a timely and definitive basis, represents one of the biggest achievements of the Uruguay Round negotiations. This mechanism has been effectively used by its members in resolving trade disputes, as shown in Table 14.1. Among the total of 220 cases filed by the end of 2000, 86 cases were pending for consultation with the governments involved, 17 were under active investigation, 43 had been investigated and ruled on by the DSB Panel or Appellate Body and the rest were either adopted for implementation or had been closed. This dispute resolution mechanism is well recognized as unique and effective among international institutions (Grady and Macmillan, 1999: 135).

Since the implementation of the WTO dispute settlement procedure in 1995, the patterns of trade conflict have changed significantly in comparison with those under the GATT. First, more dispute cases are being brought to the Dispute Settlement Body (DSB) of the WTO. During the 47-year existence of the GATT, there were altogether 236 dispute cases filed with an average of roughly five cases per year (Kim, 1996). However there were 220 cases filed (with 168 distinct matters) during 1995–2000 according to the Overview of the State-of-play of WTO Disputes. On average there have been 37 complaints reported to the WTO annually, which is seven times the

Table 14.1: Statistical Overview of the WTO Dispute Settlement Mechanism

Cases (From 1 January 1995 to 15 January 2001)	Number
Consultation requests (complaints referred to the WTO; 168 involve distinct matters)	220*
Pending and consultations	86
Active cases (including pending or suspended panel proceedings or appellate review proceedings) on reporting date	17
Appellate Body and Panel reports adopted before 1 January 2001 (including requests resulting from DSU 21.5 proceedings)	43
Implementation status of adopted reports	27
Cases settled or inactive	36

Note: The figures presented in this table do not add due to the fact that many of the cases have multiple parties or can be recorded at more than one stage of resolution. In some cases, there is more than one complaining country to a respondent country. Therefore the total number of respondents can be greater than the total number of complaining countries. The tabulation in Table 14.1 is based on the total number of respondent countries.

Source: Overview of the WTO State-of-play of WTO Disputes, 15 January 2001

number reported to the GATT annually, as shown in Table 14.2. One positive explanation is that 'the increasing number of disputes is simply the result of expanding world trade and stricter rules negotiated in the Uruguay Round and the fact that more disputes are coming to the WTO reflects a growing faith in the system' (WTO website, 1998). Such a dramatic increase in the number of dispute cases brought to the WTO might be largely due to the WTO's more powerful and effective dispute settlement system. It indicates that the DSB of the WTO is more effective than that of the GATT in the sense that the panel report of the DSB is automatically accepted unless all WTO members unanimously disapprove of the report. Furthermore the WTO is able to enforce implementation of its decision through the threat of imposing retaliatory trade barriers against the offending country if that country does not abide by the WTO's decision. In effect then the dispute settlement system is structured with greater discipline than the old GATT system.

A second difference is that more trade dispute cases involve developing countries under the WTO than was the case under the GATT. Table 14.2 shows the composition of developed countries and developing countries in

Table 14.2: Number of Trade Dispute Complaints under GATT and WTO

Complaining country	Respondent country	GATT Number of cases	%	WTO Number of cases	%
Developed	Developed	174	73.7	87	39.5
	Developing	24	10.2	64	29.1
Developing	Developed	35	14.8	43*	19.5
	Developing	3	1.3	26	11.8
Total		236	100	220	100

Note: Including 11 cases (five distinct matters) filed by both developed and developing country members against the EC (nine cases) and Hungary (one case). The tabulation of Table 14.1 is based on the total number of respondent countries.

Source: Overview of the State-of-play of WTO Disputes

the trade dispute cases reported to the WTO. Approximately three-quarters of all trade disputes reported to the GATT were disputes among developed countries. Only the remaining one quarter were disputes involving developing countries. However under the WTO about one half of all disputes involved developing countries as either complaining party or respondent. In particular, a higher proportion of the total disputes were developing countries being subject to complaint by developed countries. Under the old GATT system, most of the complaints were directed at developed countries and many developing countries enjoyed 'special and differential' treatment from the developed countries. In other words, developed countries were more or less generous towards developing countries in international trade under the old system. Under WTO, however, developing countries have been increasingly involved in trade disputes as competition has intensified in the global market and as the developing countries have begun to lose their trade privileges.

Third, more non-tariff barriers (NTB) were employed during the WTO era. Under the GATT, it was mostly either tariff barriers or quantitative import restrictions that hindered free trade between countries. While these tariff barriers had constantly been lowered through repeated rounds of multilateral negotiations, more non-tariff barriers such as standards barriers, subsidies, intellectual property rights violations, dumping, discriminatory domestic taxes, government procurement, and measures related to investment were used under the WTO.[1] Table 14.3 summarizes the types of

Table 14.3: Types of Trade Barriers

Type	Number of complaint cases
Subsidy & countervailing duties	23
Anti-dumping restriction	22
Quantitative restriction	20
Tariff, custom duties	19
Intellectual property rights measure	18
Domestic tax measures	12
Technical barriers	11
Safeguard measures, quota	11
Import/export procedures	11
Investment measures	5
Government procurement	5
Service restriction measures	3
Service, subsidy	2
Others	22
Total	184

Source: Overview of the State-of-play of WTO Disputes (1 February 2000).

trade barriers reported to the WTO by complaining countries during 1995–99. As shown in the table, conventional trade barriers such as tariff and quantitative restrictions (such as quotas and import bans) were used less frequently. Instead, NTB, such as subsidies, dumping, intellectual property rights, domestic taxes, technical barriers and service measures were more often used.

In addition to the above observations, Lee (2000) conducted a statistical analysis of 897 bilateral trade cases involving 45 WTO country members during 1995–99 and found the following conventional economic factors that tend to be related to trade disputes.

1. Trade disputes are positively related to trade volume. This conforms to common reasoning: the more trade a country conducts, the more conflicts and frictions it is likely to encounter. However there are some empirical exceptions. For example, even though India was the 22nd largest country in terms of trade volume, it was ranked as the 4th largest country in terms of the number of trade disputes in which it was involved.

2. A country is more likely to be involved in trade disputes if its trade volume, income and trade deficits are large and if its trade regime is less open.
3. Two countries are more likely to engage in trade disputes when there is a gap in income and their trade imbalance is large.
4. Trade disputes between two countries will be less if their trade relations are complementary.

Having not yet become a member of the WTO, China has not been a party to the trade disputes discussed above. However the pattern of trade disputes presented above is highly relevant for China. Based on the above observations and analysis, China should not expect to have a smooth phase-in period in fulfilling all its commitments made for full WTO membership and it should not expect to be immune from trade conflicts with its trade partners. Instead, it should be well prepared for trade disputes in the short term and in the long term as well. The following section will discuss why and in what way China is most likely to be involved in trade conflicts.

CHINA'S TRADE STATUS AND POTENTIAL TRADE CONFLICTS

Given this discussion of factors contributing to trade disputes, China may perhaps come to face more trade conflicts than many other WTO members. Specific reasons include its high trade volume, its developing country status, its relatively high formal and informal trade barriers and its large trade surplus with its major trade partners. China may also face some country-specific difficulties in integrating its trade regime with that of the world economy and this too may give rise to trade conflicts.

Conventional Sources of Trade Disputes

First, China is now the world's seventh largest national economy and tenth largest trading nation. Its annual foreign trade rose from a mere $21 billion in 1978 to $338 billion in 1998, with an annual average growth rate of 15 per cent, which is much higher than the average growth rate of world trade (as shown in Table 14.4). More dramatically, China has been very successful in attracting foreign capital from near zero in 1978 to a high of $110 billion in 1993. China became second only to the US, as a largest recipient of foreign direct investment in the early and mid-1990s. In the last ten years or so, China has actively participated in international financial and capital markets through issuing stocks and bonds and buying foreign

Table 14.4: China's International Trade Statistics, 1986–99

Year	Exports US $ billion	Growth %	Imports US $ billion	Growth %	Total US $ billion	Growth %
1986	30.9	---	42.9	---	73.8	---
1987	39.5	28	43.2	1	82.7	12
1988	47.5	20	55.3	28	102.8	24
1989	52.5	11	59.1	7	111.6	9
1990	62.1	18	53.3	– 10	115.4	3
1991	71.9	16	63.8	20	135.6	18
1992	84.9	18	80.6	26	165.5	22
1993	91.7	8	104.0	29	195.7	18
1994	121.0	32	115.6	11	236.6	21
1995	148.8	23	132.1	14	280.9	19
1996	151.1	2	138.8	5	289.9	3
1997	182.8	21	142.4	3	325.1	12
1998	183.8	5	140.2	– 2	324.0	0
1999	194.9	6	165.7	18	360.6	11
2000	249.2	28	225.1	36	474.3	32

Sources: China Statistics Yearbook, 2000; China's Customs Monthly; 2000 Country Reports on Economic Policy and Trade Practices, the Bureau of Economic and Business Affairs, US Department of State.

securities in the international markets. The pace of integration of the Chinese economy into the world economy is widely expected to be faster after its WTO accession. The rapid growth in international business engagement and anticipated increase in business volume may result in more commercial disputes.

Second, following the point made in last section, China as a developing country may be involved in more trade disputes than developed countries under the WTO system. Over the eight rounds of GATT multilateral trade negotiations, great progress was made in creating easier market access. Developed countries lowered their tariff rates on manufacturing goods from an average of 40 per cent in the 1960s to less than 4 per cent in 1999, whereas the applied tariff rates for many developing countries, such as Mexico and Turkey, were reduced to around 14 to 10 per cent on average (Grady and Macmillan, 1999: 18–19). In the case of China, considerable progress had been made. China had slashed the average tariff rates on imports from 24.6 per cent in 1997 to 17 per cent in 1998. In addition the

Chinese government announced its intention to achieve an average tariff rate of 15 per cent in 2000 (Yin, 1999a). However these stiffer tariff targets are yet to be achieved. Under the WTO agreement, China committed to reduce further its tariffs on industrial goods to an average of 9.4 per cent, with zero tariffs for some specified chemical and electronic products by 2005. This will present a major challenge for China to meet the phase-in requirements on tariffs. Other challenges China will face are in non-tariff areas, such as anti-dumping, intellectual property rights protection, market opening in services and in the financial industries and restrictions on subsidies (Yin, 1999b). In the process of implementing the WTO agreement (of the Uruguay Round), developing countries experienced various difficulties and had increasing conflicts with developed countries on those issues. The failure of the Seattle Millennium Round negotiation in 1999 demonstrated that significant gaps existed on a wide range of issues between developing and developed economies. Without question, China will have to face the same or even tougher a challenge than many other WTO developing country members in its dealings with developed economies.

Third, as discussed above, large trade imbalances can be a source of trade disputes. China has five major trading partners, the US, Japan, the EU, the ASEAN and South Korea, not counting Hong Kong and Taiwan. Of these five, China has maintained a relatively balanced trade relationship with the ASEAN, Japan, and the EU. Even though China has experienced a chronic trade deficit with Korea, it is very unlikely that it will have major trade disputes with Korea due to the complementary nature of the bilateral trade structure between these two countries (Yin, 1999c).

Trade Dispute Estimation

Based on the conventional constraints discussed above, we applied the linear model developed in an empirical study conducted by Lee (2000) to estimate the number of trade disputes that China might be involved in once it becomes a member of the WTO. According to Lee's model, the six explanatory variables employed can explain 97 per cent of the variation in the numbers (cases) of trade disputes (the 'R-square' was 0.973). The empirical coefficients for the six variables can be expressed as follows:

TD = 1.203 + 0.047 TV − 0.125 TB − 0.0083 HCI − 0.0069 PRI
    − 00397 TR + 0.307 TA

where:

TD is the total number (cases) of trade disputes a country has been involved with since the establishment of the WTO;

TV is the average trade volume of a country between 1995 and 98;

TB is the trade balance of the two countries in dispute;

HCI is the average ratio of exports of heavy and chemical industries to total exports;

PRI is the ratio of primary industry to GDP;

TR is the average ratio of trade to GDP; and

TA is the tariff rate.

Using this equation and inserting China's data for 1998 into each explanatory variable, we can make a rough estimate of the number of trade disputes that China would be involved with if it had been a member of the WTO. This calculation suggests that China would have had 19 trade dispute cases with the rest of the world if it had been a member of the WTO. This would place China in fifth place in the world in terms of number of trade disputes and as such, can probably be considered a reasonable projection.

Country-specific Sources of Trade Disputes

In addition to the above-mentioned conventional sources of trade conflicts, China has its own country-specific problems that may create more difficulties for itself in complying with the WTO rules after its accession.

Transitional economies

The GATT/WTO was enacted on an implicit premise of trade between countries which follow free-market practices in their domestic economies. But the GATT never lived up these free-market principles and failed to come up with acceptable standards for dealing with former socialist countries with planned economies, such as China, Russia and the other Eastern European countries. Although the GATT included members with socialist regimes and large-scale state ownership and government control over major sectors, such as Poland and Romania, its rules did not anticipate the prospect of many members whose entire economies were based on state ownership and state trading principles. 'Now, with the imminent arrival on the WTO doorstep of seventeen former Communist, state-controlled economies, a major challenge looms for fundamental WTO principles and rules' (Groombridge and Barfield, 1999: 43).   The absence of clear standards for dealing with non-market economies complicated China's WTO accession process (it took 14 years for the negotiations) and it will complicate the dispute settlement procedure.

It remains a major challenge for China to transform fully its planned economy to a market economy. In fact, under pressure to comply with WTO rules and standards, China has achieved remarkable progress in economic transition and trade liberalization. The quest to become a WTO member has been an impetus for China to establish a market-oriented economy. Despite the changes in the Chinese economy, China still has a long way to go to complete its market economy reform.

State-owned enterprises
The centerpiece of China's economic transition is the reform of the state-owned enterprises (SOE), including the state trading companies. Although the share of industrial output from the SOEs has declined steadily over the past 20 years, from 80 per cent in 1980 to 28 per cent in 1998, the SOEs will continuously play a prominent role in the Chinese economy for years to come. State enterprises still roughly employ two-thirds of the urban industrial workforce and are in the controlling position in the overall economic activity of the country. The primary concern of foreign companies with respect to the state-controlled enterprises has been the degree to which those companies exercise monopolistic power in handling imports and exports and whether their decisions are solely based on commercial considerations, such as price, quality, availability, and marketability, as required by the WTO Agreements. Although considerable progress has been made in SOE reform, it is clear that commercial factors are interacting with many other political, social, legal and economic factors in the reform process. The Chinese political leaders are very reluctant to relax control of China's strategic resources and industrial sectors for free market competition.

Administrative and judicial reform
Another major concern is transparency of government policies, the implementation process and the judicial system overseeing business conduct in China. It is clear that new administrative and judicial systems, compatible with WTO rules, must be in place to resolve business disputes within China and disputes regarding China's obligations as a WTO member. However China has a long journey to reform its legal and administrative systems. As a legacy of traditional Chinese culture, China has a long history of subordinating law to government policy. The law is used as an instrument to achieve the goals of the government, which is under the control of the ruling Communist Party, instead of subjecting everybody (including the government and the ruling party) to the same law (i.e. rule by law rather than rule of law). In addition, the socialist commercial law, under the Chinese Communist Party and planned economy, reflects the primacy of the

collectivist norms rather than market-oriented decision-making by the economic actors themselves (Groombridge and Barfield, 1999: 21). Third, a lack of uniformity of law presents another dimension to the concerns relating to business dealings in China. For instance, under China's Arbitration Law (1994), arbitration committees are established to handle economic disputes in a number of areas. The arbitration process, although often fair and objective, suffers from political intervention by the Party and local authorities, ex parte contracts with disputants, and lack of cooperation from other agencies once judgements are rendered (Mora, 1995). The rudimentary nature of China's administrative and legal systems, the absence of an equitable review system for administrative decisions, and weak ruling enforcement mechanisms would be among the core obstacles for China in fulfilling its obligations as a WTO member.

US–China Trade Relationship

The US is China's most important trade partner but the trade relationship has not been smooth. As shown in Table 14.5, according the US Department of Commerce (USDOC), the US trade deficit with China has been escalating for the last ten years. The trade deficit issue has often been one of the major disputes discussed in the US–China commercial relationship. The two countries could not even agree on the trade figures. For example, the 1998 bilateral trade deficit was $56.9 billion according to USDOC and it was $21 billion according to the *China Statistical Yearbook*. Such a major discrepancy in calculating the trade volume reflects conflicts of interests in bilateral trading. The US government complained that China was not opening its market wide enough for US products and pressed China to liberalize further its trade regime. On the other side, China argued that the US had enjoyed a growing surplus in its trade in services with China that was not included in the calculation and that the value-added to Chinese products in Hong Kong prior to their export to the US should be deducted from China's export figures. China also blamed the US for import restrictions on textiles and apparel from China.

Besides the argument involving the trade deficit, more trade conflicts in the US–China trade relationship can be noted in the Office of US Trade Representative's Annual Report of Foreign Trade Barriers. These can also be noted in its Special 301 Provision annual reviews of its trade partners on violations of US intellectual property rights (Yin, 1999b). In its 25-page report on trade barriers in China for 1998, the USTR detailed China's tariff and non-tariff barriers, including import and export licenses, import quotas, export subsidies, lack of transparency, trading rights and other restrictions.

Table 14.5: China's Exports to and Imports from US (in billions of US dollars)

Year	US data			China data		
	China exp (cif)	China imp (fas)	Trade surplus (deficit)	China exp (cif)	China imp (fas)	Trade surplus (deficit)
1982	2.5	2.9	– 0.4	1.8	4.3	– 2.5
1985	4.2	3.9	0.3		5.1	– 2.7
1990	16.3	4.8	11.5	5.2	6.6	– 1.4
1991	19.0	6.2	12.8	6.2	8.0	– 1.8
1992	25.7	7.5	18.2	8.7	8.9	– 0.2
1993	31.5	8.8	22.7	17.0	10.7	6.3
1994	38.8	9.3	29.5	21.5	14.0	7.5
1995	45.6	11.8	33.8	24.7	16.1	8.6
1996	51.5	12.0	39.5	26.7	16.2	10.5
1997	62.5	12.8	49.7	32.7	16.3	16.4
1998	71.2	14.3	56.9	38.9	17.0	21.0
1999	81.9	15.0	66.9	41.9	19.5	22.4

Note: The China import/export data for 1982 were originally in yuan (RMB) and the official exchange rate was 1.89 yuan/dollar; all other data were in US dollars.

Sources: The US Department of *Commerce* (www.uschina.org/press/trade*);* 1999 'Country Reports on Economic Policy and Trade Practices', the Bureau of Economic and Business Affairs, US Department of State; *China Statistical Yearbook 1983–1999*. The China data are from the *China Statistical Yearbook.*

Furthermore the report elaborated on the issue of services barriers by complaining that China's 'restrictive investment laws, lack of transparency in administrative procedures and arbitrary application of regulations and laws severely limit US service exports and investment in China, especially in the financial services, telecommunications, audio-visual, distribution, professional services and travel and tourism sectors' (USTR, 1999: 62). As to intellectual property rights protection, the report recognized the Chinese government's extensive efforts in establishing a functioning system to combat IPR piracy. However it claimed 'US industry estimates of intellectual property losses in China due to counterfeiting, piracy and export to the third countries have exceeded USD 2 billion' (USTR, 1999: 62). It warned China that the destructive effect of counterfeiting has discouraged additional foreign direct investment and threatened the long-term viability of some US business operations in China.

The four dimensions of country-specific factors also suggest that China will find itself engaged in trade disputes with its trade partners and with the US in particular

ANALYSIS OF CHINA'S TRADE COMPLEMENTARITY

In order to analyze the future of China's trade, trade complementarity indices (TCI) between China and its major trading partners were calculated, using a trade complementarity index model in Yoon, Park and Oh (1998). According to the model, the trade complementarity index (TCI) for country i to export to country j can be calculated in equation:

$$C_{ij} = \frac{X_i^{'} M_i}{\|X_i\| \circ \|M_i\|}, \text{ where}$$

C_{ij} = the TCI between country i and j ;

X_i = proportional vector of country i's export;

M_j = proportional vector of country j's import;

$\|X_i\|$ = inner product square root of X_i ;

$\|M_j\|$ = inner product square root of M_j .

The categories of import and export data on bilateral trade were based on the 2-digit Standard International Trade Classification (SITC) of all countries from the Commercial Trade Database 2000, the United Nations.

The TCIs for China are summarized in Table 14.6. As shown in the table, China's TCIs for exports to US, Japan, and Germany were above 0.60. This indicates that China's export structure is more complementary to the import structures of developed countries than to those of developing countries. These relative high complementarity indices indicate that China's exports fit better with the import needs of developed economies. The complementarities between exports from China and the imports of the developed economies are very important because they will help China to reduce its potential trade conflicts due to its exports to these nations and to find mutually beneficial resolutions. However the TCIs for China's exports to Korea and Malaysia

Table 14.6: Trade Complementarity Indices between China and Its Major Trade Partners (1999)

	US	Japan	Germany	Malaysia	Korea
TCI between China's exports and each country's import structures	0.686	0.683	0.610	0.493	0.493
TCI between China's imports and each country's export structures	0.785	0.694	0.612	0.763	0.884

Source: SITC 2-digit trade data classified by the United Nations (2000).

were under 0.50. The relatively low TCIs for China's exports to Korea and Malaysia suggests a competitive relationship between China and other developing nations. This might create more trade conflicts if China targets these other developing countries as markets for its exports.

Nonetheless the TCIs for China's imports from both the developed economies such as the US, Japan and Germany and the developing economies such as Malaysia and Korea were all above 0.60. This indicates that the complementarities of China's imports with the exports from other nations will ensure more constructive trade relations. In other words, the growing Chinese economy will be able to absorb foreign exports and investment without much friction.

STRATEGIC OPTIONS FOR CHINA AFTER ITS ACCESSION TO THE WTO

WTO membership will grant China three privileges. First, China will have a voice in the decision-making process to protect its interests in world trade. Second, through gaining most favored nation status, China will have permanent assurance of non-discrimination in international trade. And third, through participation in a legally binding dispute settlement system, China will be less subject to unilateral trade sanctions and retaliation. However these privileges will not insulate China from trade disputes. Instead, for both conventional and country-specific reasons, meeting the obligations of full WTO membership will remain a challenge for China and it is more likely to be involved in trade disputes than many other developing countries in its phase-in period and thereafter. China needs to formulate its strategy early on to be fully prepared for the anticipated disputes. Based on the above analysis, we think the following suggestions worth consideration.

Bringing the Chinese Economy into Line with WTO Obligations.

Having signed bilateral agreements with the US and its other trade partners, China now has to complete its negotiations to develop a final Protocol of Accession that will take the concerns of all WTO members into account. Although the protocol is to come, the US–China agreement on WTO accession has laid out a substantial set of commitments that China will have to meet. The key components of the commitments include opening China's agricultural market to foreign competition; phasing out trade barriers for industrial goods; eliminating most foreign equity and geographic restrictions in all major service categories (including telecommunication and financial services) and phasing-out broadly defined trading and distribution rights (for example, wholesaling, retailing, franchising, maintenance, and transportation, etc.) to foreign trade partners within three to five years. These commitments represent much greater market access for foreign capital and goods and services and imply that the Chinese government will need to bring its economy in line with its WTO obligations. The early stages of the phase-in period could be disruptive, especially for those with the most entrenched positions. The Chinese government needs to be prepared for this and needs to make great efforts to follow through on its commitments, including the development of a legal environment to support contract enforcement and dispute adjudication in all areas of the country.

Continue reform of economic and trade regimes
Fundamentally, the lack of compatibility for China's economic system and the WTO's premise of free-market operations would lead to trade fraction and dispute. China should take its WTO accession as an opportunity to push ahead its economic reform and to restructure its trade regimes to make them compatible with the world trade system. The WTO membership will give Chinese enterprises greater access to foreign goods, capital, technology, and market opportunities. It will also create job opportunities in various sectors, particularly in labor-intensive service industries. Chinese companies, either state- or privately owned, will be under unprecedented pressure to become more efficient and more market-oriented to be competitive in open market. One major concern for open-market competition is that many local enterprises, especially state-owned enterprises that are severely inefficient and plagued with over-capacity and indebtedness, would not be able to survive the competition. Consequently, many local enterprises will be out of

business and many workers will be out of jobs. The Chinese government needs to take proper measures to make sure that the WTO entry will create new job opportunities to reallocate the unemployed workers and to gradually enhance the competitiveness of Chinese enterprises in open market competition.

Fully participate in WTO functions
The development experience of a set of developing countries that achieved rapid and sustained economic growth since the 1960s provides a broad profile of what type of trade and associated policies could be appropriate for other developing countries. The rapidly increased share in the world trade in manufacturing goods of the newly industrialized developing countries enhanced both their 'right' and 'leverage' to participate in the GATT/WTO negotiations. Corresponding to their enhanced rights to negotiate was the need for those newly industrialized developing countries to participate fully in the Uruguay Round (UR) negotiations to protect their trade interests. The experience of those countries may set an example for China. The rapidly growing Chinese economy and its capability to compete in international market will enhance China's bargaining power in the new Millennium Round trade negotiation. The more active its participation, the better its interests will be reflected in the new trading rules. Subsequently it is more likely that trade conflicts between China and its trade partners will be reduced. In addition, after joining the WTO, China will be able to ally itself with other developing countries to gain more bargaining power in setting rules of the game.

Active use of the WTO dispute settlement proceedings
The WTO dispute settlement procedures have become increasingly important and are increasingly utilized. It is well expected that both the volume of complaints and the complexity of cases will increase. China should establish a strong dispute settlement team as soon as possible. This team should learn quickly the dispute settlement rules and procedures and be fully prepared for dispute litigation, consultation, and settlement. China needs to be a fast learner to overcome its inexperience in international litigation and conciliation. China should learn fast how to seize the opportunities to litigate cases within the WTO dispute settlement system, as done by many other developing countries. China should realize that the increase in cases makes the private counsel play an important role in settling disputes. Hiring private counsel should be a practical alternative for China in resolving its disputes with its trade partners. It might be particularly useful in the early stage of its WTO accession and in its dealings with the US and European Union who have large and experienced legal teams.

Focusing its strategic attention on disputes with developed countries

As analyzed earlier, China should mainly focus on handling trade disputes with its trade partners from developed world. Regarding what has happened in the past, Japan, the European Union, and Canada often followed in the footsteps of the US in formulating their diplomatic and economic policies on China. This kind of strategic alliance on their China policy will be much weakened after China's accession because China will have the permanent assurance of non-discrimination, its own voice in the trade club and equal access to the dispute settlement system. It is also because the EU, Japan and Canada may have more conflicts of interest in competing in the Chinese market. But the US–China trade relationship will most likely remain a model for other developed countries. If China can manage to have a constructive trade relationship with the US, it will be in a favorable position to prevent and/or reduce its trade friction with the other developed countries. Therefore, China's international trade policy should concentrate on establishing a constructive and mutually beneficial relationship with the US. This strategic objective is achievable given the complementarities of the trade and shared economic interests in Asia and the world between those two economic giants.

STRATEGIC OPTIONS FOR MULTINATIONALS

It is clear that China's WTO membership provides great opportunities for foreign companies. But it is premature to make concrete projection about the impact of China's WTO accession on multinational corporations (MNC) and disputes they may have with Chinese counterparts. However, it is proper to make suggestions on the possible WTO-induced changes that MNCs may face and strategies MNCs should consider for entering into the Chinese market and for handling trade disputes.

First of all, MNCs will have stronger confidence in doing business in China when the WTO's dispute settlement mechanism becomes an option for resolving trade disputes with Chinese trading partners. The business environment will be more predictable when China's trade and investment policies are more transparent and when its legal systems incorporate WTO norms and rules. With key laws and enforcement procedures in place, China's legal system will offer MNCs another channel to resolve their bilateral trade disputes. This will be a great opportunity for MNCs to participate in trade and investment in China. Once the WTO provisions are phased in, MNCs will be in a better position to rationalize operations in China to make these more efficient through restructuring internal information system, transportation, and warehousing facilities. They will be in better position to integrate China more fully into their global operations through centralized management of production, sales, marketing and finance. However, the transparency and due process in the Chinese legal system will not meet the WTO standards for a considerably long time period. This is not only because the rapid change is taking place in China but also because China's entry comes at a time that the WTO is facing a challenge of making a major structural change in its own jurisdiction.

We are optimistic that China will gradually improve its business and legal environment and eventually meet the WTO standards, but we are less optimistic that this will quickly lead to the type of dramatic change that many Westerners envisioned. One concern that many MNCs doing business in China have been sharing is the uniformity of law and regulatory policies given the high degree of regional disparity. MNCs should realize that while the central government takes the right market opening moves, the local government might ignore central decrees for local interests. After 20 years of reform, the central government's power has been decentralized significantly; the local-level bureaucrats have developed their own basis of power and do not feel obliged to listen to the central authority (Groombridge and Barfield, 1999: 22). This might complicate the process of dispute settlement. Therefore, MNCs should not miss the opportunity to compete in the Chinese market but should also adopt a pragmatic approach in doing business with China even after China's accession.

Local Partnership

MNCs will be able to use the phase-in schedules to better understand the changes of business environment in China and develop their strategies for their business engagement in China. Since the WTO provisions will provide more freedom to set up wholly foreign owned subsidiaries in China, some companies may seek buyout opportunities including buying state-owned enterprises in China to integrate China into their global marketing and/or operation strategy. However, more MNCs will look for local partners to penetrate telecommunications, insurance, banking and security industries, in which minority equity ownership (less than 50 per cent) is required even after the phased-in period, according to US–China WTO Accession Agreement. Choosing a right local partner might be a real challenge to many MNCs. In the past, many MNCs had little choice but to partner with state-owned enterprises for reasons such as overcoming local bureaucracy and non-tariff barriers. Now the restricted industries are still mostly state owned but much less monopolistic and less protective than before. This change provides more choices for MNCs in seeking their local partners. Nonetheless, once China completes its phase-in commitments, MNCs might find themselves encountering greater competition from local and foreign competitors.

CONCLUSIONS

The WTO is now serving as a tribunal for arbitrating trade disputes and monitoring the trade policies of its member countries through its Trade Dispute Settlement system. Better understanding of the nature of international trade disputes and the dispute settlement system is critically important for China when it is becoming a new WTO member. The analysis indicates that China, as a developing country, a large trading partner with a big trade imbalance with its major trade partners, and a transitional economy without a complete market mechanism in place, is most likely to be heavily involved in trade disputes after its WTO accession. But, fortunately, the complementarities between China and its major trade partners will help China ease trade friction and find solutions after its WTO accession.

As one of the fastest growing economies and the seventh largest trading nation in the world, China's WTO entry will have significant impacts not only on its own economy and trading policies, but also on the way the WTO operates from now on. It deserves serious research work from different dimensions and at various levels. This chapter represents an initial effort to explore the causal relationship of trade disputes. This study is limited by preliminary statistical reference on trade disputes China might be involved and by a small sample group of countries in analysis of complementarities. However, we believe this kind of pioneering work is necessary and important and we hope it will lead to more thorough conceptual and empirical studies such as trade disputes in relation to the complementary nature of trade between partners and trade dispute management.

NOTES

1. When the GATT was founded in 1947, the average tariff rate on manufactured goods of developed countries was around 40 per cent. However, a series of efforts by GATT such as the Kennedy Round (1964–67) and the Tokyo Round (1973–79) lowered this rate to roughly 5 per cent by 1990. For example, as a result of the Tokyo Round, the average tariff rate on manufactured goods of the nine biggest developed countries was cut from 7 per cent to 4.7 per cent. By 2000, this rate was expected to be less than 4 per cent. Refer to *The Economist* (1990/9/22, 1998/5/16, 1998/10/3).

REFERENCES

August, R. (1999). *International Business Law: Text, Cases, and Readings* (3rd edition), New Jersey: Prentice Hall, pp. 109–133, 354–385.

Grady, P. and K. Macmillan (1999), *Seattle and Beyond: The WTO Millennium Round*, Ottawa, Ontario, Canada: Global Economics Ltd.

Groombridge M. A. and C. E. Barfield (1999), *Tiger by the Tail: China and the World Trade Organization*, Washington DC: The AEI Press.

Kim, J. (in Korean, 1996), 'Comparative Study between the System and Cases of WTO Dispute Settlement', *Journal of Korea Trade Association*, 24(1).

Lee, Doowon (2000), 'Causes of Trade Conflict: Korean Case vis-à-vis the global trade', *Journal of International Trade and Industrial Studies*, 5(1).

Mora, Alberto (1995), 'The Revpower Dispute: China's Breach of the New York Convention?', in *Dispute Resolution in the PRC: A Practical Guide to Litigation and Arbitration in China*, Hong Kong, pp. 155ff.

Ruggiero, R. (1997), 'Settling disputes: the WTO's most individual contribution', *About the WTO*, www.wto.org/dispute/dsu.htm

USTR (1999), 'Foreign Trade Barriers: People's Republic of China', pp. 53–68.

World Trade Organization (Various years), 'WTO Dispute Settlement Understanding', www.wto.org/wto/dispute/dsu.htm.

WTO Dispute Settlement Body, 'Overview of the State-of Play of WTO disputes'

Yin, J. Z. (1999a), 'China's Quest for the WTO: Barriers and Strategic Options', *Applied Management and Entrepreneurship*, 10(3), pp. 95–109.

Yin, Jason Z. (1999b), 'The WTO: What Next for China?', in Andrew J. Nathan and Zhaohui Hong (eds), *Dilemmas of Reform in Jiang Zemin's China*, pp. 91–106.

Yin, Jason Z. (1999c), 'Competition and Complementarity: An Assessment of Sino-South Korean Economic Relations', in Doowon Lee and Jason Z. Yin (eds), *Comparison of Korean and Chinese Economic Development*, Seoul, South Korea: Yonsei University Press, pp. 275–292.

Yoon, Bo-Il, Park, Sang-Won, and Oh, Ho-Il (1998), 'The Complementary and Competitive Relation of Korea's Trade with Its Major Trading Partners', *Monthly Bulletin*, The Bank of Korea, 11, pp. 3–24 (in Korean).

Index